THE
SUGGESTIBILITY
OF
CHILDREN'S
RECOLLECTIONS

THE SUGGESTIBILITY OF CHILDREN'S RECOLLECTIONS

EDITED
BY
JOHN DORIS

American Psychological Association
Washington, DC

First Printing July 1991
Second Printing November 1991
Third Printing December 1992

Published by
American Psychological Association
750 First Street, NE
Washington, DC 20002

Copies may be ordered from
APA Order Department
P.O. Box 2710
Hyattsville, MD 20784

Designed by Margaret Scott
Typeset by Harper Graphics, Waldorf, MD
Printed by BookCrafters, Inc., Chelsea, MI
Technical editing by Deanna D'Errico
Production coordinated by Nancy Niemann

Library of Congress Cataloging-in-Publication Data

The Suggestibility of children's recollections : implications for eyewitness testimony /
   edited by John Doris.
      p.   cm.
   Proceedings of the Cornell Conference on the Suggestibility of Children's
Recollections, held June 1989 at Cornell University.
   Includes index.
   ISBN 1-55798-118-3 (acid-free paper): $40.00
   1. Children as witnesses—United States—Congresses.   2. Child abuse—Law and
legislation—United States—Congresses.   3. Psychology, Forensic—Congresses.
I. Doris, John, 1923–   .   II. Cornell Conference on the Suggestibility of
Children's Recollections (1989)
KF9672.A75S84   1991
347.73'066'083—dc20
[347.30766083]   91-16649
                                                                                      CIP

Printed in the United States of America.

CONTENTS

CONTRIBUTORS

Charles J. Brainerd, *University of Arizona*
John C. Brigham, *Florida State University*
Ray Bull, *Glasgow College, Scotland, UK*
Stephen J. Ceci, *Cornell University*
Alison Clarke-Stewart, *University of California at Irvine*
Graham Davies, *Polytechnic of East London, London, UK*
Helen R. Dent, *University of Birmingham, Birmingham, UK*
John Doris, *Cornell University*
Phillip W. Esplin, *St. Luke's Medical Office Building, Phoenix, AZ*
Rhona Flin, *RGIT-Hilton Place, Aberdeen, Scotland*
Gail S. Goodman, *SUNY-Buffalo*
Marc Lindberg, *Marshall University, Huntington, WV*
Elizabeth F. Loftus, *University of Washington*
Lucy S. McGough, *Louisiana State University, Paul M. Herbert Law Center*
Peter A. Ornstein, *University of North Carolina*
Douglas P. Peters, *University of North Dakota*
David C. Raskin, *University of Utah*
Max Steller, *Free University of Berlin, Institute for Forensic Psychiatry, Berlin, Germany*
Michael P. Toglia, *SUNY-Cortland*
Amye Warren-Leubecker, *University of Tennessee*
Gary L. Wells, *Iowa State University*
John C. Yuille, *University of British Columbia, Vancouver, BC, Canada*
Maria S. Zaragoza, *Kent State University, Kent, OH*

FOREWORD

One of the most invigorating aspects of the scientific endeavor is the active debate that so frequently accompanies controversy. Such an engagement can be stimulating and highly informative: We broaden our views by learning about the different methods and approaches of others. Debate and disagreement among colleagues may be disconcerting to some, but it is part and parcel of the scientific process and should not be stifled.

This volume includes contributions from psychology's leading authorities on the suggestibility of children's recollections, a subject already known to be controversial because of issues related to the believability of children as witnesses. This book is not a statement of the American Psychological Association (APA) policy on a particular topic, nor are other APA-published scholarly books. This book represents scientific exchange and debate. We do not hide the differences of opinion among these scholars, but rather seek to inform the debate by affording opportunities for disagreement. The researchers whose work is presented here differ in the methods they use, and certainly disagree in the interpretation of results. However, all would agree, we believe, that further incisive research is needed to resolve the major empirical and practical issues.

Federal research agencies stopped most support of investigator-initiated state-of-the-art research conferences in scientific psychology over a decade ago. During this period, however, scientific psychology has continued to grow, and scientific psychologists have adapted their talents to diverse areas. Yet, there have been few opportunities for investigators in new and promising research areas to convene in special settings to discuss their findings. As part of its continuing effort to enhance the dissemination of scientific knowledge in psychology, the American Psychological Association established in 1988, in its Science Directorate, the Scientific Conferences program. An annual call for proposals is issued by the APA Science Directorate to solicit conference ideas. Proposals from all areas of psychological research are welcome. From the inception of this program through mid-1991, 19 conferences have been funded, with a total outlay of more than $250,000.

This volume is based in part on a June 1989 conference entitled "The Suggestibility of Children's Recollections," held at Cornell University. Topics include development of memory; effects of stress on the child witness; and suggestibility of children's testimony, especially as it relates to sexual abuse investigations. Leading scholars with differing points of view debated current issues of scientific controversy and considered specific topics for future research. The APA is pleased to have sponsored this conference and now to make these originial chapters and accompanying dialogue available in book form.

The conferences funded thus far through this APA Science Directorate program include:

Research Community Psychology: Integrating Theories and Methodologies, September 1988

The Psychological Well-Being of Captive Primates, September 1988

Psychological Research on Organ Donation, October 1988

Arizona Conference on Sleep and Cognition, January 1989

Socially Shared Cognition, February 1989

Taste, Experience, and Feeding, April 1989

Perception of Structure, May 1989

Suggestibility of Children's Recollections, June 1989

Best Methods of Analysis of Change, October 1989

Conceptualization and Measurement of Organism-Enviornment Interactions, November 1989

Cognitive Bases of Musical Communication, April 1990

Conference on Hostility, Coping/Support, and Health, November 1990

Psychological Testing of Hispanics, February 1991

Study of Cognition: Conceptual and Methodological Issues, February 1991

Cardiovascular Reactivity to Psychological Stress and Cardiovascular Disease: A Conference on the Evidence, April 1991

Developmental Psychoacoustics, August 1991

Maintaining and Promoting Integrity in Behavioral Science Research, October 1991

The Contributions of Psychology to Mathematics and Science Education, October 1991

Lives Through Time: Assessment and Theory in Personality Psychology from a Longitudinal Perspective, November 1991

Lewis P. Lipsitt, Ph.D.   Virginia E. Holt
Executive Director for Science   Manager, Scientific Conferences Program

PREFACE

The impetus for the Cornell Conference on the Suggestibility of Children's Recollections began with the organizers' awareness that the legal system, concerned with the investigation and adjudication of cases of sexual abuse of children, was with increasing frequency turning to the behavioral and clinical sciences for guidance on issues relevant to the reliability of children's eyewitness testimony.[1] How good, in both absolute and relative terms, is the memory of children for eyewitnessed or experienced events? How do the child's memory functions change with age? How is a child's recall of events best facilitated and least contaminated?

These and similar questions appear to be appropriately addressed to psychologists. Unfortunately, the state of our field is such that we do not answer with one voice. The result is the danger that those seeking help will dismiss our collective or individual claims for expertise as the confusion of Babel, the pretensions of a pseudo-science, or, even more discreditably, as the advertisements of guns for hire, and they will shop about our field not for truth but expediency. That our answers differ is not strange. Although much is known, much is unknown. Plain facts have a way of shifting their plain meaning as they are moved from one context to another, and theories are always fuzzy at the growing edge even if not flawed at birth.

In such circumstances it seemed to us that there was great need for psychologists to talk among themselves, to step back and see the problem of children's eyewitness memory in the broader context of child development and cognitive science. We would not be completely unmindful of the courtroom and the legal context but that would not be the focus. The background issues needed clarification. We dreamed but did not expect any consensus. We set as a goal the clarification of issues—the juxtaposition of conflicting views. If we would provide no simple response to the question addressed to us, we would clarify for ourselves,

---

[1] The organizers of this conference included Drs. Stephen Ceci, John Doris, Gail Goodman, David Raskin, Michael Toglia and John Yuille.

and, hopefully for the questioner as well, why the answer cannot be simple. Indeed, the question itself has only a deceptive appearance of simplicity.

Therefore, we need to broaden the base from which we respond, and the questioner must take care that the question be not narrowly framed. In asking about eyewitness memory in the legal context, it must be remembered that most cases of sexual abuse never reach the courtroom. The concerned parent, the social worker, the police, the physician, the prosecutor, all with earlier involvement and latitude for disposition, must be equally concerned with those questions that the court raises. Justice or injustice for child or alleged perpetrator may be effected long before the open forum of the court is reached, if indeed it ever is.

We as psychologists have the right to think we can individually and collectively be of some help now, if we honestly apply our craft and do not reach above its limits. We may be of more help later when time and the commitment of resources have nurtured the growth of knowledge. Meanwhile we trust this published outcome of our conference, which reflects the content of the presented papers as well as the professional exchanges that they provoked, may advance our limited goal of clarifying issues, presenting the range of expert opinion, and roughly mapping out the terrain yet to be crossed. If its does that, much has been accomplished both for ourselves and for those desperate enough to seek our aid.

I would like to extend personal thanks, as well as that of all participants, to those who made the conference possible:

- ☑ The Science Directorate of the American Psychological Association, for providing indispensable matched funding;
- ☑ Virginia Holt, who represented the Directorate with encouraging warmth and support in the development and presentation of the conference;
- ☑ Tom Hanna and Michael Nunno of the professional staff of the Family Life Development Center, who problem-solved at all stages of planning and execution;
- ☑ Dean Francille Firebaugh of the New York State College of Human Ecology who graciously provided the funds for our travelers from Europe and Canada, for without their presence the conference would have been parochial in its scope and vision; and
- ☑ The State of New York for the establishment in 1974, and its continuing support, of the Family Life Development Center with its mission of teaching, extension, and research activities relevant to families under stress and particularly to the most dysfunctional symptom of stress—child abuse.

Special acknowledgement and thanks are also in order for: Madeline Dean, our Administrative Supervisor and our Executive Staff Assistant; Brenda Wolcott-

Aume, who provided logistical support before, during, and after the conference; Colleen Bushnell and Karen Arnold, for secretarial support; and graduate students Michelle DeSimone and Marybeth Putnick, who provided valuable volunteer services during the actual presention of the symposium.

John Doris

CHAPTER 1

SOME OVERARCHING ISSUES IN THE CHILDREN'S SUGGESTIBILITY DEBATE

STEPHEN J. CECI

The backdrop against which planning for this conference, Suggestibility of Children's Recollections (June, 1989), began was the contradictory findings—both in the literature and in conference presentations—that I first became aware of a couple years ago. My awareness was brought to a head at the 1988 American Psychology–Law Society meeting in Miami, where it seemed as if one child memory researcher after another ascended the podium to report conflicting, sometimes even opposite, findings from those of his or her predecessor. There was no attempt at synthesis or integration of these conflicting reports. I found the whole ordeal troubling. Lest one imagine that these contradictions were apparent only to me, suffice to say that at one paper session several individuals who became contributors to this volume commented to me regarding their similar perceptions. At that time several people asked whether Cornell University would consider hosting a conference that would have as its aim the exploration of the sources of this conflict. I agreed to discuss this with colleagues at Cornell upon my return. The end result was a proposal to the Office of the Science Directorate of the American Psychological Association that interested parties meet and grapple, in the true spirit of scientific cooperation, with the methods, procedures, and constructs that have given rise to so much disagreement in this field.

IS CONSENSUS POSSIBLE?

My hope at the time of preparing the proposal to the Science Directorate to hold the conference on which this volume is based was an alluringly simple-minded idea: If only the empirical researchers in this field would sit down for three days and review each others' arguments, data, and methods, it would be possible to arrive at a consensus—both on points for which there is broad agreement and points for which there is not. In discussing this goal with colleagues, I realized that my optimism that a consensus was achievable was not universally shared. Some, perhaps many, are of the opinion that the field of children's memory research is so split on every level that it is premature to look for consensus areas.

I believe that most of the disagreements that riddle the field of children's memory are not true disagreements at all. That is, they are not failures to replicate the work of others, under highly similar conditions. The sole exception to this claim that I am aware of is the disparity between the findings of Zaragoza's laboratory and the results from the Cornell laboratory. And even here I feel that progress in understanding this disparity is being made as newly designed studies by both labs get under way. Based on my analysis of the literature in this area, I believe that the majority of the disagreements that plague the field of children's memory result because researchers use dissimilar vocabulary, constructs, and procedures. Thus the reader is forced to compare apples and oranges in an attempt to make sense of the disagreements. My hope is that the noncomparability of procedures, vocabulary, and constructs will become evident as the authors of this volume help us wade through the empirical bases of their conclusions.

In my own view, some issues are widely shared by the authors of this book. Of course, there are other issues about which disagreement will still exist. Only someone unfamiliar with the practice and passions of science would imagine that if all of the empirical researchers got together and shared their data and arguments the result would be a single shared view of what the research says. I trust that I am not this naive about the way science works. But this does not mean that we should not try to achieve consensus on those points that are within reach and present them, along with their rationale, in addition to an explicit indication of those points about which we cannot reach consensus, and their rationale as well. If this strikes you as reaching too high, then I would regard this as preferable to the converse. As that most cognitive of all 19th-century English poets, Robert Browning, once remarked, "Ah, but a man's reach should exceed his grasp, or what's a heaven for."

I have assembled a list of what I call "overarching issues" because of their presumed relevance to arguments that I anticipate will crosscut many of these chapters. My discussing them at this time is not meant to forestall their later discussion but rather to encourage their elaboration and refinement. Here are the issues that I predict will be revisited in the chapters of this book many times. If I am correct, this volume will reflect a turning point in the area of the suggestibility of children's memory, because investigators will begin to tame their conclusions, consistent with the need to recognize threats to the external validity (i.e., generalizability) as well as the noncomparability of methods and constructs.

ECOLOGICAL VALIDITY

It has become an unfortunate habit for researchers on both sides of the suggestibility debate to hurl charges of lack of ecological validity at the other side's research. So, let me begin by asking: What does ecological validity mean, anyway? It is a term that has come into fashion again this past decade, especially in developmental psychology. Cornell has been the home to ecological psychology from its very beginnings in this country, from the time of Frank Angell at the turn of the century, to the more recent formulations of James and Eleanor Gibson, Ulric Neisser, and Urie Bronfenbrenner. The first debate over the definition of ecological validity was reported in the *Psychological Review* in 1943 by Brunswick and Lewin, the latter himself also a member of the Cornell faculty at that time. Lewin and Brunswick argued about the relation between a distal object and its proximal cue. Brunswick had interrupted a woman doing her daily activities to ask her to make size judgments of objects of various shapes, at various distances, at various times of the day. At issue was whether it was necessary to demonstrate a co-occurrence of some object with a visual cue (e.g., the retinal size of the object) across a sample of not just subjects but also situations, to "possess generality with regard to normal life conditions" (Brunswick, 1943). Since their debate, this construct of ecological validity has come into and out of fashion in psychology, and it presently appears once again to be in fashion, propelled by methodological treatments of the related (and ecompassing) concept of external validity. In their essence, both ecological and external validity have to do with how far one can generalize from the procedures and subjects of one study to some target population. Consider some representative comments on external validity from methodology textbooks:

> Would the same effect be obtained with individuals other than those who participated in the study? Would the same effect be obtained in other settings? If another researcher defined the independent or dependent variables slightly differently, would the same effect be obtained, or is the effect limited to the persons, settings, and operations that this particular researcher used? How far can the experimental effect be generalized? What are the limits on the generalization of the study findings? (Smith & Glass, 1987, p. 144)

> Making generalizations is the essence of external validity. . . . The major point . . . is that external validity is concerned with specifying the contin-

gencies on which a causal relationship depends and all such specifications
have important implications for the generalizability and nature of causal relationships. (Cook & Campbell, 1979, pp. 81–82)

As can be seen, the concept of external validity encompasses that of ecological validity, the latter being more concerned with the fine-grained analysis of
the settings, people, and treatments themselves. Although both constructs have
been used quite differently by various researchers, no researcher, to my knowledge,
has ever used either one to suggest that systematic laboratory research is unwarranted, invalid, or undesirable. The problem is not whether a study is done in a
laboratory or nonlaboratory setting, but rather the extent to which the causal
mechanisms under study are illuminated by the study's setting and the integration
of laboratory findings with observations of real-world events as they unfold in
natural settings. In the field of children's suggestibility this becomes a spark point
because of the past insistence of some researchers that entire research traditions
have little to offer our understanding of children's recollections in, say, courts of
law. More about this later. First, I want to return to ecological validity and how
it does not mean that we ought to be studying contexts at the expense of processes
that are at work in those contexts.

Bronfenbrenner (1989) has decried the almost mindless rush to study behavior in context because it has come to mean the study of contexts without an
understanding of the basic processes that support behavior. You might imagine
from this statement that Bronfenbrenner, a leader of the revived interest in ecological validity in this country, favors laboratory studies. To make that claim
would be to carry his beliefs further than is warranted. But Bronfenbrenner has
been a clear and articulate voice on the need to include laboratory work as an
important ecological contrast whenever one does work in the field. In some of
the work he and I have done together he has referred to the "unexploited potential
of the laboratory as an ecological contrast" (Ceci & Bronfenbrenner, 1985), and
elsewhere he has referred to himself and his ideas about ecological validity as a
"victim of his own success" (Bronfenbrenner, 1989), because some have interpreted it to mean that what is really important is the study of contexts rather than
processes. All of this is my way of saying that ecological validity ought not be
the starting point of each specific study but rather the end point for an entire
program of research. To craft each specific study with the idea of transplanting
it into the real-world context of interest is likely to yield little in the way of
scientific leverage, a leverage built on careful disentanglement of variables that
are frequently co-linear or confounded in naturalistic field studies and in need of
systematic laboratory-like research.

So, if ecological validity is not synonymous with field research, what is it
synonymous with? Again, I turn to Bronfenbrenner for an answer:

> Ecological validity refers to the extent to which the environment experienced by the subjects in a scientific investigation has the properties it is supposed or assumed to have by the investigator. . . . The ecological validity of any scientific effort is called into question whenever there is discrepancy between the subject's perception of the research situation and the conditions assumed by the investigator. (1979, pp. 28–30)

Thus Bronfenbrenner comes to a position that is similar to that of Neisser's view of ecological validity. To rephrase Neisser, it means we ought not build laboratory models of phenomena that have no real-world counterpart. And when we talk of real-world counterparts we should keep in mind Bronfenbrenner's caution that the real world is perceived or constructed by individuals, and therefore it is important to understand how they perceive the situations, including the threats, motives, inducements, and suggestions that inhere in these situations. This notion of ecological validity gets at the heart of what is a strong and at times acrimonious debate among researchers, namely, what it is that one takes to be the real-world analog that one wishes to understand and predict? There are lots of phenomena that one might wish to understand, but if the construct of ecological validity is to guide our understanding as opposed to merely being a rallying cry for the recruits of one side or another in the suggestibility debate, then I suggest we attempt to make clear exactly what real-world analog is being referred to, because what is valid for one class of phenomena might not be for another. Moreover, what is valid for one subtype within one class of phenomena may not even be valid for other subtypes within this same class. Let me give a couple examples of what I mean.

For psycholegal researchers interested in children's recollections in a sex abuse case, the real-world analog might be a set of circumstances that includes bodily victimization in the context of high levels of arousal; personal embarrassment; and a web of motives, threats, inducements, and suggestions that might tilt the odds one way or another that the victim will tell others what happened and tell them accurately or inaccurately. Moreover, there are frequently—even typically—multiple interviews and interventions in the aftermath of such acts. (Putting aside the fact that for researchers interested in other types of autobiographical memory the constellation of forces operating may be quite different from those just described, even within this class of sexual abuse events, there is considerable diversity.) No single program of research that I am aware of sufficiently illuminates this diversity. In fact, most studies that purport to say something about the suggestibility of children's recollections of sexual abuse events have omitted all consideration of the strong motives, threats, and inducements that are often part of the aftermath of abuse. Any one of these motivational forces can be used to reverse the findings that have been reported in the literature. So, a prediction I make is that the authors of this book will acknowledge the limits to the relevance of their work for sexual abuse, something that they have neglected to do in the past.

DIVERSITY OF CASES

A second but related overarching point that I wish to make concerns the diversity that exists within samples and situations. To prepare these remarks, and with the help of two researchers from the Cornell University Family Life Development Center, I examined two data sets involving reports of sexual abuse made to the New York Central Register for Child Abuse and Maltreatment that were subsequently investigated. One data set is from a major metropolitan center, and the other is from a small city. Hard as I tried to find the modal pattern of variables that co-occur in these sexual abuse cases, I came up empty. Although many cases share a few characteristics, only a handful of them share more than a few characteristics.

For instance, in these two data sets there are almost as many different scenarios as there are cases; in many a boyfriend or stepparent is the alleged perpetrator, but in others it is someone unconnected with the family, including a stranger in 12% of the cases and a daycare provider in 9%. In some cases high levels of arousal may not have been a part of the ordeal, whereas in others it would almost certainly have been a part. The point of this exercise is that there is no single constellation of variables that characterizes all of these cases or even most of them. What may be ecologically valid research for understanding some types of abuse may not be for understanding others. And in all cases, we need to know not just the variables that occur in a particular context but also the way these variables are perceived by the individuals in these contexts.

But I realize that some child memory researchers, like myself, have contexts and analogs in mind that differ from those of sexual abuse in many ways. By dwelling on the context of sexual abuse, I do not want to give the impression that I think that this is the only, or even the most important, context for looking at the suggestibility of children's recollections. I recently participated in a death row case that involved testimony about a rather mundane observation a girl had made. Not only was there no heightened arousal during her initial observation (she did not even realize that a crime had been committed until two weeks after her observation), but also there was not the tangle of personal embarrassment and ego defenses that occur in some sexual abuse cases. In the aftermath of this girl's observation, various adults vigorously interrogated her, pursuing every answer with a battery of leading and potentially distorting questions.

Her testimony nearly was responsible for sending the defendant to the electric chair, were it not for the fact that several years later (one month before the scheduled execution) she offered a complete recantation, explaining how confused she became because of the incessant questioning coupled with her desire to help authority figures. No reliable figures exist as to how many cases involve child witnesses of mundane events (in this case, witnessing a man washing his hands) in capital felonies, but they are probably quite rare. But it is becoming increasingly common for child witnesses to offer their recollections in domestic violence and custody cases, something my attorney wife sees with growing frequency in her own practice. Naturally, these sorts of contexts differ enormously from each other and from sexual abuse contexts.

Anyway, I predict that the issue of ecological validity will permeate the following chapters, and it may help if we are clear about the contexts to which we are trying to generalize, and how applicable our research methods and measures are to the real-world events that are of interest. Of particular importance is a consideration of the role that motives and social forces might play in children's recollections of events. Here I speak of motives in the broadest sense of that term, including threats, inducements, suggestions, rewards, and so forth. It is rare for our studies to capture the potency of such motives. But for some real-world contexts, such as sexual abuse, their elucidation strikes me as important, maybe critically so.

DISTORTION OF RECOLLECTION

For other researchers, of course, there is no need to discuss real-world contexts in the proximal sense that I have been discussing them. Their main concern is with elucidating the basic mnemonic characteristics themselves. And this brings me to another overarching issue, namely the distinction between distortion of one's recollection that is due to genuinely mnemonic processes versus distortion that is the result of nonmnemonic sources, for lack of a better term. The first source, mnemonic processes, are those that posit some alteration or erasure of the original trace for an event. For example, if a postevent suggestion leads to an alteration of the trace, then that trace should be difficult or even impossible to recover in all retrieval environments. Various analytic tools exist to test this hypothesis, and Brainerd and Ornstein's chapter (Chapter 2) should elucidate the role that encoding time processes, in particular, might play, since suggestibility problems at this locus would result in irreversible trace alteration. By definition, genuinely mnemonic distortion is unconscious. The people doing the recollecting have no intention of withholding or misleading, and they have no idea when and if their reports are false. Finally, they should have little awareness that the source of their faulty memory was some erroneous postevent suggestion.

In contrast to mnemonic distortion, one can speak of cases in which a false report is false precisely because the people doing the reporting are aware of its falsity. Perhaps someone in a powerful position has threatened, cajoled, bribed, persuaded, or otherwise induced them to falsify their account. This is a quite different phenomenon from mnemonic distortion, both in its underlying dynamics and in its phenotypic attributes. If I am correct in thinking that this distinction will prove central to some of the chapters in this book, then I urge all of us to make clear what type of distortion we are referring to when we make statements about the suggestibility of children's memory: Trace alteration, or socially or emotionally induced confabulations of which the subject is fully aware. Both are forms of suggestibility, but they are very different.

GRAPPLING WITH THE PROBLEM

I should say something in closing about the political, emotional, and social turmoil that attends a discussion of children's suggestibility. Conflict is not easy to live with. But, at least in science, that does not make it an undesirable or unhelpful companion. Earlier I mentioned some Cornell colleagues from a bygone era to make a point about ecological validity. Now I want to mention another Cornellian from a bygone era. In his paper on controversy and adversity in science, Boring stated:

> After much thought on the matter, I have come reluctantly to the conclu-
> sion that scientific truth . . . must come about by controversy. . . . It
> seems that scientific truth . . . lies in its greatest minds being brilliantly
> and determinedly wrong . . . with some third, eclectically minded, middle-
> of-the-road nonentity seizing the prize . . . running off with it, and sticking
> it into a textbook for sophomores written from no point of view and in
> defense of nothing whatsoever. I hate this view, for it is not dramatic and
> it is not fair; and yet I believe that it is the verdict of the history of science
> . . . [thus] without fighting you get science nowhere; you are just the cau-
> tious critic who is afraid to venture. (1963, p. 68)

So, although it may not be pleasant to grapple with ideas that are inimical to our own, doing so can be a valuable enterprise for science even if the temporary conflict is ugly and unpleasant. With apologies to Shakespeare's words in the guise of the Banished Duke buffeted by the winter's wind in the Forest of Arden,

> "Sweet are the uses of [conflict,]
> Which like the toad, ugly and venomous,
> Wears yet a precious jewel in his head"
> (As You Like It, 2.1. 12–14).

I trust that beginning this book with a reference to reaching for the heavens and ending it with a reference to toads, does not portend the path readers shall take as they navigate through the Scylla and Charybdis of datum and argument. In this regard, my colleagues and I have been filming preschoolers as they attempt to report events such as whether they were kissed while being bathed (Ceci,

DeSimone, Putnick, Lee, & Toglia, 1990). Prior to eliciting their statements, an interviewer conveys to the children that it is naughty for adults to kiss them while the children's clothes are off. Not surprisingly, against such a backdrop the children falsely reported that they were not kissed in the tub. This is just one of five motives (the desire to avoid embarrassment) that we have examined so far, and evidence exists that preschoolers are susceptible to four of the motives. We have not examined developmental trends in this type of false reporting yet, but we now know that claims to the effect that children never lie or that children never falsely report events about their own bodies are overly simplistic. Under conditions that approximate naturalistic levels of motivation to lie, children will at the very least commit errors of omission. We are now exploring errors of commission under similar motivational inducements. We expect that they will succumb to such pressures, as they are, after all, members of the human race!

References

Boring, E. (1963). The psychology of controversy. In *History, psychology, and science: Selected papers*. New York: Wiley.

Bronfenbrenner, U. (1989). Ecological systems theory. *Annals of Child Development, 6*, 187–249.

Brunswick, E. (1943). Organismic achievement and environmental probability. *Psychological Review, 50*, 255–272.

Ceci, S J., & Bronfenbrenner, U. (1985). Don't forget to take the cupcakes out of the oven: Prospective memory, strategic time-monitoring, and context. *Child Development, 56*, 150–165.

Ceci, S. J., DeSimone, M., Putnick, M. B., Lee, J. M., & Toglia, M. P. (1990, March). *The role of motives in children's reports*. Paper presented at the meeting of the American Psychology–Law Society, Williamsburg, VA.

Cook, T. D., & Campbell, D. T. (1979). *Quasi-experimentation: Design and analysis issues for field settings*. Chicago: Rand McNally.

Lewin, K. (1943). Defining the "field" at a given time. *Psychological Review, 50*, 292–310.

Smith, M. L., & Glass, G. V. (1987). *Research and evaluation in education and the social sciences*. Englewood Cliffs, NJ: Prentice-Hall.

CHAPTER 2

CHILDREN'S MEMORY FOR WITNESSED EVENTS:
THE DEVELOPMENTAL BACKDROP

CHARLES BRAINERD AND PETER A. ORNSTEIN

Our goal is to set the stage, both empirically and theoretically, for applying research on memory to interpreting children's testimony. To do this, we examine selected topics from the literature on the development of memory in children. From our perspective, many factors may affect children's testimony, but most fundamentally, we are dealing with an issue of memory. Thus, although information on emotional, social, and physical development is clearly relevant, interviews, depositions, and court testimony are ultimately tests of children's memories about events and experiences. Simply put, children cannot provide information about events that cannot be remembered. Moreover, because children's memories of events in the distant past are those most often being interrogated, research on the development of retention and forgetting is most relevant.

SOME UNDERLYING ASSUMPTIONS

In the space available, it is impossible to explore the development of memory in depth, especially when it comes to adding the sorts of qualifications and provisos that usually figure in academic tracts. Instead, the best we can do is to make a few general, and, we hope, nontrivial, remarks about each of a number of topics and then point readers to the relevant primary references or to other, more in-depth overviews that we have prepared (e.g., Howe & Brainerd, in press; Ornstein,

Gordon, & Baker-Ward, in press). This means that the validity of our remarks depends rather more heavily on auctorial judgment than is typical in scholarly writing. Thus it behooves us to clarify the principles that have guided both our selection of topics and our interpretations.

1. We are firmly opposed to know-nothingism, which can masquerade as expert opinion, experienced professionalism, and the like. If the goal is to be able to provide sound advice to legal and law-enforcement professionals, based on the research literature, it is critical to know the facts. And these facts are derived from the basic research literature in cognitive development. Thus it is important to understand the relevant research on children's memory, and it is equally essential to be clear about what we as a field do not yet know. Anything else is a recipe for disaster.

2. Asseverations about ecological validity notwithstanding, laboratory-based research is of fundamental importance in understanding children's testimony. The unsurpassed value of the laboratory derives from the opportunities it affords for precise experimental control over the myriad factors that may affect children's performance. Of course, it is essential to think creatively about bridging the gap between the laboratory context in which information is gathered and the real-world setting to which it must be applied. Yet, in many cases, the basic principles of memory that are illuminated by laboratory research have direct implications for application in extralaboratory contexts. And in others, principles derived in the laboratory can set the research agenda for applied investigations that are directly relevant to the issue of testimony.

3. Special significance attaches to variables that are known to have powerful effects on children's retention and that also happen to be variables that can be manipulated, for good or questionable purposes, by those who question child witnesses. Although it is important to keep in mind the factors that affect children's initial acquisition of information, these may ultimately be less important than those that influence children's forgetting and the recovery of previously acquired information. Indeed, because testimony is given at some distance from the witnessed events, variables that operate during the long retention interval most clearly satisfy both conditions just described.

We have used these guiding principles to select for discussion salient topics in the literature on memory. However, before we present our overview, it is important that we emphasize that there are many different kinds of memory (e.g., short-term, long-term, visual, verbal, deliberate, incidental, etc.) and that we must clearly identify those types of memory that are operative in situations involving testimony.

What Kind of Memory is Involved?

Testimony involves an interesting combination of incidental and deliberate memory that can be both spontaneous and prompted. When a child first reports an incident or is questioned about one, we are dealing with a case of incidental recall. Clearly, he or she was not told in advance that there would be a deliberate memory test and thus was not engaged in particular strategies to increase the likelihood of storing the information. So, we are asking about the retention of information that was acquired earlier in an incidental fashion. Of course, later on, this incidental recall turns into a deliberate memory task, as the child is questioned repeatedly and even implored to try to remember. Under these conditions, strategies for retrieval may be involved, but what got into memory and is, in principle, accessible was picked up incidentally.

It also must be emphasized that when children are questioned in a legal context, the memories under consideration are those that typically involve the recall of personally experienced (either as a participant or eyewitness) and highly salient or meaningful events. These events contrast sharply with the stimulus materials (e.g., words, pictures, even stories) that are often employed in studies of memory. In addition, testimony typically involves remembering over very long intervals—frequently years—during which children may undergo significant intellectual and social development. Moreover, these intervals are routinely filled with experiences that can potentially alter—for better or worse—memory of the initial event. Thus, for example, questions from attorneys and social workers can have an impact, as can psychotherapy, and can help a child to overcome a traumatic experience.

Retention and Forgetting

Questions of retention and forgetting—whether in the laboratory or the real world— typically can be viewed in terms of some variation on the Ebbinghaus long-term retention paradigm. In the laboratory, children study some material to be remembered during an acquisition session. They then resume their daily lives for some time and finally return to the laboratory for a retention session in which their memories of acquisition-phase information are tested. Additional delayed retention tests are sometimes given as well. Outside of the laboratory, of course, there is no formal acquisition session. Rather, as suggested earlier, children typically experience some event in an incidental fashion, and then, following a delay interval, retention is probed in a formal laboratory assessment or an interview.

In its ideal form, the measurement of retention and forgetting involves a comparison of performance at the end of the aquisition session with that at the delayed test. Indeed, forgetting is often characterized by the slope of the line connecting measures of performance at initial and delayed assessments. Although this measurement is readily accomplished in laboratory studies, it can be somewhat problematic outside of the laboratory when there is no acquisition session to provide an index of baseline performance. When there are assessments at multiple delay intervals, however, it may be possible to use performance at an early delay as a substitute for a missing acquisition session. Moreover, if an accumulated data base concerning children's retention is established (something that is thus far not available), it would be possible to overcome this measurement problem by extrapolating forgetting functions obtained in the laboratory.

Admittedly, the classic literature on children's long-term retention and forgetting is quite sparse, but in recent years research activity has been on the increase. As a result, we now have evidence that children's memory for salient, meaningful experiences—for example, a class trip (Fivush, Hudson, & Nelson, 1984); a visit to the dentist (Peters, 1987); a physical examination (Ornstein, Gordon, & Braddy, in press); or an inoculation (Goodman, Aman, & Hirschman, 1987)—can be quite good over extended periods of time. Ornstein, Gordon, and Braddy (in press), for example, studied 3- and 6-year-olds' retention of the details of a visit to the pediatrician for a physical examination. Children at both ages remembered most of the features of the check-up on an immediate test. Moreover, the performance of the 3-year-olds decreased over delay intervals of one and three weeks, but was nonetheless still impressive, whereas that of the older children was constant over this period.

Although this research suggests that children's long-term retention can be quite good, it is important to point out its limitations. In general, it seems that there exist demonstrations of surprisingly good retention only after several days and weeks, but little is known about the course of forgetting over extended intervals of months and years. Little is known also about how children's performance varies as a function of the type of events or materials that need to be remembered. And little is known about age differences in retention, particularly when performance is corrected for differences in the initial acquisition of information. In short, what is missing is a systematic exploration of the characteristics of children's retention and forgetting over varied intervals, intervals that are not neutral, but rather are filled with potentially interfering events.

IMPLICATIONS OF RESEARCH ON MEMORY FOR ASSESSING CHILDREN'S TESTIMONY

Given the limited nature of the knowledge base, what can we say about the variables that affect children's memory over the long term? What do we know about procedures that can be followed to facilitate children's remembering? How can the extant literature be applied to a consideration of issues affecting children's testimony? Our position is that although there is not a great deal of work that is directly applicable—in the sense of a thorough set of studies exploring children's long-term retention of personally meaningful, salient events—the existing literature nonetheless offers important guides to thinking about children in the legal context. Moreover, this literature can easily be extended by a series of coordinating studies, so as to be directly applicable to the legal context. In the remaining sections of this chapter, we focus on a number of features of the literature that have implications for thinking about these issues.

The Role of Knowledge and the Constructive Nature of Remembering

It is clear that interviewers cannot manipulate what children know about events that are being remembered, and laboratory researchers can do this in only a limited fashion. Nonetheless, because memory performance is strongly affected by prior knowledge, understanding what children bring to the interview context is of critical importance for all who work with children. Both classic (e.g., Bartlett, 1932; Binet & Henri, 1894) and current (e.g., Chi, 1978; Chi & Ceci, 1987) research indicate that prior knowledge affects how one monitors the world, how information is coded and placed in memory, and how it is subsequently retrieved. Thus age-related changes in children's knowledge and understanding can be important determinants of developmental differences in long-term retention and forgetting.

One implication of the literature on children's knowledge is that with the passage of time, information in memory can be altered and interpreted more consistently in the light of prior knowledge. Memory, in short, may become more reconstructive and less reproductive. Moreover, given that young children are readily able to construct scripts or event representations of familiar routines (e.g., Fivush, 1984; Nelson, 1986; Nelson, Fivush, Hudson, & Lucariello, 1983), one must be especially concerned with the possibility that their delayed memory reports may be generated on the basis of this underlying knowledge. Simply put, with the passage of time, the details of a particular day in school may be lost, and a child's recollections may quite unconsciously be governed by his or her general knowledge of the routines of school (see, e.g., Myles-Worsley, Cromer, & Dodd, 1986).

What Happens in the Delay?

The delay interval is not neutral. Events that take place during this period—including interaction with experimenters and interviewers—can have a profound effect on what children are able to remember. Two categories of events must be considered: those that have the potential to facilitate remembering and those that serve to distort memory. Perhaps the most fundamental principle of memory is that repetition facilitates performance! At least since the time of Aristotle, it has been known that exposure to a particular event or set of materials after its initial presentation will increase the probability of subsequent successful recall. So too will partial exposure to the original stimulus situation. For example, a certain amount of experience between initial exposure and subsequent test can serve as a booster shot to maintain memory over a delay interval (e.g., Campbell & Jaynes, 1966; Rovee-Collier & Hayne, 1987). The experience is insufficient for new learning, but it can serve as an inoculation against forgetting. Thus repeated discussion of a previously experienced event can serve to maintain it, but so can partial repetitions of the experience (e.g., visits to the scene, etc.). And recent evidence suggests that testing memory for an event in close proximity to that event can have a dramatic inoculation effect on later recall (Brainerd, Reyna, Kingma, & Howe, 1989).

In contrast to the facilitative effects of repetition and testing, certain intervening activities have the potential to lead to distortions in memory. For example, if an individual has some uncertainty about the details of a particular event, exposure to other accounts of it can lead to an alteration of the memory for the episode. And to the extent that younger children's initial encoding of events is less complete than that of older individuals, the likelihood of such alteration is inversely associated with age. Furthermore, this same alteration process can be induced by the form of questions that are directed to the individual attempting to remember. Indeed, research on the effects of misleading post-event information (e.g., Ceci, Ross, & Toglia, 1987a, 1987b) indicates that misleading questions can easily distort children's memory, even though there is considerable debate as to whether the initial memory trace is altered as a result of questioning (Loftus, Miller, & Burns, 1978; McCloskey & Zaragoza, 1985; Zaragoza, 1987).

Test-Induced Recovery

A related issue concerns what happens at the end of a delay interval, namely, at a final test of memory. Just as repeated questioning following an event can facilitate subsequent retention, there is evidence to suggest that repeated testing after a lengthy forgetting interval may have positive effects on the recovery of information. Indeed, children seem to be able to refurbish their memories of witnessed events purely as a consequence of having those memories tested. Moreover, the evidence suggests that children demonstrate as much improvement as a function of repeated testing as do adults.

Support for these statements comes from a large corpus of data obtained from a series of laboratory studies on the forgetting of verbal materials (see, e.g., Brainerd, 1985; Brainerd, Kingma, & Howe, 1985; Brainerd et al., 1989; Howe

& Brainerd, 1989). In these experiments, children and adults were given a series of four retention tests at intervals of one to two weeks after the target material had originally been acquired, and recall performance improved approximately 10% across the tests. However, it must be emphasized that the positive effects of repeated testing will be likely to turn to negative consequences if the experimenter or interviewer attempts to mislead the subject. Moreover, it is also possible that the obtained effects may vary as a function of the materials or events to be remembered.

Storage Failures Versus Retrieval Failures

We turn now to two fundamental theoretical issues about the nature of forgetting and the fate of lost memories that can have profound implications for understanding children's testimony after long delays. The first issue deals with the basic characterization of forgetting. Once information has been acquired, does forgetting arise from storage failures, that is, the loss of memory traces from long-term memory? Or can forgetting be viewed in terms of retrieval failures, that is, the inability to gain access to the target traces on memory tests? The second, related issue depends on a resolution of the first question: If forgetting involves substantial amounts of loss from storage, how shall this process be characterized? Is it chiefly a matter of trace destruction or of trace fading?

Interest in such questions originated in a debate between associationists and Gestalt psychologists that has been in progress for most of this century (Bower & Hilgard, 1981). Barring subsequent neurological insults, associationists thought that a memory trace remains intact once it is deposited in long-term memory. By process of elimination, forgetting must be a growing inability to access these intact traces. Atkinson and Shiffrin's (1968) claim that long-term memory is a permanent storage system and a labile retrieval system is the archetypal crystallization of this position. Gestalt psychologists, on the other hand, thought that the traces themselves are destroyed with time. The destruction process that they envisioned was a sort of spontaneous mental rewriting of history.

It was the associationist view that became the textbook interpretation of forgetting throughout most of this century. However, there is a minority position favoring storage failure, and, importantly, this position has been very influential in research on eyewitness testimony. It has been vigorously espoused in connection with adults by Loftus and her associates (e.g., Loftus, 1979), and it has been advanced in connection with children by Ceci and his colleagues (e.g., Ceci et al., 1987a, 1987b). These investigators' working hypothesis is that subsequent experience, of which the well-known misinformation effect of leading questions is a special case, supplants or destructively updates previously stored traces, a hypothesis that obviously comports well with Gestalt thinking.

Let us now consider what the developmental data indicate about these questions concerning the characterization of forgetting. To examine these issues, it is necessary to be able to analyze long-term retention data so as to differentiate between processes such as storage and retrieval failure, and to identify the extent to which children might be able to regenerate and refurbish memory traces long after they have been deposited. Although such measurement is indeed difficult, it can be facilitated somewhat with the use of recently developed mathematical models that have been applied to the data obtained in the series of laboratory studies of forgetting that were previously mentioned (e.g., Brainerd, 1985; Brainerd et al., 1985; Brainerd et al., 1989; Howe & Brainerd, 1989). A discussion of how these models work is, of course, far beyond the scope of this chapter. For present purposes, the only critical features of the models are that they (a) are stochastic and (b) contain specific parameters that give the possibilities of storage failure and retrieval failure across a retention interval, as well as the probabilities of restorage and retrieval relearning on a series of retention tests.

Repeated applications of these models with subjects who range in age from late preschool to early adulthood have indicated that the rate of storage failure is routinely higher than the rate of retrieval failure, and that the incidence of each type of forgetting declines with age. Moreover, throughout this age range, storage failure seems to be a matter of trace fading rather than trace destruction, because subjects display an ability to restore failed traces on retention tests despite the fact that they are not permitted to restudy the target material. This ability improves with age. Of course, we must add the caveat that at this point in time, our inferences may turn out to be quite dependent on the specific assumptions of the models. In addition, as we have suggested, it is necessary to extend these laboratory-based models to experiments involving children's retention of real-world events. It is possible that under these conditions, the use of cues and prompts may indicate that greater amounts of forgetting result from difficulties in retrieval.

IMPLICATIONS AND RECOMMENDATIONS

Given the importance of prior knowledge as a determinant of subsequent memory, it becomes very important to have detailed information concerning just what it is that young children know about salient domains in their experience. Moreover, because of the increasing frequency with which children are called upon to testify in proceedings concerning allegations of sexual abuse, it is most necessary to learn what children of different ages know about human anatomy and sexual behavior. Gordon, Ornstein, and Schroeder (1989) have provided an initial account of the sexual knowledge of children between 2 and 7 years of age, but additional research is clearly necessary.

The consequences of repetition and questioning are of considerable importance for the handling of children in the context of the legal system. From one perspective, children's testimony would be expected to be facilitated as a consequence of repetition, repeated questioning, and reinstatement operations. And when it comes to repeated questioning, it would seem that numerous opportunities are built into the system. Just consider the frequency with which a child may be interviewed by police, lawyers, nurses, social workers, and psychologists, during the period before a court appearance.

Yet, there is an obvious caveat about the effects of repetition, and this concerns the issue of suggestibility. Clearly, memory tests and interviews can have the opposite effect if they are intentionally designed to mislead and misinform. Moreover, it seems quite likely that the individuals who interact with a child do not have to be deliberately motivated to mislead in order for their questions to have a negative influence on the child's subsequent retention. Again consider the child's multiple contacts with police, lawyers, social workers, and so forth and the way in which the perspectives of these individuals may gradually weave their way into the child's version of his or her own story. Given both the positive and negative consequences of questioning, it seems important to keep in mind those who interact with the child during the period between a critical event and the subsequent treatment of this event in a legal context. Ideally, it would be most worthwhile to develop guidelines for interviewing children that would increase the likelihood of maintaining but not distorting memory.

Similar issues arise in considering the implications of the facilitation of memory by repeated testing after a delay. If a police officer interviews a witness or an attorney takes a deposition, it might seem advisable to interrogate about critical facts repeatedly, perhaps separated by questions on other, less critical matters. To some extent, these multiple inquiries can induce recovery of the target memories. Yet, it is also important to guard against the possibility that the repeated questioning itself may contribute to an alteration in the content of the reported memories. Of course, this can most obviously be seen when there is a deliberate attempt to mislead or misinform. Nonetheless, even without an attempt to misinform, repeated questioning—particularly by high-status adult interviewers—can result in children spontaneously changing their reports. Given this, the development of guidelines is a high priority.

At first glance, the evidence suggesting that forgetting over long delays can be viewed primarily in terms of storage failures, as opposed to retrieval failures, would lead to a pessimistic view of children's abilities to provide testimony. If children forget at faster rates than do adults—and laboratory studies (Brainerd et al., 1985; Brainerd & Reyna, 1990) suggest that they do—they should not be able to regenerate lost memories if the traces themselves have failed in some way. However, the implications for children's testimony are less serious than might be imagined because the storage failure seems to be of an impermanent, fading variety. In this connection, even very young children have been found to regenerate traces long after acquisition, simply by virtue of being interrogated about their memories. Of course, repeated assessments of memory are also potential opportunities for suggestion, and it is critical that these tests be carried out in as neutral a fashion as possible.

We close with a recommendation that underlies our view of the process of applying the findings of the cognitive development literature to the legal context: More research is needed! As suggested here, research on developmental changes in remembering and forgetting is directly relevant to our understanding of children's abilities to provide reliable testimony. The extant literature provides important insights for our conceptualization of the testimony process, some of which have been outlined here. Yet much additional research is necessary, with children of different ages presented with real-world materials over very long delays, before the gap between the laboratory and the courtroom can be closed. The necessary work will take some time, but it will certainly have great payoff in terms of the management of children in the context of the legal system.

References

Atkinson, R. C., & Shiffrin, R. M. (1968). Human memory: A proposed system and its control processes. In K. W. Spence & J. T. Spence (Eds.), *The psychology of learning and motivation* (Vol. 2, pp. 89–195). New York: Academic Press.

Bartlett, F. C. (1932). *Remembering: A study in experimental and social psychology.* Cambridge, England: Cambridge University Press.

Binet, A., & Henri, V. (1894). La memoire des phrases (memoire des idees). *L'Annee Psychologique, 1,* 24–59.

Bower, G. H., & Hilgard, E. R. (1981). *Theories of learning.* Englewood Cliffs, NJ: Prentice-Hall.

Brainerd, C. J. (1985). Model-based approaches to storage and retrieval development. In C. J. Brainerd & M. Pressley (Eds.), *Basic processes in memory development* (pp. 143–208). New York: Springer-Verlag.

Brainerd, C. J., Kingma, J., & Howe, M. J. (1985). On the development of forgetting. *Child Development, 56,* 1103–1119.

Brainerd, C. J., & Reyna, V. F. (1990). Can age × learnability interactions explain the development of forgetting? *Developmental Psychology, 26,* 194–203.

Brainerd, C. J., Reyna, V. F., Kingma, J., & Howe, M. L. (1989). *Development of reminiscence and forgetting: Evaluating the disintegration/redintegration hypothesis.* Manuscript submitted for publication.

Campbell, B., & Jaynes, J. (1966). Reinstatement. *Psychological review, 73,* 478–480.

Ceci, S. J., Ross, D. F., & Toglia, M. P. (Eds.) (1987a). Age differences in suggestibility: Narrowing the uncertainties. In S. J. Ceci, D. F. Ross, & M. P. Toglia (Eds.), *Children's eyewitness memory* (pp. 79–91). New York: Springer-Verlag.

Ceci, S. J., Ross, D. F., & Toglia, M. P. (1987b). Suggestibility in children's memory: Psycholegal issues. *Journal of Experimental Psychology: General, 116,* 39–49.

Chi, M. T. H. (1978). Knowledge structures and memory development. In R. Siegler (Ed.), *Children's thinking: What develops?* Hillsdale, NJ: Erlbaum.

Chi, M. T. H., & Ceci, S. J. (1987). Content knowledge: Its role, representation, and restructuring in memory development. In H. W. Reese (Ed.), *Advances in child development and behavior* (Vol. 20, pp. 91–142). New York: Academic Press.

Fivush, R. (1984). Learning about school: The development of kindergarteners' school scripts. *Child Development, 55*, 1697–1709.

Fivush, R., Hudson, J., & Nelson, K. (1984). Children's long-term memory for a novel event: An exploratory study. *Merrill-Palmer Quarterly, 30*, 303–316.

Goodman, G. S., Aman, C., & Hirschman, J. (1987). Child sexual and physical abuse: Children's testimony. In S. J. Ceci, M. P. Toglia, & D. F. Ross (Eds.), *Children's eyewitness memory* (pp. 1–23). New York: Springer-Verlag.

Gordon, B. N., Ornstein, P. A., & Schroeder, C. S. (1989, August). *Children's testimony in sexual abuse cases: Implications of prior knowledge and interview procedures.* Paper presented at the meeting of the American Psychological Association, New Orleans.

Howe, M. L., & Brainerd, C. J. (1989). Development of children's long-term retention. *Developmental Review, 9*, 301–340.

Loftus, E. F. (1979). *Eyewitness testimony.* Cambridge, MA: Harvard University Press.

Loftus, E. F., Miller, D. G., & Burns, H. J. (1978). Semantics integration of verbal information into a visual memory. *Journal of Experimental Psychology: Human Learning and Memory, 4*, 19–31.

McCloskey, M., & Zaragoza, M. (1985). Misleading postevent information and memory for events: Arguments and evidence against memory impairment hypotheses. *Journal of Experimental Psychology: General, 114*, 1–16.

Myles-Worsley, M., Cromer, C., & Dodd, D. (1986). Children's preschool script reconstruction: Reliance on general knowledge as memory fades. *Developmental Psychology, 22*, 2–30.

Nelson, K. (1986). *Event knowledge: Structure and function in development.* Hillsdale, NJ: Erlbaum.

Nelson, K., Fivush, R., Hudson, J., & Lucariello, J. (1983). Scripts and development of memory. In M. T. H. Chi (Ed.), *Trends in memory development research: Contributions to human development* (Vol. 9, pp. 52–70). Basel, Switzerland: Karger.

Ornstein, P.A., Gordon, B. N., & Baker-Ward, L. E. (in press). Children's memory for salient events: Implications for testimony. In M. L. Howe, C. J. Brainerd, & V. F. Reyna (Eds.), *Development of long-term retention.* New York: Academic Press.

Ornstein, P. A., Gordon, B. N., & Braddy, D. (in press). Children's memory for a personally experienced event: Implications for testimony. *Applied Cognitive Psychology.*

Peters, D. P. (1987). The impact of naturally occurring stress on children's memory. In S. J. Ceci, M. P. Toglia, & D. F. Ross (Eds.), *Children's eyewitness memory* (pp. 122–141). New York: Springer-Verlag.

Rovee-Collier, C., & Hayne, H. (1987). Reactivation of infant memory: Implications for cognitive development. In H. W. Reese (Ed.), *Advances in child development and behavior* (Vol. 20, pp. 185–238). New York: Academic Press.

Zaragoza, M. (1987). Memory, suggestibility, and eyewitness testimony in children and adults. In S. J. Ceci, M. P. Toglia, & D. F. Ross (Eds.), *Children's eyewitness memory* (pp. 53–78). New York: Springer-Verlag.

COMMENTARY: A GRAND MEMORY FOR FORGETTING

RHONA FLIN

What can developmental psychology offer those professionals who are faced with the difficult task of gathering and testing children's evidence? Brainerd and Ornstein have tackled this question by surveying the literature and identifying those research data that can enhance our understanding of children's ability to give accurate testimony. They focus their attention on children's memory development, specifically examining the processes of forgetting and retrieval. These topics have obvious implications for legislation on children's evidence and for the improvement of interviewing techniques. My comments address the forensic applications that they have outlined.

First, they highlight the influence of prior knowledge on memory performance. This clearly merits attention, particularly in terms of specific event categories, such as sexual behavior. The essential point here is not only that underlying knowledge can influence the encoding and storage of events, but also that age-inappropriate knowledge can be a critical test of the credibility of witnesses' statements. Another aspect of knowledge that may affect a child's memory performance in a police investigation or in court is the child's comprehension of his or her role in the legal process (Cashmore & Bussey 1990; Flin, Stevenson, & Davies, 1989). Consequent anxiety due to fear of the unknown can also influence the quality of recall.

Second, their emphasis on the need to understand more fully the process of forgetting is entirely appropriate. In Scotland, child witnesses wait an average of six months between witnessing a crime and being examined in court (Flin, Davies, & Tarrant, 1988). With few exceptions (e.g., Goodman, Rudy, Bottoms, & Aman, 1989) the majority of developmental studies have used very short delays, at best weeks rather than months. Even after a one-week delay, the observed age differences in a laboratory face-recognition task diminish, and care should be taken in drawing developmental conclusions based on single delay intervals (Ellis & Flin, 1990). My colleagues and I are currently measuring children's memory for a live event over a five-month interval (Flin, Boon, Knox, & Bull, in press), and more work of this type is required.

Third, a delay does not occur with the child in a vacuum, and Brainerd and Ornstein also consider the impact of questioning on memory. In serious crimes this is a significant problem, as the child can be interviewed repeatedly by parents, police, social workers, doctors, and lawyers. They suggest, somewhat surprisingly, that multiple interviews can actually enhance memory for a witnessed event, a conclusion that seems to have been drawn principally from laboratory studies of children learning lists of words, as there is no reliable body of data from children watching live events to indicate any such effect. (Perhaps the term *event* is rather ambiguous; it is not a label I would apply to most laboratory learning tasks.) They also use the phrase ''repeated testing.'' But in a criminal investigation the tests may be highly variable, the interviewers do not know what transpired, and questioning will be geared to the agenda of a particular professional. Although facilitation may occur in the sterile conditions of the laboratory with word lists, I doubt that this finding can or should be applied to the practice of interviewing child witnesses.

In its present form, their suggestion does not acknowledge the strong consensus of expert opinion that repeated questioning of witnesses can be both damaging to the emotional well-being of the witnesses and to the quality of their evidence. All the recent guidelines issued to professionals who interview child victims emphasize the need to minimize the number of times the child is questioned. Notwithstanding the risks of contaminating evidence during multiple interviews, there are ethical, emotional, and motivational factors to be considered. First, repeated questioning can be highly stressful for the witness, resulting in impairment of performance, an effect unlikely to be observed in the laboratory. Reporting a list of unrelated words is somewhat lacking in the emotional intensity of relating the intimate details of a sexual assault. Second, child witnesses can become unmotivated and uncooperative following repeated questioning. This can result in the child refusing to give additional statements or even evidence in court because he or she has recounted the events several times before. Third, over-rehearsing a witness may diminish the credibility of the testimony in the eyes of a jury.

This is not to say that I disagree with Brainerd and Ornstein's other recommendations. They balance their remarks by raising the problem of suggestibility, which does appear to present some degree of risk. However, the degree has not yet been quantified: Suggestibility may be due to social compliance or to a mnemonic effect. It is not clear to what extent suggestibility occurs when children report personally significant events, nor do we know whether child witnesses are more suggestible than adults. The importance of interviewing the witness as early as possible is generally accepted, and their advocacy of reinstatement is well supported by techniques such as cognitive interviewing or returning the witness to the scene of the crime.

Brainerd and Ornstein present a strong case for the central role of controlled laboratory research; however, an equal argument could be tendered for the superior validity of both forensically realistic experimental paradigms and studies of actual child witnesses during their involvement in legal proceedings. These are not mutually exclusive methodologies, and, in essence, the issue is which approach is seen as primary. Their contention that the value of the laboratory is "unsurpassed" could certainly be debated, and they themselves comment that "there is not a great deal of work that is directly applicable." We need to acquire a more systematized and sophisticated knowledge of the cognitive and emotional demands placed on child victims and witnesses before we can begin testing precise mnemonic effects in the laboratory. I concur with their plea for more research but add the proviso that conclusions derived solely from laboratory experiments should be applied with circumspection.

Developmental memory research can enhance and improve current knowledge of children's competence to act as witnesses. Furthermore, certain legal rules and procedures are based on an inaccurate or outmoded knowledge of developmental psychology (see Spencer & Flin, 1990), and established research findings need to be made available to both legal practitioners and policy makers. Developmentalists need to emphasize the broad range of individual differences within age levels, while being more specific about age when referring to children. There is also a need to stress the powerful effects of contextual factors in any given crime, and the developmental backdrop should be the incompetence and fallibility of adult eyewitnesses who have, to paraphrase Robert Louis Stevenson (1886), grand memories for forgetting.

References

Cashmore, J., & Bussey, K. (1990). Children's constructions of court proceedings. In J. Spencer, G. Nicholson, R. Flin, & R. Bull (Eds.), *Children's evidence in legal proceedings* (pp. 137–145) Cambridge, England: Cambridge University Law Faculty.

Ellis, H., & Flin, R. (1990). Encoding and storage effects in 7 year olds' and 10 year olds' memory for faces. *British Journal of Developmental Psychology, 8*, 77–92.

Flin, R., Boon, J., Knox, A., & Bull, R. (in press). The effect of a five month delay on children's and adults' eyewitness memory. *British Journal of Psychology*.

Flin, R., Davies, G., & Tarrant, A. (1988). *Children as witnesses*. Edinburgh: Scottish Home and Health Department.

Flin, R., Stevenson, Y., & Davies, G. (1989). Children's knowledge of court proceedings. *British Journal of Psychology, 80*, 285–297.

Goodman, G. S., Rudy, L., Bottoms, B. L., & Aman, C. (1989). Children's concerns and memory: Ecological issues in the study of children's eyewitness memory. In R. Fivush & J. Hudson (Eds.), *What young children remember and why* (pp. 189–206). Cambridge, England: Cambridge University Press.

Spencer, J., & Flin, R. (1990). *The evidence of children*. London: Blackstone.

Stephenson, R. L. (1886). *Kidnapped*. London: Cassell.

COMMENTARY: DEVELOPMENT OF EVENT MEMORIES OR EVENT REPORTS?

AMYE WARREN-LEUBECKER

Brainerd and Ornstein eloquently and effectively argue that current laboratory research on the development of memory has much to contribute to our understanding of children's eyewitness testimony. They further assert that future laboratory memory research, although it "will take some time," will "certainly have great payoff in terms of the management of children in the context of the legal system." Apparently undaunted by the myriad factors that "may" affect children's testimony (they refer only in passing to emotional, social, and physical development), Brainerd and Ornstein confidently assert that "interviews, depositions, and court testimony are ultimately tests of children's memories. . . . Simply put, children cannot provide information about events that cannot be remembered."

Although I wholeheartedly support their appeal for more laboratory research, from my perspective the issue of children's testimony is not simply a question of the development of event memory. Rather, it is a question of the development of event reporting. Children, in fact, can and probably do report information about events that cannot be remembered—however fabricated, suggested, reconstructed, or inferred—most likely upon request from adults. In contrast, events that children remember perfectly clearly and completely may be reported vaguely and partially, depending upon the social context of the report; the children's interpretation of that context; their current knowledge base and level of cognitive, social, emotional, and communicative development; the level of those same skills at the time of the event; experiences and changes occurring during the delay between event and reports; and more. This lengthy, yet still incomplete, list of both memorial and nonmemorial factors should suffice to illustrate the point that reports of events, or reports of memories of events, are not made in a vacuum. Even in a simple laboratory study of memory, a remarkably rich context exists. Thus our minimal unit of study is not a pure event memory, but an event report.

To highlight my distinction between an event report and an event memory more clearly, I use the example of a 6-year-old subject I call Laura, who was questioned regarding her memory of the space shuttle accident two weeks, two months, and again two years following the event (Warren-Leubecker, Bradley, & Hinton, 1988).

> Interrogator: "How did you find out about the shuttle accident for the very first time?"
>
> Laura: "I saw it on the news."
>
> Interrogator: "Can you tell me everything you remember about when you very first heard about the space shuttle exploding?"
>
> Laura: "It interrupted my show, *Price is Right.*"
>
> Interrogator: "Can you tell me anything else you remember?"
>
> Laura: "I like the Smurfs on Saturday morning."

Two months after the accident, Laura responded in this manner to the same questions: "I saw it on TV. I was watching TV." When asked, "Do you remember anything else?" she answered "Well, no." Two years later, she responded to the identical questions as follows:

> "I was watching *The Price is Right* and at the very end for the showcase to come on, it went off because the rocket exploded. I was upset, but when I heard about it I felt sorry for them. I really felt sorry for the teacher. But when I kept seeing the news on all of my shows I got tired of it but that was the only thing to watch, so I kept watching it. I will never forget that story in my whole life. I really feel so sorry for them I wish it did not happen. But I am still disappointed about not getting to see who won the showcase. I'm going to always feel sorry for them."

What factors are responsible for the enormous difference in Laura's initial and final reports? We could first look to memory processes for possible explanations. Laura was repeatedly questioned, and her memory/report was apparently facilitated—a simple rehearsal effect? Interestingly, in comparing repeatedly questioned children like Laura with those first questioned at the two-year postevent mark, a significant rehearsal effect is evident (which interacts with age, in that some age groups perform best with single as opposed to multiple interrogations). Could Laura be reconstructing her report? As is often the case in children's testimony, her report cannot be verified (with the exception of confirming that the space shuttle accident did occur during *The Price is Right*). How did her prior knowledge of the space program or of disasters affect her original encoding and report of the event (and conversely, how has subsequently gained knowledge affected her prior memory)?

Moving to nonmemorial processes, is it possible that Laura's underlying memory for the event has not changed, but her expressive language skills have developed to allow greater report elaboration? If so, perhaps young children questioned during periods of rapid linguistic growth exhibit greater change over time in their event reports than do older children. What of Laura's receptive language and her interpretation of the questions posed to her? How do the syntactic and semantic complexity of the questions themselves affect children of varying ages (Walker, 1987)? Pragmatic development most assuredly is involved as well. Is Laura simply adapting her report to her audience over time? Do older children possess greater skill in adapting their event reports to their various adult interviewers (e.g., social worker vs. police detective)? How does their knowledge of their audiences' social roles and status (e.g., judge or jury) affect their communicative success (e.g., Warren-Leubecker, Tate, Hinton, & Ozbek, 1989)?

Again, my list of factors potentially affecting Laura's reports, or any child's testimony, is far from complete. My aim in presenting this list is neither to needlessly complicate the tasks of or dissuade those undertaking children's memory research, nor to decry laboratory work in favor of more ecologically valid studies. Indeed, I echo the recent words of Benaji and Crowder (1989): "The complexity of a phenomenon is a compelling reason to seek, not abandon, the laboratory (p. 1192).

In my comments thus far, I have unfairly (albeit purposely) depicted Brainerd and Ornstein as being naive and overly optimistic, believing that more laboratory-based memory development research alone will cure all ills. A thorough examination of their chapter reveals otherwise. They are fully cognizant of the pitfalls of current laboratory-based memory research and its limited utility in the real world of children's testimony. As just one example, after asserting that repeated questioning facilitates memory, they quickly acknowledge that misinformation presented in subsequent questioning can have detrimental effects. Their frequent allusions to what happens during the interval/delay between events and reports and to the importance of prior knowledge for subsequent memory also indicate awareness of the multifactorial nature of event reporting. Finally, they conclude that research including children of different ages presented with real-world materials over very long delays is necessary "before the gap between the laboratory and the courtroom can be closed." I fully agree but hasten to add that while we continue investigating memory development, I hope that we do not neglect other equally important aspects of the development of children's event reports, or the laboratory–courtroom gap will remain.

References

Benaji, M., & Crowder, R. G. (1989). The bankruptcy of everyday memory. *American Psychologist, 44*, 1185–1193.

Walker, A. G. (1987, June). *Questioning young children in court: A case study*. Paper presented at the meeting of the Law and Society Association, Washington, DC.

Warren-Leubecker, A., Bradley, C., & Hinton, I. (1988, March). *Scripts and the development of flashbulb memories*. Paper presented at the meeting of the Conference on Human Development, Charleston, SC.

Warren-Leubecker, A., Tate, C. S., Hinton, I. V., & Ozbek, I. N. (1989). What do children know about the legal system and when do they know it? First steps down a less-traveled path in child witness research. In S. J. Ceci, D. F. Ross, & M. P. Toglia (Eds.), *Perspectives on children's testimony* (pp. 158–183). New York: Springer-Verlag.

CHAPTER 3

PRESCHOOL CHILDREN'S SUSCEPTIBILITY TO MEMORY IMPAIRMENT

MARIA S. ZARAGOZA

In recent years, the courts have seen a growing number of cases in which children serve as witnesses. Attempts to prosecute such cases have raised concerns about the accuracy and reliability of children's testimony. One potentially serious source of inaccuracies in children's testimony is the suggestibility of their memory. Through interviews with parents, child care workers, law enforcement officials, and attorneys, children are often exposed to new information, some of which may be erroneous or misleading. Even innocent attempts to elicit information from a child can lead to unintentional exposure to the biases and preconceived notions of the interviewer. Hence, there is good reason to be concerned about the effects this questioning might have on a child's memory.

Preparation of this chapter was supported by National Institute of Mental Health Grant MH43581 to Maria S. Zaragoza.

The study reported in this chapter was made possible through the cooperation of many day care centers throughout northeast Ohio. The assistance of these centers and the parents of the children who participated in the study is greatly appreciated. I would also like to thank Diana Wilson, Donna Dahlgren, Jean Muench, Mimi Watt, David Delmonico, and Mary French for their assistance with this project.

THE RELATION BETWEEN MEMORY IMPAIRMENT AND SUGGESTIBILITY

To what extent can children's memories be altered by suggestion? Can children be led to remember things that are different from those they actually saw? These issues have been investigated in research on the *memory impairment hypothesis* (see Loftus, Miller, & Burns, 1978). According to the memory impairment hypothesis, when children are exposed to misleading suggestions (or misinformation) about an event they have witnessed, these suggestions will impair their ability to remember the events they saw. This impairment may come about because the original memory representation is altered by the misinformation (e.g., Loftus & Loftus, 1980) or because the misinformation has rendered the original memory difficult or impossible to retrieve (Bekerian & Bowers, 1983; Christiaansen & Ochalek, 1983). The memory impairment hypothesis further assumes that as a consequence of this impaired memory for original details, children will remember the misleading suggestions instead of the events they actually witnessed.

The claim that children are suggestible can mean many things, not all of which are encompassed by the memory impairment claim. Memory impairment refers to those situations in which misinformation alters or otherwise impairs a child's ability to remember previously stored information. However, there are a number of other ways in which children might be suggestible. For example, in some cases suggested information may merely supplement and embellish information already in memory, or fill gaps in memory, without actually impairing a child's ability to remember originally stored details. In addition, some types of suggestibility are entirely unrelated to memory, such as the tendency to conform or comply with the suggestions provided by an adult authority figure. Children may conform to suggestion because they are anxious to please an authority figure, feel pressure to conform to an adult's suggestions, or simply trust the information provided by an adult authority figure more than their own memory.

Thus the mere fact that children's testimony is influenced by suggestion does not necessarily imply that their ability to remember the witnessed event is impaired. Consequently, in order to assess whether children's memory is impaired by misleading suggestions, special test procedures are needed. In particular, what is needed are procedures that can assess the effects of misinformation on a child's ability to remember the original details independent of the child's tendency to go along with the misinformation.

EXPERIMENTAL PROCEDURES FOR ASSESSING SUGGESTIBILITY

Laboratory studies of children's suggestibility have typically employed a three-phase procedure whereby children first view some event (e.g., a story illustrated

Table 1.

EXAMPLES OF THE ORIGINAL TEST AND MODIFIED TEST PROCEDURES

| Condition | Original test procedure | | |
	Original item (seen)	Misinformation (heard twice)	Test (asked to choose)
misled	rabbit	dog	rabbit or dog?
control	rabbit	—	rabbit or dog?
	Modified test procedure		
misled	rabbit	dog	rabbit or bear?
control	rabbit	—	rabbit or bear?

by pictures), are later asked leading or misleading questions about some aspects of the original event, and finally are tested on their memory for the originally seen details. One widely used version of this three-stage procedure is the Original Test developed by Loftus et al. (1978), illustrated in the top half of Table 1. In this example, all subjects first view a series of slides depicting a little girl playing with a toy rabbit. Later, children in the misled group are told incorrectly that the girl had been playing with a toy dog, whereas subjects in the control group are not given any misinformation about the stuffed animal. Finally, when tested on their memory for the stuffed animal they saw in the slides, subjects in both groups are given a forced choice between the original item (rabbit) and the item provided as misinformation for subjects in the misled group (dog). The typical finding is that subjects in the misled group perform more poorly than do subjects in the control group, because misled subjects are more likely to report the misinformation. In a study that my colleagues and I conducted with preschoolers who were given the Original Test (Zaragoza, 1987), performance in the misled condition (54% correct) was much poorer than performance in the control condition (77% correct).

Why do misled subjects perform so poorly on this test? One possibility is that their ability to remember the original item has been impaired by the misinformation. Another possibility, however, is that misled subjects are conforming to the misleading suggestion even though their memory has not been impaired. It is also likely that some of the errors are due to misled subjects who have forgotten the original detail even before they were misled, and are selecting the misleading item because it is the only response that is familiar to them. In contrast, control subjects who fail to remember the original item are much less likely to select the misleading response because they were never exposed to that information. Hence, the Original Test does not provide a direct measure of memory impairment.

The bottom half of Table 1 illustrates a procedure developed by McCloskey and Zaragoza (1985a) that provides a clearer test of the memory impairment claim. This procedure is known as the Modified Test. The Modified Test procedure is identical to the Original Test precedure with the exception that the misleading item is not a choice on the test. Instead, subjects are asked to choose between the original item (e.g., rabbit) and a new item (e.g., bear). Because the misinformation is not a choice on this test, it eliminates the social pressure to agree with the experimenter's suggestion. In addition, it eliminates the bias toward the misleading response among misled subjects who fail to remember the orginal detail. Thus, with this procedure, misled subjects will perform more poorly than control subjects if, and only if, their ability to remember the original details is impaired (see McCloskey & Zaragoza, 1985a, 1985b, for a more detailed analysis and discussion of this procedure).

In the foregoing discussion, subjects are described as either remembering or not remembering the original information. However, this is not meant to imply that memory impairment is an all-or-none phenomenon. It is possible that exposure to misinformation merely reduces the strength or accessibility of the original information. It is important to note, however, that even if misinformation merely reduces the strength of original information, this will result in impaired performance on the Modified Test. It can be assumed that there is a strength threshold for recognition memory such that strengths above the threshold are sufficient to permit a correct response on a recognition test, and strengths below the threshold are not. It can also be assumed that across subjects the initial strength of the original information is distributed along a strength continuum, such that some items fall above the recognition threshold, and some items fall below. If misleading information reduces the strength of the original information, it will shift the distribution downward relative to the strength threshold. This will cause some items (though not all) to shift from above threshold to below threshold and will therefore impair performance on the recognition test. It follows, therefore, that the Modified Test should be sensitive to possible strength-reducing effects of the misinformation, just as it is sensitive to complete loss of information from memory.

TESTS OF CHILDREN'S SUSCEPTIBILITY TO MEMORY IMPAIRMENT

Several studies have employed the Modified Test (or variants of this test) in an effort to assess adults' susceptibility to memory impairment following misinformation. These studies have consistently shown that adults are quite resistant to memory impairment (Bowman & Zaragoza, 1989; McCloskey & Zaragoza, 1985a;

Zaragoza, McCloskey, & Jamis, 1987). In contrast, only two studies have assessed young children's susceptibility to memory impairment, and these studies have produced contradictory results.

Ceci, Ross, and Toglia (1987, Experiment 4) used the Modified Test with preschool children 3 to 4 years of age who were first presented with a story about a school carnival, and through later questioning were presented with misinformation about two of the items they had seen (type of fruit and the color of a balloon). In this case, misinformation impaired subjects' ability to remember the originally seen details, as evidenced by the fact that performance in the control group (88% correct) was significantly better than performance in the misled group (72% correct).

My colleagues and I conducted a very similar study (Zaragoza, 1987) with preschoolers 3 to 6 years of age, but we obtained very different results. Subjects viewed a series of slides depicting a little girl in a city park and received misinformation about various details. When later tested with the Modified Test, performance in the misled condition (74% correct) was as accurate as performance in the control condition (71% correct). In a second study in which the children were misled twice, the same result was obtained: Misled subjects (69% correct) were as accurate as control subjects (70% correct). In contrast, a second group of subjects tested with the Original Test showed marked decrements in misled performance.

Ceci et al.'s (1987) finding that young preschoolers can be susceptible to memory impairment is particularly important in light of the fact that analogous studies with adults have uniformly failed to show evidence of memory impairment. Although direct comparisons across studies cannot be made, the Ceci et al. results suggest that susceptibility to memory impairment may be one important way in which children's memory and suggestibility differ from those of adults. Nevertheless, my failure to replicate this finding under very similar conditions (Zaragoza, 1987) raises some questions about the pervasiveness of this memory impairment effect.

In summary, the available research on children does not provide a clear indication of the extent to which young children are susceptible to memory impairment. Nevertheless, this is an important issue, the resolution of which has considerable theoretical and practical implications. To the extent that young children differ from adults in their susceptibility to memory impairment, the accuracy of their testimony is sure to differ as well. This is not to say that memory is the sole determinant of accurate testimony; a child's testimony may be inaccurate for a number of reasons other than memory impairment. Nonetheless, the information that children provide in their testimony can only be as complete and accurate as their memory permits, and susceptibility to memory impairment is one factor that can compromise children's ability to remember events they have witnessed.

STUDIES OF FACTORS CONTRIBUTING TO
MEMORY IMPAIRMENT

In an effort to assess preschool children's susceptibility to memory impairment, my colleagues and I have conducted four studies aimed at resolving the discrepancy between the results of the Ceci et al. (1987) and Zaragoza (1987) studies. The goal of this reserch was to identify the conditions under which misinformation causes memory impairment in preschoolers and thus gain some insight into the mechanisms underlying susceptibility to memory impairment. In this way we hoped to gain some insight into the reasons for this susceptibility and thus be better able to predict the circumstances under which such impairment is likely to occur.

All of the experiments to be discussed were conducted with children between the ages of 3 and 5, and all experiments employed the same general procedure. Children first viewed a series of color slides depicting a live event, a young girl spending a typical day at home (e.g., eating, picking up toys, playing with a friend, etc.). The slides were accompanied by a story narrated by the experimenter. The slide sequence contained four critical slides on which subjects would later be tested. The critical slides were a fruit (apple, orange, or banana), a stuffed animal (rabbit, dog, or bear), a toy musical instrument (piano, drum, guitar), and a toy vehicle (airplane, truck, or boat). Following the slides, the experimenter provided a synopsis of the story "to make sure the child could remember the story." For each subject the synopsis provided misinformation about two of the critical details and no information about the other two details. In addition, in each experiment the experimenter went over the synopsis twice, so that in effect all subjects were misled twice. Finally, subjects were tested with the Modified Test. In all but one of the experiments, we also tested a second group of subjects with the Original Test procedure, to ensure that we could replicate the misleading effect reported in the literature.

The Original Test results from Experiments 1, 2, and 4 are shown in Table 2. The important finding here is that in every experiment, and across different age groups, children performed significantly worse in the misled condition than in the control condition. They performed more poorly, of course, because they selected the misleading item on the test. These findings are important because they assure us that subjects in our experiments were indeed attending to and encoding the misinformation. Once more, it is important to note that the results of this Original Test procedure cannot be attributed to memory impairment, because it is impossible to determine to what extent subjects are merely conforming to the misinformation. Having shown that we could replicate the misinformation effect obtained in previous studies, we proceeded to test the hypotheses of interest.

Table 2.

PERFORMANCE OF PRESCHOOLERS IN ORIGINAL TEST GROUPS OF
EXPERIMENTS 1, 2, AND 4

Subjects	Mean percentage of correct responses		
	Misled condition	Control condition	Difference
Experiment 1			
3-year-olds ($n = 36$)	65	82	17*
5-year-olds ($n = 24$)	79	95	16*
Experiment 2			
3-year-olds ($n = 36$)	69	86	17*
4-year-olds ($n = 24$)	71	94	23*
Experiment 4			
4- to 5-year-olds ($n = 24$)	49	78	29*

*$p < .05$

Experiment 1: Is Memory Impairment Age Dependent?

The first hypothesis we investigated was the possibility that memory impairment is age dependent. It so happens that the subjects in Ceci et al.'s study were approximately one year younger ($M = 3$ years, 8 months) than subjects in the Zaragoza (1987) study ($M = 4$ years, 11 months). One possibility is that memory impairment is more likely to occur in very young preschoolers than in older children. In order to test this hypothesis, we compared the performance of sixty 3-year-olds on the Modified Test with the thirty-six 5-year-olds.

The results provided no evidence that 3-year-olds are more susceptible to memory impairment than 5-year-olds; in fact, there was no evidence of memory impairment in either age group. In both groups, misled and control performance did not differ significantly. In the 3-year-old group, performance was 71% correct in the misled condition and 73% correct in the control condition, and in the 5-year-old group, performance was 94% correct in the misled condition and 97% correct in the control condition (both $ps > .05$).

Experiment 2: Memory Impairment and Strength of Original Memory

The second experiment we conducted was designed to investigate whether there is a relationship between memory impairment and the strength of the original memory. In the initial studies we conducted with the Modified Test (Zaragoza, 1987), control performance was between 70% and 73%, approximately halfway between ceiling (100%) and guessing (50%). Although this intermediate level of memory would seem to be ideal for assessing potential memory impairing effects of misinformation, it is possible that memory impairment is dependent on the level of memory for the original information. It is not at all clear, however, what the relation between strength of original memory and susceptibility to memory impairment should be. On the one hand, one might expect that the poorer the memory for the original information, the more susceptible it would be to impairment effects. On the other hand, if few subjects can remember the orignal information even before they are exposed to misleading information, there are few subjects whose memories can be potentially impaired by misinformation. With regard to this latter point it is interesting to note that the level of control performance in Ceci et al.'s study was 88%, even though subjects were tested three days after viewing the original event.

One possibility, then, is that moderately high levels of control performance are necessary for memory impairment effects to be observed: The more subjects who remember the original details, the more subjects whose memories are likely to be impaired, and the greater the chances of observing a memory impairment effect (see Chandler, 1989, for a similar proposal). In order to investigate this hypothesis, we tested a group of forty-eight 3-year-olds and a group of twenty-four 4-year-olds in experiments identical to those just described with the exception that two changes were made in an attempt to improve subjects' memory for the original slides. First, the number of filler slides in the sequence was reduced from 45 to 12 and, second the exposure duration of the slides was increased from 4 s to 8 s.

The results provided no support for the hypothesis that memory impairment is more likely to be observed at high levels of control performance. Although the manipulations were effective in raising levels of control performance, there was no evidence of memory impairment in either age group. In both groups misled and control performance did not differ. In the 3-year-old group, performance was 76% correct in the misled condition and 82% correct in the control condition, and in the 4-year-old group, performance was 96% correct in the misled condition and 98% correct in the control condition (both $ps > .05$).

Experiment 3: Memory Impairment and Retention Interval

A third potentially important difference between the Ceci et al. and Zaragoza studies was the retention interval involved. In the Ceci et al. study, subjects were misled one day after the original story, and were tested two days after the presentation of the misinformation. In contrast, in the Zaragoza study, the entire experiment was conducted in a single 20-minute session. One possibility is that misinformation has a greater impact on memory if it is presented after a lag of a few days instead of a short retention interval. In order to test this idea, we conducted an experiment with forty-eight 4-year-olds in which presentation of the misinformation occurred two day after the original event, and testing occurred shortly after presentation of the misinformation. The results provided no support for the hypothesis that subjects would be more susceptible to memory impairment if misinformation was presented after a delay of a few days. Performance in the misled condition (69% correct) did not differ from performance in the control condition (73% correct; $p > .05$).

Experiment 4: Memory Impairment and Recall

Having failed to obtain evidence of memory impairment with the Modified Test, we conducted a fourth experiment with a different test. This experiment was designed to investigate the possibility that memory impairment in preschoolers would be more readily observed when children are tested with a recall rather than a recognition test procedure. A recall precedure has the advantage of providing fewer retrieval cues and therefore being a more sensitive measure of possible memory impairment. In addition, a recall procedure is more likely than the Modified Test to detect small memory impairment effects because the probability of guessing correctly on a recall test is much lower. Because subjects who cannot remember the original information have a 50% probability of responding correctly on the Modified Test (a two-alternative forced choice), half the subjects whose memories are impaired can be expected to respond correctly by chance (cf. Loftus, Schooler, & Wagenaar, 1985). With a recall procedure, the probability of guessing correctly is likely to be much lower, and larger differences between misled and control preformance can therefore be expected.

A group of 48 children 4 to 5 years of age were tested with a cued recall precedure analogous to one we have developed for use in studies with adults (see Zaragoza, McCloskey, & Jamis, 1987, for a more extensive discussion of this procedure). The results of this experiment showed that even with a test that was better able to detect memory impairment, there was no evidence of memory impairment in children 4 to 5 years of age. In fact, misled subjects performed slightly better than control subjects, although not significantly so. Performance in the misled condition was 32% correct, and performance in the control condition was 30% correct ($p > .05$).

DISCUSSION

After four experiments involving more than 260 subjects, we have not been able to identify any factors or circumstances that are likely to produce memory impairment in preschool children. This is not to say, of course, that memory impairment never occurs, or even that children are resistant to memory impairment under most circumstances. Instead, we have documented several cases in which memory impairment in preschoolers does not occur.

The four experiments reported here were conducted with the same stimulus materials involving the same four critical items (although the Zaragoza, 1987, study, which also failed to find evidence of memory impairment, was conducted with a different stimulus set involving different critical items). Without further empirical work it is difficult to know to what extent the results will generalize to other types of stimulus materials, items, and so forth. In addition, there is one remaining difference between the Ceci et al. (1987) study and those reported here, and its potential contribution to memory impairment has yet to be tested directly. In the Ceci et al. study, exposure to misleading information was manipulated between subjects, that is, one group of subjects received misinformation about two items and a second group of subjects (the control group) received no misinformation. In contrast, in the experiments reported here (as well as those reported in Zaragoza, 1987), all subjects received misinformation about some of the critical details and no information about others. One possibility is that exposure to misleading information has a general effect on subjects' memory performance that is not restricted to the specific times subjects are misled about. If this were true, our failure to observe a memory impairment effect could be due to the fact that performance in our control conditions was in fact lower than it would have been had our subjects not been exposed to any misinformation. We are currently investigating this possibility.

Given the early stage of research on children's susceptibility to memory impairment, it is perhaps not all that surprising that there are inconsistencies in the research findings. Nevertheless, it can be said that the available evidence in support of the claim that misinformation leads to memory impairment in children is far from impressive. Although it is always difficult to argue the null effect—that children are not susceptible to memory impairment—the available evidence provides little support for the hypothesis that young children are susceptible to memory impairment. Without additional evidence in support of the memory impairment claim, the reliability and generality of this effect remains open to question. Certainly there is insufficient evidence to support the general claim that children are more susceptible to memory impairment than are adults.

CONCLUSIONS AND DIRECTIONS FOR FUTURE RESEARCH

Clearly, the susceptibility of children's memory to impairment is an issue in need of further investigation. Further research must first establish with greater precision the magnitude and generality of the memory impairment effect and the factors responsible for susceptibility to memory impairment. There is also need for additional, more analytic work aimed at identifying the types of information that might be (or might not be) susceptible to impairment. For example, much of the current work has examined children's memory for peripheral details; it is not known whether memory for central and meaningful aspects of an event are susceptible to memory impairment in the same way. Furthermore, there is great need for developmental work aimed at assessing susceptibility to memory impairment for different age groups and understanding how the factors that affect susceptibility to memory impairment interact with age. Finally, no studies have assessed children's (or adults) susceptibility to memory impairment when they are misled repeatedly, and over long periods of time, as might occur in real-world situations in which a child is witness to a crime. It is entirely possible that children are not very susceptible to memory impairment when misled on a single occasion (the procedure employed in all previous studies), but would be susceptible to memory impairment under conditions that more closely mimic the repeated and extended questioning children undergo in the real world.

In addition to continued work on the memory impairment hypothesis, there is a great need for research on other mnemonic sources of suggestibility. The memory impairment hypothesis focuses on an error of omission, the inability to remember originally seen details. Equally important, if not more so, are errors of commission, whereby children might come to believe they remember seeing things they never actually saw. Of particular relevance here is the possibility that children might come to believe they remember witnessing events that were only suggested to them through questioning, a possibility that has begun to receive some attention in work with adults (Lindsay & Johnson, 1989; Zaragoza & Koshmider, 1989). As we have seen, errors of commission can occur in the absence of any memory impairment particularly if children receive misinformation that merely supplements, rather than contradicts, some aspect of the originally witnessed event. Other errors of commission may be brought about by misinformation that leads children to reinterpret ambiguous events already stored in memory (see, e.g., Chapter 6, this volume).

Although no studies have examined the extent to which children confuse items that were merely suggested to them for those they actually saw, there is evidence from a related line of work to suggest that young children might be more susceptible to this type of error. Johnson and Foley (1984) have examined developmental differences in *reality monitoring*, the ability to distinguish between perceived and imagined events. Their results suggest that under some circumstances young children (less than 8 years of age) have more difficulty than do older children and adults in distinguishing between imagined events and those they actually perceived. Given the greater tendency to confuse imagination with perception, young children might also be more likely to confuse items that were only suggested to them with those they actually perceived.

Finally, there is also need for further research on the social and individual factors that contribute to susceptibility to suggestion. For example, there is some evidence that children's suggestibility will depend heavily on factors such as the perceived authority of the person providing the suggestions (Ceci, Ross, & Toglia, 1987, Experiment 2). Much more research is needed to understand the roles that these factors play in children's susceptibility to suggestion, and the extent to which these factors vary across situations, individuals, and age groups.

In the opening comments at the Cornell Conference on the Suggestibility of Children's Recollections, Ceci stated that the goal of research on this topic should be generalizability to situations in the real world. The approach we have taken to achieving generalizability is to conduct systematic laboratory research aimed at identifying the general principles that underlie children's memory performance. The goal was to discover the variables that are relevant to the occurrence of memory impairment effects and the circumstances under which these effects are likely to occur. Clearly, our understanding of children's susceptibility to memory impairment is still incomplete given that we have not yet determined the conditions under which memory impairment effects might be observed. Further work to characterize the mechanisms underlying memory impairment effects is necessary before it will be possible to adequately assess and predict the reliability of children's memory in natural settings.

References

Bekerian, D. A., & Bowers, J. M. (1983). Eyewitness testimony: Were we misled? *Journal of Experimental Psychology: Learning, Memory, and Cognition, 9*, 139–145.

Bowman, L. L., & Zaragoza, M. S. (1989). Similarity of encoding context does not influence resistance to memory impairment following misinformation. *American Jounal of Psychology, 102*, 249–264.

Ceci, S. J., Ross, D. F., & Toglia, M. P. (1987). Suggestibility of children's memory: Psycholegal implications. *Journal of Experimental Psychology: General, 116*, 38–49.

Chandler, C. C. (1989). Specific retroactive interference in modified recognition tests: Evidence for an unknown cause of interference. *Journal of Experimental Psychology: Learning, Memory, and Cognition, 15*, 256–265.

Christiaansen, R. E., & Ochalek, K. (1983). Editing misleading information from memory: Evidence for the coexistence of original and postevent information. *Memory & Cognition, 11*, 467–475.

Johnson, M. K., & Foley, M. A. (1984). Differentiating fact from fantasy: The reliability of children's memory. *Journal of Social Issues, 40*, 33–50.

Lindsay, D. S., & Johnson, M. K. (1989). The eyewitness suggestibility effect and memory for source. *Memory & Cognition, 17*, 349–358.

Loftus, E. F., & Loftus, G. R. (1980). On the permanence of stored information in the human brain. *American Psychologist, 35*, 409–420.

Loftus, E. F., Miller, D. G., & Burns, H. J. (1978). Semantic integration of verbal information into a visual memory. *Journal of Experimental Psychology: Human Learning and Memory, 4*, 19–31.

Loftus, E. F., Schooler, J. W., & Wagenaar, W. (1985). The fate of memory: Comment on McCloskey and Zaragoza. *Journal of Experimental Psychology: General, 114,* 375–380.

McCloskey, M., & Zaragoza, M. (1985a). Misleading postevent information and memory for events: Arguments and evidence against memory impairment hypotheses. *Journal of Experimental Psychology: General, 114,* 3–18.

McCloskey, M., & Zaragoza, M. (1985b). Postevent information and memory: Reply to Loftus, Schooler, and Wagenaar. *Journal of Experimental Psychology: General, 114,* 381–387.

Zaragoza, M. S. (1987). Memory, suggestibility, and eyewitness testimony in children and adults. In S. J. Ceci, M. P. Toglia, & D. F. Ross, (Eds.), *Children's eyewitness memory* (pp. 53–78). New York: Springer-Verlag.

Zaragoza, M. S., & Koshmider, J. W. (1989). Misled subjects may know more than their performance implies. *Journal of Experimental Psychology: Learning, Memory, and Cognition, 15,* 246–255.

Zaragoza, M. S., McCloskey, M., & Jamis, M. (1987). Misleading postevent information and recall of the original event: Further evidence against the memory impairment hypothesis. *Journal of Experimental Psychology: Learning, Memory, and Cognition, 13,* 36–44.

COMMENTARY: MEMORY IMPAIRMENT—IT IS MORE COMMON THAN YOU THINK

MICHAEL P. TOGLIA

Since the time of Ebbinghaus, memory researchers have shown, in a variety of paradigms, that memory is fallible and sometimes highly susceptible to forgetting. More recently, theories of forgetting have been influenced by Tulving's distinction between episodic and semantic memory (Tulving, 1972, 1986). It is now generally accepted that episodic traces are fragile memory representations that are vulnerable to interference and subject to possible modification. The fact that many sensory experiences or episodes are not remembered is not surprising, as some information that we seek or that we find ourselves confronted by will be deemed unimportant. As intelligent human information processors, we can choose to devote varying depths of processing to incoming stimulus events depending on our goals and intentions at any given moment. To a degree, then, forgetting is adaptive, the significance of which the mnemonist S, who was frequently frustrated by his inability to forget, was painfully aware (Luria, 1968).

The emphasis on episodic, personal memory is because an eyewitness to an event stores a series of episodic traces, and therefore the contents of semantic memory may influence the encoding, storage, and retrieval of a witnessed event in either a facilitory or an inhibitory fashion. Thus memory failures may involve more than just lack of sufficiently deep processing. Furthermore, memory impairment and subsequent forgetting of some aspects of witnessed events may also be due to some form of interference. Interference theory, a longstanding approach to understanding forgetting, is significant to the present discussion because most studies on the influence of postevent misinformation on eyewitness memory conform to the standard retroactive interference paradigm (cf. Brainerd & Reyna, 1988). That is, an event (sometimes a film) is presented, followed by misleading information or questions, and then subjects are tested for their retention of aspects of the original event. These procedures were pioneered by Loftus in a series of studies with adults over the last 15 years (e.g., Loftus, 1975; Loftus & Davies, 1984; Loftus, Miller, & Burns, 1978; Loftus & Palmer, 1974; Loftus, Schooler, & Wagenaar, 1985).

Loftus and her colleagues have argued that misleading postevent information competes with original information in such a manner that it alters or transforms the underlying memory, producing changes in the recollection of the event. Thus the original memory is said to be "erased" through a destructive updating process such that memory impairment is equated with trace distortion. Another interpretation of the influence of misleading postevent information suggests that memory impairment reflects retrieval failure. This position, sometimes referred to as the "coexistence hypothesis," contends that memory traces for the original and biased information coexist in memory and that the presence of the misinformation makes the process of retrieving the original information more difficult. However, a strong version of the coexistence hypothesis has been advanced by McCloskey and Zaragoza (1985a, 1985b). They have claimed that misleading postevent information has no effect at all on memory for the original episode, neither erasing it nor competing with it for retrieval.

More recently, the debate regarding the suggestibility of memory has been extended from adults to children. Ceci, Ross, and Toglia (1987b, Experiments 3 and 4), using both the standard (original) test and the modified test described in detail by Zaragoza in the preceding chapter, found evidence that postevent misleading information caused some form of memory impairment in preschoolers. However, Zaragoza (1987) studied slightly older children and found no indication that misinformation impaired memory. In Chapter 3 Zaragoza reports a series of four experiments with results that are consistent with her earlier work with older children. The main purpose of these experiments was to examine some factors that may have been responsible for why she (Zaragoza, 1987) observed different results than did Ceci et al. (1987b).

In each of the four experiments reported by Zaragoza, the event (involving a young girl spending a typical day at home) was presented in a series of color slides. The critical items consisted of fruit the girl ate and three toys that she played with during the day. The event was followed by a synopsis (presented twice) that contained misleading information about two of the critical items. Finally, subjects were tested using the modified recognition testing procedure.

In the first experiment, Zaragoza found that neither 3- nor 5-year-old children were susceptible to memory impairment. For both age levels there was a nonsignificant effect of 2% or 3% in terms of the difference between the control and the modified condition. The conclusion is that susceptibility (or lack thereof) to misleading suggestions is age invariant. Of course, to be certain of this a wider age range must be examined, and Zaragoza makes essentially this point when she calls for developmental work in her discussion of directions for future research. It is during this discussion that we discover in part, I believe, why memory impairment was not observed in her first and succeeding studies. That is, the issue of whether susceptibility to memory impairment might vary as a function of peripheral versus central details was raised because of the concern that investigators have primarily studied children's recollection of peripheral details. It is difficult to believe that this concern applies to the studies reported by Zaragoza in this volume, because it is quite likely that the critical items employed in the four experiments were very high in centrality. Recall that three of the four items were toys, which are particularly salient to young children. It should come as no surprise, then, that it might be very difficult to bias a child's memory about such items (i.e., telling him or her that a stuffed rabbit was a stuffed bear or that an airplane was a boat). In fact, the level of control performance across studies in the original and modified testing conditions was 87% and 85% correct, respectively.

Level of control performance was the focus of Zaragoza's second study, in which she examined whether or not moderately high levels of control performance are necessary to observe memory impairment. Compared to the first study, control performance increased by 9%. Of interest is that the control minus modified difference also increased (although not significantly) from about 2% to 6%. A close examination of the published literature strongly indicates that there is in fact a relationship (correlation) between control level of recognition performance and the difference in accuracy between the control and the modified (misled) conditions.

For example, for the six experiments with adults reported by McCloskey and Zaragoza (1985a) this correlation is $r = .69$. When additional data points are obtained from other studies in which the modified condition has been used (Bowman & Zaragoza, 1989, 2 data points; Ceci, Ross, & Toglia, 1987b, 2 data points; Chandler, 1989, 4 data points; Loftus, Donders, Hoffman, & Schooler, 1989, 2 data points), the correlation increases somewhat to $r = .73$. Furthermore, if you recompute the Pearson correlation with the data points provided by Zaragoza (this volume), r remains at .73. (Only 3 of her data points were used because for the other 2 points the control performance, nearly 100%, was clearly at ceiling. But even if these extreme points are included the relationship remains significant at $r = .53$). All of the researchers I have mentioned, with the exception of Zaragoza and her colleagues, demonstrated with various indices that control performance was in fact reliably better than performance in modified condition, thus indicating the presence of memory impairment.

Retention interval was addressed in Zaragoza's third study, wherein there was a two-day lag prior to the presentation of misleading information. Performance on the recognition test, administered shortly after the biasing manipulation, did not provide support for the existence of memory impairment. Procedurally, this study differs in an important way from the retention-interval studies reported by Ceci et al. (1987b). In those experiments, subjects were biased one day after the original event and tested two days following the presentation of the misleading postevent information. Clearly, a several-day retention interval applied to *both* the original and the postevent information in the Ceci et al. (1987b) work, but not in Zaragoza's third study. Arguably, retrieval difficulties and opportunities for trace confusions are much greater when retention interval potentially can affect both the original and biased events, as opposed to just the original episode. Therefore, any memory impairment that might be present is less likely to be observed under the conditions employed in Zaragoza's study. In fact, administering the test shortly following the biasing might aid or interfere with memory for the original details, depending on the strength of the traces for those details (cf., Ceci, Ross, & Toglia, 1987a). On the positive side, juxtaposing biasing and testing may more closely mimic some real-life instances of suggestibility, such as its introduction during the interviewing of a witness.

In addition to the manner in which Zaragoza manipulated retention interval, her studies differed from the prototypical Ceci et al. (1987b) experiment along other important dimensions. One such difference is that she employed adult biasers, whereas Ceci et al. had a 7-year-old provide the misinformation. And with a child biaser, Ceci et al. observed memory impairment. Still another point of contrast, noted by Zaragoza, involves the experimental design. The control versus misled manipulation has alway been within-subjects in Zaragoza's work and always between-subjects in the Ceci et al. studies. If misinformation has a "spreading effect," not just influencing critical items, such an effect would be evident only in a repeated-measures design. This is certainly a good possibility; however, in a study with adults, Bonto and Payne (1989) employed McCloskey and Zaragoza's (1985a) materials and a within-group manipulation of biasing and reported a reliable memory impairment effect.

A final issue to be addressed is, how pervasive is memory impairment? Clearly, Zaragoza has demonstrated that children's memories are not always impaired. Ceci et al. (1987b) realized this when they noted "Our own data indicate that very young children's memories *can be* distorted through postevent suggestions, not that they inevitably *will be*." When memory is degraded it may result from distortion of traces, interference with retrieval, or both. This is consonant with a large body of literature that indicates that both storage and retrieval factors promote forgetting. The view that retrieval mechanisms are solely responsible for forgetting is consistent with most versions of the coexistence hypothesis, in which it is assumed that all traces survive, such that postevent suggestions may make original memories less accessible, although still potentially retrievable at some time.

The claim that memory traces are permanent has not, however, gone unchallenged. Long ago Bartlett (1932) outlined a reconstructive view of memory and asserted that memories were susceptible to distortion. Modern-day extensions of Bartlett's work have resulted in schema theories of memory that emphasize that forgetting results from some kind of alteration of what is stored. Alteration is a major aspect of storage accounts of forgetting, implying an actual loss of information from memory. Evidence of reconstructive impairments of memory with adults and children abound, as is exemplified by studies of semantic integration (Bransford & Franks, 1971), story comprehension (Paris & Upton, 1976), memory blending (Belli, 1988), and pragmatic inference (Barclay, Toglia, & Chevalier, 1984).

Furthermore, recent work by Reyna and Brainerd (1989) has shown that forgetting based on storage failures is very common in list-learning studies with children. Consistent with the idea that storage and retrieval factors may cause impairment is the model presented by Lindberg (Chapter 4, this volume), in which he proposes not only that memory processes (encoding, storage, and retrieval) are responsible for suggestibility, but also that a complete theory of retention and memory impairment must also take into account subject characteristics and the focus of the study (i.e., memory for details, inferences, gist, etc.).

Overall, then, memory impairment in some form occurs in a wide variety of memory contexts. Yet despite contextual variability, sometimes the impairment effect is strikingly similar. For example, the acceptance by misled subjects of a novel event that bears a resemblance to the original event is not unlike the errors subjects make in studies examining memory for everyday autobiographical events. For instance, Barclay and Wellman (1986) demonstrated that after long delays people recognize a substantial number of novel events as their own memories! They argued that this suggests that we may not have direct access to stored memory traces for autobiographical memories. In a similar vein, the belief that there might be some memories that are unusually accurate, vividly retained, and highly re-sistant to forgetting, as in the case of flashbulbs memories, has been seriously questioned (McCloskey, Wible, & Cohen, 1988). McCloskey et al. concluded that flashbulb memories, like other memories, are "subject to reconstructive errors" and can be understood "in terms of ordinary memory mechanisms."

And so, is there reason to believe that there is something special about memory in the postevent misinformation paradigm? Are eyewitnesses somehow inoculated against reconstructive errors and other forms of memory impairment that are common in other memorial situations? On both counts, I must conclude that the answer is no. Although this is an important conclusion, many challenges remain in understanding susceptibility to misleading information. Clearly, there is a need to further document the conditions under which it occurs, as well as to determine the extent to which mechanisms responsible for memory impairment in adults are the same for children.

References

Barclay, C. R., Toglia, M. P., & Chevalier, D. S. (1984). Pragmatic inferences and type of processing. *American Journal of Psychology, 97*, 285–296.

Barclay, C. R., & Wellman, H. M. (1986). Accuracies and inaccuracies in autobiographical memories. *Journal of Memory and Language, 25*, 93–103.

Bartlett, F. C. (1932). *Remembering: A study in experimental and social psychology.* Cambridge, England: Cambridge University Press.

Belli, R. F. (1988). Color blend retrievals: Compromise memories or deliberate compromise responses? *Memory & Cognition, 16*, 314–326.

Bonto, M. A., & Payne, D. G. (1989, April). *Effects of misleading postevent information on accessibility of original memories.* Paper presented at the meeting of the Eastern Psychological Association, Boston, MA.

Bowman, L. L., & Zaragoza, M. S. (1989). Similarity of encoding context does not influence resistance to memory impairment following misinformation. *American Journal of Psychology, 102*, 249–264.

Brainerd, C. J., & Reyna, V. F. (1988). Memory loci of suggestibility development: Comment on Ceci, Ross, and Toglia (1987). *Journal of Experimental Psychology: General, 117*, 208–211.

Bransford, J. D., & Franks, J. J. (1971). The abstraction of linguistic ideas. *Cognitive Psychology, 2*, 331–350.

Ceci, S. J., Ross, D. F., & Toglia, M. P. (1987a). Age differences in suggestibility: Narrowing the uncertainties. In S. J. Ceci, M. P. Toglia, & D. F. Ross (Ed.), *Children's eyewitness memory* (pp. 79–91). New York: Springer-Verlag.

Ceci, S. J., Ross, D. F., & Toglia, M. P. (1987b). Suggestibility of children's memory: Psycholegal implications. *Journal of Experimental Psychology: General, 116*, 38–49.

Chandler, C. C. (1989). Specific retroactive interference in modified recognition tests: Evidence for unknown cause of interference. *Journal of Experimental Psychology: Learning, Memory, and Cognition, 15*, 256–265.

Loftus, E. F. (1975). Leading questions and the eyewitness report. *Cognitive Psychology, 7*, 560–572.

Loftus, E. F., & Davies, G. M. (1984). Distortions in the memory of children. *Journal of Social Issues, 40*, 51–67.

Loftus, E. F., Donders, D., Hoffman, H. G., & Schooler, J. W. (1989). Creating new memories that are quickly accessed and confidently held. *Memory & Cognition, 17*, 607–616.

Loftus, E. F., Miller, D. G., & Burns, H. J. (1978). Semantic integration of verbal information into a visual memory. *Journal of Experimental Psychology: Human Learning and Memory, 4*, 19–31.

Loftus, E. F., & Palmer, J. C. (1974). Reconstruction of automobile destruction: An example of the interaction between language and memory. *Journal of Verbal Learning and Verbal Behavior, 13*, 585–589.

Loftus, E. F., Schooler, J., & Wagenaar, W. (1985). The fate of memory: Comment on McCloskey and Zaragoza. *Journal of Experimental Psychology: General, 114*, 375–380.

Luria, A. R. (1968). *The mind of a mnemonist.* New York: Basic Books.

McCloskey, M., Wible, C. G., & Cohen, N. J. (1988). Is there a special flashbulb memory mechanism? *Journal of Experimental Psychology: General, 117*, 171–181.

McCloskey, M., & Zaragoza, M. (1985a). Misleading postevent information and memory for events: Arguments and evidence against memory impairment hypotheses. *Journal of Experimental Psychology: General, 114*, 1–16.

McCloskey, M., & Zaragoza, M. (1985b). Postevent information and memory: Reply to Loftus, Schooler, and Wagenaar. *Journal of Experimental Psychology: General, 114*, 381–387.

Paris, S. G., & Upton, L. (1976). Children's memory for inferential comprehension. *Child Development, 47*, 660–668.

Reyna, V. F., & Brainerd, C. J. (1989, April). *Development of forgetting: A disintegration/ redisintegration theory*. Paper presented at the meeting of the Society for Research in Child Development, Kansas City, MO.

Tulving, E. (1972). Episodic and semantic memory. In E. Tulving & W. Donaldson (Eds.), *Organization of memory* (pp. 382–403). New York: Academic Press.

Tulving, E. (1986). What kind of hypothesis is the distinction between episodic and semantic memory? *Journal of Experimental Psychology: Learning, Memory, and Cognition, 12*, 307–311.

Zaragoza, M. S. (1987). Memory suggestibility and eyewitness testimony in children and adults. In S. J. Ceci, M. P. Toglia, & D. F. Ross (Eds.), *Children's eyewitness memory* (pp. 53–78). New York: Springer-Verlag.

CHAPTER 4

AN INTERACTIVE APPROACH TO ASSESSING THE SUGGESTIBILITY AND TESTIMONY OF EYEWITNESSES

MARC LINDBERG

In 1884 a man was accused of attempting to rape two girls from a small French town. The girls' testimony was, however, somewhat contradictory. One girl said that there was something red on his penis, and the other girl said that there was something blue on his penis. As in many cases of sexual abuse, their testimony was the only evidence against the man. Should the judge have trusted their testimonies and convicted the man, or should the judge have set the man free? This question relates to the broader questions of whether we should trust the courtroom testimony of children who have witnessed crimes against themselves or others. Can young children accurately report a witnessed event or provide accurate identifications of assailants? In comparison to adults' memories, are children's memories more suggestible?

As can easily be shown, these questions about childhood memories are older that scientific psychology itself. These issues were pivotal in Freud's development of psychoanalysis. Furthermore, they helped initiate one of the more substantial research fronts in experimental psychology with such notables as Binet, Stern, Whipple, Borst, Lipmann, and Munsterberg being active leaders of this research front. Did these early experimentalists and psychoanalysts disagree on this issue of childhood suggestibility in memory? No! They all concluded that the memories of children were very prone to the effects of suggestion.

Where are we today in this controversy? Even on the notion of developmental differences in suggestibility the answer seems less clear, and it is doubtful that psychology has much more to offer the courts than it did 100 years ago. In spite of the recent deluge of studies on the psychology of courtroom testimony focusing on the malleability of memory, there is not a sound theoretical taxonomy that can organize the data on the development of suggestibility in memory performance. All we know is that under different conditions, children's memories are sometimes more suggestible, in others, less suggestible, and in still others, they do not differ from adults. Thus, although we have a long and honored history of studying these important issues, we still do not have any theoretical organization that can state the boundary conditions for consistent descriptions, let alone predictions in this confusing array of divergent data.

It could be the case that the major reason why little clarity has been offered is that different investigators have chosen to analytically explore particular variables one at a time. Although this approach has resulted in the required isolation of parameters of interest, something still seems to be missing. If there are interactions between the important variables of interest, then the study of one aspect at the expense of the others will produce an area of main effects that do not reflect the most parsimonious and heuristic level—the level of interactions between several impacting variables (see Jenkins, 1978).

A TAXONOMY OF VARIABLES AFFECTING SUGGESTIBILITY

It is my purpose in this chapter to offer such a descriptive taxonomy and then discuss it in terms of how we can organize the data and complexities in the field within a common terminology. From the outset, it should be emphasized that this is merely a descriptive taxonomy, not a predictive model. In line with most developments in a science, I believe that we must first be able to describe the phenomena of interest using a common operational vocabulary before we are able to generate more concise predictive models for phenomena within the taxonomy.

The taxonomy illustrated in Figure 1 distinguishes three major interacting classes of variables: memory processes, focus of study, and subject's characteristics. Distinguishing memory processes as one class of variables, taken from Melton (1962), raises the possibility that suggestibility can operate differentially during trace encoding, storage, or retrieval. The second distinction is that of the appropriate focus of study, which involves the type of memory being tested, that is, episodic memory for details or semantic memory for inferences, scripts, the gist, and so forth. Another dependent variable distinction that must be considered within the category of focus of study is Postman's (1964) distinction between memory for central versus peripherial information. The third theoretical class of variables has to do with the subject's characteristics and focuses on the memory

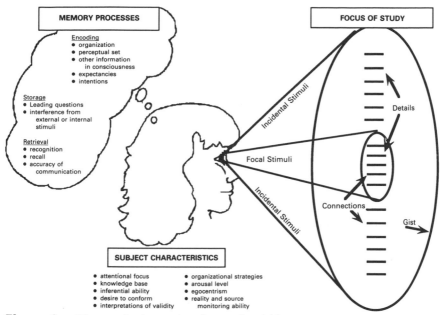

Figure 1.   Three major interacting classes of variables.

and personality characteristics displayed by children of different ages. If these main effects and their interactions can be adequately articulated, then an initial descriptive taxonomic structure can be offered that can lead to greater clarity in the suggestion literature. The present experiment was designed to manipulate some of the variables as a demonstration of the need to consider these three classes of constructs in interaction.

METHOD

The subject variable studied was that of age. There were 254 subjects consisting of third graders, sixth graders, and college students. The subjects were tested on their memories for a five-minute film about "a group of students who were taking a test." Memory process was studied by means of manipulations made either before the film, after the film, or at the time of test. Thus memory process was defined in terms of the typical retroactive inhibition design. I manipulated trace encoding (manipulations occurring before the presentation of material) by telling one group of subjects of each age that the students in the film taking the test were a group of known cheaters, the encode-cheat condition, and the other half were just told that these were students taking a test, the encode-neutral condition. Storage was manipulated by giving half of the subjects leading questions about cheating after they had seen the film (storage-cheat condition), whereas the other half were not given leading questions (storage-neutral condition). These manipulations produced a 2 × 2 × 3 (Encoding × Storage × Grade) design and permitted qualitatively different dependent variables, measurements that will now be considered.

I examined the third class of variables, those dealing with the focus of study, by asking different kinds of questions. The definitions in this class of dependent variables were borrowed from Tulving's (1972) distinctions between episodic and semantic memory. As used here, *details* refer to Tulving's notions of episodic memory whereby memory for an event from a single perceptual experience is tested—people, things, and actions that constitute perceptual units and their spatial, temporal, and perceptual attributes. That is, they are memories from only one encoded source, and they do not involve the capabilities of inferential reasoning or generalizations, or the application of rules and formulas (see Tulving, 1972). Semantic memory involves objects, concepts, and relations that are detached from autobiographical reference. Thus memories for inferences, scripts, and the gist of what happened in the film fall under this heading.

In examining the focus-of-study variables, I also made a distinction between central versus peripheral information (see Postman, 1964), whereby central information is defined as those perceived events and their attributes that are relevant to the instructed central learning task, and incidental information is defined as those perceived events and their attributes that are irrelevant to attending to the instructions. Because of the instructions given in this study, central information centered around the students and their actions and attributes, whereas incidental information referred to aspects of the situation that were independent of the student's actions—such as the actions of the teacher or the things on the back of the classroom wall. In contrast to Zaragoza's study (Chapter 3, this volume), my approach to studying suggestibility in memory is broader. In my study I maintain that memory is something that can vary qualitatively and that the essence of memory is dependent on interactions among the three classes of variables described.

RESULTS AND DISCUSSION

As I suggested earlier, these results are most understandable if they are approached in terms of the relation among the three major constructs. I first present the data on memory for the gist. Memories for the gist were studied in terms of an overall impression of the film, in this case by asking the subjects to estimate the total amount of cheating they felt went on in the film. Subjects could circle a number ranging from 0 to 8 cheaters. I found that the encoding manipulations were stronger than the storage manipulations and that these two memory processes interacted with age. When cheating was implied in both the encode and storage phases, the encode-cheat/storage-cheat condition, the third graders said that 4.10 people cheated and the college students said that 2.52 people cheated, whereas both groups held that less than 2 people cheated in the purely neutral condition (encode-neutral/storage/neutral).

What is most interesting is that the encoding and storage manipulations seemed to combine differently for the different ages. The combined encode-cheat/storage-cheat condition was much greater than either the encode-cheat/storage-neutral or the encode-neutral/storage-cheat manipulations taken alone for the children. This result was not found for the college students, for whom the combined encode-cheat/storage-cheat condition was no greater than the encode-cheat/storage neutral condition. Thus this testimony for the gist in young subjects seems to conform to Bartlett's (1932) notion that memories can interact together to produce a picture of the composite, whereas they do not seem to combine in a similar manner for college students. This also shows that manipulations at encoding and storage can combine in testimony for children and that just because one manipulates a particular memory stage, this does not mean that it is the only stage at which testimony can be influenced.

It is important to note that this particular dependent variable for the gist may not have been the best to consider. In a follow-up experiment with college students, it was found that 68% of the subjects reported that they based their judgments of the total number of cheaters on an overall impression, and the remaining 32% based it on a specific count. Thus, although a clear majority based their decisions on an overall impression, a better measure seems to be called for. One example of a more valid measure is to ask subjects to give an overall impression of what happened in their own words (i.e., a free report.)

The next focus-of-study issue involved memories for specific inferences about details in semantic memory. The first question I will deal with is whether the student who turned her test in last had cheated. Subjects in the leading questions conditions were led to believe that this student cheated; they were asked where the girl was sitting who "turned in her test last, and cheated by changing her answer after looking at the tests on the desk." It was found that younger subjects were more likely to say that this person had cheated. Whereas in the previous question on memory for the gist the encoding manipulations had the greatest effects, in this question focusing on memories for inferences about details, the storage manipulations had the greatest effects.

One can also discuss this recollection of guilt in terms of its pragmatic significance and whether these psychological manipulations can change a witness's judgment of guilt versus innocence. Although the subjects rated the item on a 6-point scale (1 = positive, she did not cheat, and 6 = positive, she did cheat), the notion of guilt versus innocence is really a 2-point decision whereby 3.5 is the midpoint. Those subjects in the encode-neutral/storage-neutral condition averaged 3.17 "innocent," whereas those in the other three conditions in which cheating was suggested averaged 4.48 "guilty." Thus this study clearly shows that memory manipulations are sufficient to alter subjects' recollections of whether they saw a crime or not.

A pure conformity hypothesis may not be the best explanation of these data. This suggestion is based on the data that emerged when subjects were asked the hypothetical question about whether looking at someone else's work would be cheating. It was found that the third graders in the storage-cheat/encode-neutral condition were significantly less confident that cheating occurred. Thus, rather than saying that the subjects became more compliant to the suggestions of the experimenter, it seems as though the storage suggestions made them adopt a more cautious strategy of saying what cheating involved. It should also be pointed out, however, that these effects were small and subjects from each grade averaged 5 or higher on the 6-point scale.

If we extend the results and conclusions from the inferential literature (cf. Paris & Lindauer, 1977), then it might be expected that older subjects would be more prone to the effects of suggestion if they use a more elaborate knowledge base to encode the information in the film. This prediction was confirmed by the question dealing with the person who asked for the time of day. Whereas the sixth graders and college students in the previous questions were less confident that cheating occurred, they tended to be more confident that this other student had cheated in the encode-cheat/storage-neutral condition. At first, this finding was surprising to the experimenters because it was assumed that this person looked quite innocent, and the question would simply serve as another baseline question. When subjects engaged in open-ended discussions after the experiment was over, the older subjects said they thought that the time question by the student was a clever cheating strategy. Thus it is obvious that one cannot make blanket statements that younger subjects are going to be more affected by suggestion. In cases such as this, older subjects can be more influenced by suggestions.

The next series of analyses explored the subjects' memories for details. A detail was operationally defined in terms of Tulving's notions of items in episodic memory. Within this class, Postman's (1964) distinction of Type II incidental learning must also be considered. According to his distinctions, central information is defined as that which the subjects were instructed to learn, and incidental information is defined as that to which they were instructed not to pay attention. According to this definition of centrality and Tulving's notion of the episodic trace as involving its spatial, temporal, and perceptual attributes, it follows that central information in the film involved anything about the students, and peripheral information involved aspects of the room and context that did not center on the students.

I first discuss a series of analyses on the central information relating to the perceptual attributes of the students in the film. In the questions about the subjects' recall of the conversations between the students, no effects of age or memory process were found because of ceiling effects. Thus it is not as if encoding and storage manipulations affect all memories for what has happened, or that children must be completely discounted on their reports of what they have seen. In this situation, in which the conversations were simple and within the comprehension of the younger subjects, all subjects displayed excellent memories.

Do these findings mean that there will be no effects of age or memory-stage manipulations on the central information, as has been suggested by some investigators (Goodman, Aman, & Hirschman, 1987)? Other findings indicate not. For example, the data on the recall of the seating arrangements of the students in the film shows that older subjects' memories were superior to young subjects.

The data on memory for details of the situation is very interesting when one examines the more incidental details of the room in which the students took their tests. It should be noted that according to Hagen, Jongeward, and Kail (1973), younger children, because of their distractibility, often show superior levels of recall for incidental items. Does this result hold for memories of eyewitnessed events? The first such analysis was performed on their recall of the teacher's instructions. It should again be pointed out that the subjects were told to pay attention to the students, not the teacher. Third graders recalled more than did sixth graders, who recalled more than did college students. Furthermore, those subjects in the neutral-encode/neutral-storage condition recalled more items than did the subjects in the other conditions. The mean recall levels were 3.63 for third graders, 3.08 for sixth graders, and 2.23 for the college students. To conclude, for this question the younger subjects had memories superior to those of older subjects, and it is again emphasized that one therefore should not automatically discount their eyewitness testimony for everything. When peripheral details are tested, or when children have excellent knowledge bases (Lindberg, 1980), their memories can be superior.

The question regarding what things were on the back of the classroom wall also tapped the subject's recall of incidental information. A significant interaction between age and storage condition was found, showing that the children performed better in the storage-neutral conditions and worse in the storage-cheat conditions relative to the college students whose recall fell between these two points. These data showing that the younger subjects were more affected by the storage manipulations seem to contradict explanations of developmental differences in suggestibility as being due to differences in measures of central versus peripheral information or trace strength. Even when encoded trace strengths could be presumed to be the same for this incidental information, it was found that younger children were more influenced by storage manipulations.

It should be noted that a follow-up experiment was conducted to empirically explore another definition of centrality. Subjects from Grade 3, Grade 6, and college rated how central they thought each of the questions were, a practice favored by other investigators (cf. Goodman et al., 1987). Different patterns of interactions on each question were found for the different ages in the different conditions tested. Furthermore, younger children displayed both better and worse retention for questions they rated as being central, and no consistent pattern emerged between the results from this rating study and the results of the present memory study. Thus the rating technique of determining centrality did not seem to work as well as the more standard definitions put forth by Postman (1964). It should also be pointed out that even if we accept what children say is most important or central to a learning task, the literature on production deficiencies suggests that younger children might not even pay attention to what they deem as central as well as do adults. Thus this other subject-defined definition of centrality does not seem to be as empirically predictive or theoretically sound.

CONCLUSION

This taxonomy for discussing the effects of suggestion on testimony performance has a number of advantages. By relating data in the fields of memory development and developmental differences in suggestibility to this tripartite taxonomy, a greater degree of order can be found. To the question, "Can we really trust the testimony of younger children?" we must answer, "It depends." It depends on the age and characteristics of the subjects, interacting with the type of memory process being manipulated and the foci under investigation.

The present study contained most of the contradictions that have been found elsewhere. If children are tested for peripheral information that they are most interested in, then developmental differences in recall may favor children over adults. However, if details central to the action are tested, then there may be differences favoring older subjects. If the inferences concerning an event are within the range of all subjects, then younger subjects may be more susceptible to the effects of suggestion at encoding. If encoding is manipulated in terms of expectancies and if the inferences are sophisticated, then older subjects may be more prone to suggestions. In comparison to testimony on the gist whereby encoding is more potent, it was found that testimony involving inferences is more affected by storage manipulations, and that these effect will be greater for children. The present data also seem to suggest that as we move from assessing testimonies for details, to assessing for inferences, to assessing to the gist, the effects of suggestions and age tend to increase. When dealing with memories for inferences, especially for the gist, it was found that encoding and storage manipulations interact in testimony for children. Thus, although we have clear definitions of encoding and storage manipulations by defining them in terms of the traditional verbal learning and cognitive literatures, it is apparent that they do not act independently of one another for the children. Although this list could go on, it is apparent that in addition to having the potential for greater pragmatic utility in discussing relations in the area of courtroom testimony, this taxonomy also has the potential advantage of better organizing data from the field theoretically. The most important aspect of this descriptive taxonomy and present data is that it is apparent that any single manipulation is meaningless in itself. On the basis of the proposed taxonomy and present data, it can be seen that it is the search for processes of interactions that will reveal the greatest pragmatic and theoretical benefits.

To conclude, let us now go back to 1884 and consider the case of the man who was accused of raping the two young girls. It can be recalled that they had conflicting testimony with regard to what they reported on the man's penis. One said that there was something blue on it, and the other said that there was something red on it. The case was solved by the clever judge who ordered the man to drop his drawers in the courtroom, displaying a red tattoo of a devil's face on the end of his penis. What this story indicated is that then, just as now, the courts will have the most advantageous posture of getting the best picture of reality in individual cases. However, I hope I have shown that knowledge of the psychology of eyewitness testimony and suggestibility can aid in that process by showing what things lead to accurate testimony and what things will lead to inaccurate testimony for different witnesses in different situations.

References

Bartlett, F. (1932). *Remembering: A study in experimental and social psychology.* Cambridge, England: Cambridge University Press.

Goodman, G. S., Aman, C., & Hirschman, J. (1987). Child sexual and physical abuse: Children's testimony. In S. J. Ceci, M. P. Toglia, & D. F. Ross (Eds.), *Children's eyewitness memory* (pp. 1–23). New York: Springer-Verlag.

Hagen, J. W., Jongeward, R. H., & Kail, E. V. (1973). Cognitive perspectives on the development of memory. In H. W. Reese (Ed.), *Advances in child development and behavior* (Vol. 10, pp. 57–101). New York: Academic Press.

Jenkins, J. J. (1978). Four points to remember: A tetrahedral model of memory experiments. In L. S. Cermak & F. I. M. Craik (Eds.), *Levels of processing and human memory (pp. 329–446).* Hillsdale, NJ: Erlbaum.

Lindberg, M. A. (1980). Is knowledge base development a necessary and sufficient condition for memory development? *Journal of Experimental Child Psychology, 30,* 401–410.

Melton, A. (1962). Implications of short-term memory for general theory of memory. *Journal of Verbal Learning and Verbal Behavior, 2,* 1–21.

Paris, S. G., & Lindauer, B. K. (1977). Constructive aspects of children's comprehension and memory. In R. V. Kail & J. W. Hagen (Eds.), *Perspectives on the development of memory and cognition* (pp. 35–60) NJ: Earlbaum.

Postman, L. (1964). Short-term memory and incidental learning. In A. W. Melton (Ed.), *Categories of human learning* (pp. 146–201). New York: Academic Press.

Tulving, E. (1972). Episodic and semantic memory. In E. Tulving & W. Donaldson (Eds.), *Organization of memory* (pp. 382–403) New York: Academic Press.

COMMENTARY:
WHEN WORDS SPEAK LOUDER
THAN ACTIONS

ELIZABETH F. LOFTUS

George saw Ann take a math test and was later questioned about what he saw. The teacher asked George a question about "the girl who turned in her test last, and cheated by changing her answer after looking at the tests on the desk." Did Ann cheat on the test? Lindberg's study bears on how George will ultimately answer this question.

Lindberg showed subjects a five-minute film of a group of students taking a test. Some subjects received an early suggestion that several students taking the test were known cheaters. Other subjects were interrogated with leading questions that implied that cheating had occurred. Lindberg showed that when interrogated with suggestive questions that implied cheating (or when led to believe in advance that known cheaters would be seen), subjects often reported that cheating is what they saw.

One of Lindberg's major interests was the timing of the suggestive information and its impact on recollection. But, unfortunately, whether suggestive information is more influential when given before the event itself or afterward cannot be readily answered by this study, because the two suggestions were quite different. When the suggestion occurred after the film, it involved supplying subjects with three tidbits of information buried (usually in a relative clause) within a list of questions: (a) some student were cheating, (b) a girl cheated by changing her answer after looking at other tests, and (c) two students in the back row cheated. To demonstrate that preevent versus postevent suggestion has different effects, one needs to design a study so that the suggestion is the same, only its timing is varied.

Lindberg was also interested in how the age of the subject influenced susceptibility to suggestion. In general, he found that suggestive questioning affected the interpretation of what happened for younger subjects (about 8 years old) more

This chapter was supported in part by National Institute of Mental Health grant MH 39575 to Elizabeth F. Loftus.

than for older ones. This is not to say that the younger subjects always performed more poorly than the older ones; in at least one case this was not so. One student in the film asked another for the time of day while the test was being taken. Was she cheating? Eight-year-olds who expected to see cheating did not see this as an instance of cheating; older subjects who expected to see cheating thought it might be a clever cheating strategy and were more likely to convict the innocent "cheater."

Another related demonstration of how words can influence the memory of actions is that of Clarke-Stewart, Thompson, and Lepore (1989). They had 5- and 6-year-old children watch an incident in which a "janitor" (affectionately dubbed Chester the Molester) followed one of two scripts while interacting with a doll. Chester either cleaned the doll or played with the doll in a rough, suggestive manner. When Chester was following the cleaning script, he engaged in various actions with the doll while saying cleaning-related words. For example, Chester sprayed the doll's face with water while uttering, "This doll is dirty. I'd better clean it." Then he looked under the doll's clothes, saying "I'd better see if it's dirty here, too." Chester also straightened the doll's arms and legs and bit off a loose thread. When Chester was following the rough-play script, his actions were essentially the same, but the words were different: "Oh goodie . . . . I like to play with dolls. I like to spray them in the face with water. I like to look under their clothes. I like to bite them and twist their arms and legs."

Like Lindberg's subjects, these children were also asked either neutral, nonsuggestive questions, or ones that were incriminating, accusing Chester of playing instead of doing his job. Finally, the children were asked to report on what they saw Chester do. The major finding was that children who were not exposed to suggestive interrogation provided answers that were reasonably accurate. However, when questioned in a suggestive manner, many of the children reported a version that was consistent with those suggestions. Chester was remembered as having played roughly with the doll when he had actually merely cleaned it.

In both studies, children witnessed an ambiguous event and then used information gained from other sources to interpret what happened. These findings are of interest because the alteration is for a recollection of actions. It has long been held that actions are special. They are the heart of many of an earlier generation of large-scale theories of meaning that were developed by cognitive psychologists (e.g., Norman & Rumelhart, 1975). And memory for actions is thought to be harder to modify than is memory for other sorts of information (Robertson, Lehnert, & Black, 1982). Yet here we see two clear instances of modification of memory for actions by the judicious use of words.

Why do children change their reports of what happened to go along with the suggestive information? Is it because their memories for what happened are distorted by the misleading suggestions? Or, are their memories intact, but social pressures induce them to provide a modified report to please the person who is asking them questions? The present studies do not shed much light on the mechanisms underlying these changes in reports.

A commonly raised question about suggestibility is whether children are more suggestible than adults. This question is typically addressed in studies in which memory for specific, concrete details is tapped. "Did Loren eat eggs at breakfast or was it cereal?" (Ceci, Ross, & Toglia, 1987). "Was a scissors used to remove a leaf or was it removed by hand?" (King & Yuille, 1987). "Was the assailant's jacket blue or black?" (Loftus, Levidow, & Duensing, 1989). In studies with critical items such as these, of which there are now many, it is common to find that young children are more influenced by suggestive misinformation than are older ones. In the three studies just cited, greater suggestibility in younger children was found, although of course this does not mean this would be true for all critical items of this type, and occasionally this result is not observed. Greater suggestibility might not be observed when the remembered detail is particularly interesting to the child or when the context is appropriately reinstated (Wilkinson, 1988).

But when it comes to the distorted interpretation of actions, new issues arise. First, very little research has been done, and any interpretations of the phenomenon of suggestibility are complicated by several considerations. Prominent among them is the fact that the child's understanding of the meaning can lack some of the features of the adult's meaning. A lovely example of this is Lindberg's finding that an adult's notion of cheating was richer and more complicated than a child's. When one student asked another for the time, an adult sometimes saw this as a clever cheating strategy, whereas for the child it seemed perfectly innocent. Differential meaning of action terms in the minds of adults and children makes it exceedingly difficult to unravel the question of who is more suggestible about what happened, and why. Wherever this line of research goes, the present step constitutes a clear demonstration that suggestive interrogations are risky: They can lead children to misinterpret what they saw.

References

Ceci, S. J., Ross, D. F., & Toglia, M. P. (1987). Suggestibility of children's memory: Psycholegal implications. *Journal of Experimental Psychology: General, 116*, 38–49.

Clarke-Stewart, A., Thompson, W., & Lepore, S. (1989, April). *Manipulating children's interpretations through interrogation.* Paper presented at the meeting of the Society for Research in Development, Kansas City, MO.

King, M. A., & Yuille, J. C. (1987) Suggestibility and the child witness. In S. J. Ceci, M. P. Toglia, & D. F. Ross (Eds.), *Children's eyewitness memory* (pp. 24–35). New York: Springer-Verlag.

Loftus, E. F., Levidow, B., & Duensing, S. (1989). *Who remembers best? Individual differences in memory for events that occurred in a science museum.* Unpublished manuscript, University of Washington.

Norman, D. A., & Rumelhart, D. E. (1975). *Explorations in cognition.* San Francisco: Freeman.

Robertson, S. P., Lehnert, W. G., & Black, J. B. (1982). *Alterations in memory for text by leading questions.* Paper presented at the meeting of the American Educational Research Association, New York.

Wilkinson, J. (1988) Context effects in children's event memory. In M. M. Gruneberg, P. E. Morris, & R. N. Sykes (Eds.), *Practical aspects of memory: current research and issues* (Vol. 1, pp. 107–111). Chichester, England: Wiley.

CHAPTER 5

THE INFLUENCE OF STRESS AND AROUSAL ON THE CHILD WITNESS

DOUGLAS P. PETERS

In the 1972 *Neil v. Biggers* decision (and later restated in the 1977 *Manson v. Bratwaite* decision), the U.S. Supreme Court specified five conditions to be considered in evaluating eyewitness evidence:

1. The opportunity of the witness to view the criminal during the crime.
2. The length of time between the crime and identification.
3. The level of certainty displayed by the witness at the time of the confrontation.
4. The past accuracy of the witness in describing the criminal.
5. The witness' degree of attention during the crime.

The research presented in this chapter was designed to investigate the influence of arousal on the eyewitness performance of children. The level of arousal experienced during the witnessed event has been viewed as relevant to the Supreme Court's degree-of-attention criterion for evaluating the likelihood of misidentification or inaccurate eyewitness evidence (Wells & Murray, 1983). In reviewing high court rulings, Ken Deffenbacher (1983) has concluded that the most common view among criminal court judges is that high arousal facilitates veridical per-

A shorter version of this manuscript, "Stress and Arousal Effects on the Child Eyewitness," was presented by the author for the symposium, Children's Ability to Remember Witnessed Events: Theoretical and Applied Perspectives, C. Brainerd (Chair), at the 1989 (April) meeting of the Society for Research in Child Development, Kansas City.

ception and thus results in better eyewitness accuracy, although in some cases the reverse opinion has been expressed, i.e., arousal degrades eyewitness memory (see Levine & Tapp, 1973). Surveys of trial attorneys and law enforcement personnel have revealed that a large majority (82%) of criminal defense lawyers and law enforcement personnel (67%) believe that high arousal leads to poorer facial recognition, while a sizeable number of the prosecutors sampled (47%) hold just the opposite view (Brigham, 1981; Brigham & Wolfskeil, 1983). Hastie's (1980) study of jury deliberations using 6-person mock juries who viewed reenactments of an actual armed-robbery trial found that stress was discussed in the context of aiding the eyewitness' accuracy in 10 of the 11 juries. However, Deffenbacher and Loftus (1982) indicated that in four different samples of laypeople, never more than 25% of those responding believed that extreme stress experienced by a crime victim would facilitate recall of the criminal act. Obviously, there seems to be some confusion among those in the criminal justice system, as well as laypersons, regarding the impact of arousal on the reliability of eyewitness testimony.

Studies with adults examining the influence of stress on eyewitness memory have produced somewhat equivocal results, with about half of the reports indicating a decrease in eyewitness accuracy as a function of increased levels of stress or arousal. Deffenbacher (1983) argues, though, that if you look only at those studies that have employed forensically relevant (i.e., high) levels of arousal, those most similar to levels experienced during criminal situations involving rape, assault, homicide, and robbery, the picture is quite clear—higher arousal levels are associated with decreased eyewitness accuracy. To explain this, the well-known Yerkes-Dodson law (Yerkes & Dodson, 1908) is invoked, which would predict that elevated levels of arousal past the optimal level for eyewitness accuracy will lead to poorer performance.

If stress and arousal experienced by an adult during an event can, in fact, impair eyewitness memory of that event, what about children? That is the question that has directed much of the research my students and I have been conducting for the past six years (e.g., Peters, 1987). We have attempted to examine young children's eyewitness memory (typically the ability to recall and recognize faces, voices, physical surroundings, and to remember actions) in the context of personally significant-meaningful events that have been known (or at least suspected) to produce elevated levels of fear or arousal in children, like a trip to the dentist, which was our first study.

STUDY 1. TRIP TO THE DENTIST

Method

Seven male dentists in Minnesota and North Dakota cooperated on this project (Peters, 1987). The subjects were 71 children (38 boys, 33 girls), 3–8 year-olds

(M = 7 years) who were visiting the dentists for the first (84%) or second (16%) time. Following their dental appointment the children were visited at their homes by a male research assistant (RA) who administered voice (through a tape player) and face (color photos) recognition tests (5-person lineups with half of the subjects receiving a target-present condition) of the dentist and his assistant, plus similar recognition tests (photos) of the dental room. A second home visit was made in which the subjects' memory of the first RA was also evaluated by voice and face recognition tests. After exposure to the targets (not significantly different in time for the two witnessing periods) memory tests were given either 24–48 hrs. or 3–4 weeks later.

Subjects gave confidence ratings (5-point Likert scale) following each memory test. Parents and dentists and dental assistants made ratings of the child's anxiety during the dental appointment, while parents and the RA provided anxiety rating for the home visits (interrater agreement: rs = .68–.78, ps < .05). Validity checks for arousal levels indicated that the children were rated (9-point Likert scale) as reliably more anxious (p < .05) during the dental visit (M = 5.8) when they were exposed to the dentist and dental assistant than during the first home (M = 4.2) visit when they interacted with the RA. (A larger absolute difference in anxiety levels would have provided a fairer test of a stress hypothesis, but in a naturalistic setting one can only hope for the best.) Would these rated differences in anxiety states affect eyewitness performance?

Results and Discussion

Since there were no significant effects of retention interval, the data were collapsed across this variable. In examining how subjects did, overall, with photo recognition (all targets combined), it is clear that target-present lineups generated more accurate responses than target-absent lineups, i.e., significantly (ps < .01) more correct identifications, 56% (true positive) versus 27% (true negative), and fewer false identifications (selecting the wrong person), 29% versus 69%. A stress effect was observed in one comparison of recognition memory for the dental visit (highest rated subject anxiety) versus the home visit (lowest rated subject anxiety). In Table 1, for target-present lineups, significantly (ps < .01) more correct identifications, 69% versus 41%, and fewer false identifications, 19% versus 39%, occurred for recognition of the research assistant versus the dentist.

A trivial association was found between anxiety ratings for the dental visit versus the home visit, r = .16, which suggests that state or situational arousal is what was being observed here and not some global or pervasive trait condition. Only for target-present lineups of the dentists and dental assistants did significant correlations (ps < .05) between anxiety level and correct identification occur, r = −.32 and −.24, respectively. When the subjects were divided into three

Table 1

PHOTO RECOGNITION AS A FUNCTION OF TARGET PRESENCE IN A LINEUP

Photo recognition		Lineup condition			
		Target present		Target absent	
		(%)		(%)	
Dentist					
	Correct response	42	(15)	26	(9)
	False ID	39	(14)	71	(25)
	False non-ID	17	(6)		
	No idea	3	(1)	3	(1)
Researcher					
	Correct response	69	(25)	28	(10)
	False ID	19	(7)	66	(23)
	False non-ID	8	(3)		
	No idea	3	(1)	6	(2)

Note. Frequencies appear in parentheses.

age groups, 7–8 ($n = 20$), 5–6 ($n = 32$), and 3–4 ($n = 19$), the oldest group was significantly more accurate ($ps < .05$), with greater correct identifications and fewer false positives, for the target-present lineups of the research assistant, than the two younger groups, which did not reliably differ. No other age or gender effects were found. Significant correlations ($ps < .05$) of confidence and recognition accuracy never got above $r = .20$. Finally, the voice recognition task (5-person, 22 s voice sample lineups equated on general voice characteristics) proved very difficult for the children. In no analysis did any voice recognition data reliably exceed chance performance.

STUDY 2: STRANGER VISITS NURSERY SCHOOL

Method

For our second study (Peters & Hagen, 1986) we went to a nursery school for 3–6-year-olds. A total of 67 children (30 boys, 37 girls) were seen by a male stranger (38-years-old) in groups of 7 to 12 each for no longer than 2 min. while being informed about a bogus health checkup that involved a procedure to measure pulse rates. Then each child was seen individually (2 min) while secretly being videotaped from across the hall as the stranger took a 1-min pulse recording (a peripheral measure of sympathetic arousal) holding the child's wrist. Following this, the children were asked some casual questions, e.g., What's your favorite TV show?, and then half (the Touched group) were vigorously rubbed on the head until they attempted to avoid the rubbing by flinching their heads away or verbally protesting. This procedure was an attempt to use a prospective design to

Table 2

SELECTED ITEMS OF THE PRESCHOOL OBSERVATIONAL SCALE OF
ANXIETY

1. Physical complaint	11. Nail-biting
2. Desire to leave	12. Sucking or chewing on objects
3. Expression of worry or fear	13. Lip licking or contortions
4. Cry with tears	14. Trembling lip
5. Scream	15. Fingers touching mouth area
6. Whine or whimper	16. Gratuitous hand, leg, foot motion
7. Trembling voice	17. Rigid posture
8. Stutter	18. Fearful facial expression
9. Whisper	19. Distraction
10. Silence to questions	20. Avoidance of eye contact

assess children's memory of physical contact with a stranger. Finally, all of the subjects were given stickers to take home and thanked for their cooperation. The exposure time for the target (stranger) was between 3–4 min.

One week later, the children were revisited at their school for memory tests that consisted of photo recognition of the stranger from 5-person lineups with half having the stranger present; voice recognition of the stranger from 5-person voice lineups with half including the stranger's voice; and asking the children if the stranger had, in addition to holding their wrist for the pulse recording, touched or rubbed them anywhere during his private meeting with them, and if so, to describe where. The interviewer was blind as to what had actually taken place.

Results and Discussion

Consistent with the results from the first study, the overall photo recognition accuracy was superior for subjects given target-present lineups versus target-absent ones, i.e., 56% (true positive) versus 18% (true negative) and 44% versus 82% false positives. The children's level of anxiety during their private meeting with the stranger was analyzed by two raters using Glennon and Weisz's (1978) Preschool Observational Scale of Anxiety, or POSA, which employs an observational methodology for recording over 20 well-defined behavioral indices of anxiety. Table 2 gives some examples. Prior use of POSA suggests that it may provide a way of evaluating situationally induced anxiety in children who are too young to accurately give verbal reports of their emotional states.

Time-sampling (20-sec intervals) of the videotape for each child was done, with anxiety-indicative behaviors being assigned a score of ''1'' for each interval in which they occurred, thus yielding a total POSA score for each child. The overall face recognition data just presented were reanalyzed using a median-split of POSA scores to divide the children into high and low anxiety groups under the target-present and target-absent conditions. These results can be seen in Table

Table 3

PHOTO RECOGNITION AS A FUNCTION OF ANXIETY LEVEL

		Target present		Target absent	
Rated anxiety		High	Low	High	Low
Correct response		37%	63%	67%	33%
	$n=$	7	12	4	2
False ID		67%	33%	48%	52%
	$n=$	10	5	13	14

3. There is a significant anxiety effect ($ps < .05$) for the subjects only in the target-present condition, where the high anxiety subjects are making more false identifications (67% vs. 33%) and fewer correct responses (37% vs. 63%).

The results of recall of physical contact revealed that for the 34 children in the Touched group a significant number (56%) made more false negative responses (did not report that the stranger had in fact touched [rubbed] their heads) than correct recall (32%) or false positives (12%) in which other parts of the body were identified ($ps < .01$). The 34 subjects in the Not Touched group were significantly more correct (79%) than incorrect (21% false positive) in their recall ($p < .001$). In looking at this data one might argue that the high rate of false negatives for those subjects who were in the Touched group, 19 of 34, reflects not a failure of memory or some motivation to lie, but rather the young child's misunderstanding or misinterpretation about the question regarding the stranger touching or rubbing him or her. Perhaps some did not consider having their heads rubbed an example of what the researcher meant by the touching-rubbing question, e.g., a "yes" answer to touching or rubbing by a stranger means more than a head rub.

To check on this possibility, we went back to the nursery and asked a similar group of children ($n = 18$) to describe the head rubbing that had happened to them. Spontaneously, without prompting, all of the children used the words "touching" or "rubbing" in their description, and when asked what would be the correct answer to the question "Did the man touch or rub you anywhere?", 17 of the children indicated that "head" would be the correct reply. One 4-year-old would not give an answer. It would thus appear that the errors the children made in recalling physical contact with the stranger were not a result of some misunderstanding of language. Recently there has been the suggestion that children may make mistakes in recalling peripheral, nonsignificant events, but they do not err when asked about things that are personally meaningful, especially actions involving their bodies (e.g., Goodman, Saywitz, Aman, & Powders, 1988). The present findings suggest that such an assertion may be somewhat premature.

Several significant correlations ($ps < .05$) were found: POSA scores and pulse rates ($r = .64$); POSA scores and correct photo identification ($r = -.27$) which indicates that the more observed anxiety the less recognition accuracy; and pulse scores and correct photo identification ($r = -.38$), suggesting that as pulse rates go up recognition accuracy decreases. It does not appear, however, that trait anxiety is what was observed. The children's teachers provided anxiety ratings of each child's overall level of anxiety and they correlated weakly with the POSA scores ($r = .24$). There was also no reliable relationship between confidence and recall or recognition accuracy.

STUDY 3: THE IMMUNIZATION CLINIC

Method

A Department of Public Health Immunization Clinic was the setting for our third stress study (Hagen, 1987). The high-stress group was comprised of 32 children who were administered shots individually in examination rooms by a nurse, while a control, low-stress group, ($n = 32$) matched for age and exposure time (5 min) were given a short talk, in small groups about immunizations. The subjects ranged in age from 3–9 years, ($M = 6.4$) years. Both groups met with the same nurse. The children who received shots counted to 10 during the immunization, while the control group children were told about the counting procedure and asked to do it once. The nurse and the children's parents made independent ratings of the child's anxiety level. Finally, the subjects were visited either 1 or 10–14 days later in their homes for memory tests.

Results and Discussion

Validity checks for arousal revealed that nurse and parent ratings of anxiety were significantly correlated ($r = .82$), and analyses of the mean ratings for the two groups of children showed a significant difference ($p < .01$) with the immunization group being perceived as more anxious, 4 points more on a 9-point Likert scale, than the no-shot control subjects. Since no significant effects of retention interval were obtained, the data were collapsed across this factor.

Recall accuracy was assessed by having the subjects provide a description of the nurse using a 12-item protocol (a modified police procedure) regarding her physical characteristics, e.g., color and length of hair. No stress effect on recall of the nurse was found. The immunization and control subjects did not differ significantly in their scores for the nurse's description. The age of the child was correlated significantly with description accuracy ($r = .41$, $p < .05$), and when the children were divided into three age groups (3–4, 5–6, 7–9 year-olds), the groups reliably differed from each other ($p < .05$) with accuracy improving with age. No significant group (stress) effects were obtained on measures of photo recognition of the nurse using 5-person lineups where target-present and target-

Table 4

ROOM RECOGNITION FOR HIGH AND LOW ANXIETY GROUPS AS A
FUNCTION OF TARGET PRESENCE IN A LINEUP

| | Lineup condition | | | |
| | Target present | | Target absent | |
Anxiety condition	High (%)	Low (%)	High (%)	Low (%)
Correct response	37.5 (6)	93.75 (15)	50 (8)	31.25 (5)
False identification	25.0 (4)	0.0 (0)	50 (8)	68.75 (11)
False nonidentification	37.5 (6)	6.25 (1)		

Note: Frequencies appear in parentheses.

absent conditions were balanced. The subjects were also given a recognition tests
of the room in which they and the nurse had interacted.

Overall, the children's eyewitness performance was much better (more correct and fewer false identifications) for the target-present condition, a common
finding in this area. There was a significant interaction ($p < .01$) of Anxiety
Condition × Lineup Condition. As shown in Table 4, with target-present lineups
the low anxiety (nonshot) group displayed 56% more correct identifications than
the high anxiety (immunization) group, 94% versus 38%, but we see a reversal
for the target-absent lineups, where the high anxiety group is slightly more accurate
(19%) but this difference is not significant, whereas the target-present difference
of 56% is ($p < .01$). For room recognition, a significant confidence-accuracy
relationship was observed ($r = .29$, $p < .05$).

STUDY 4. EVENT-STRESS AND LIVE LINEUPS

Method

In our next eyewitness study (Peters, 1988a) we decided to examine the stress
experienced at time of retrieval, in addition to that present during encoding, when
subjects witness an event. It is the only child study to date that has manipulated
in the same design both event-stress and stress during the identification procedure.
To accomplish this we employed a simulated-theft procedure. The study was
basically a 2 × 2 × 2 factorial design, with two levels of Event-Stress (staged
theft vs. no theft), two levels of Type of Lineup (live vs. photo) This is our
manipulation of stress at time of recall; Dent and Stephenson (1979) performed
a study suggesting that children's anxiety was greatly increased by having them
identify a suspect from a live lineup. Children were described as "nervous,
embarrassed, and even frightened." This reaction was not seen when they made
eyewitness identifications from photos, and two Lineup Conditions (target-present
vs. target-absent).

A total of 96 children (56 girls, 40 boys, 5–10-year-olds, $M = 7.14$ years with 90% in the 6–8-year-old range of 1st and 2nd graders) were assigned to one of the eight experimental conditions (age and gender were balanced across treatments). The subjects were left alone in a room located on the bottom floor of the Psychology Department building after finishing a card-sorting task for which they received monetary reward. The researcher and the parents left the testing room ostensibly to discuss some questions in another room as part of the study. Half of the children were told that a research assistant might come by to pick up the box containing the reward money (about $20 in coins and bills), and shortly thereafter this is what did happen.

The other half of the subjects had the money box stolen by a stranger (a 21-year-old male research assistant, or RA) who entered the room while the child was alone and, after acting surprised that the room was occupied, asked the child to show him how to do the card-sorting. While the child was distracted, the stranger grabbed the money box, slid it under his books and quickly said goodbye, making sure to shake the money box loudly as he ran out of the room. Within seconds, the researcher and the child's parent returned to the testing room. The researcher said he heard someone talking in the room, and then it sounded like someone running in the hall. He asked the child what had happened to the money box that had been on the table with the card-sorting equipment, and after being told about the stranger (all children in the theft condition reported this) the researcher ran out of the room hoping to catch the thief and recover the money. He returned two minutes later with five live lineup suspects or five color photos (explained as being found in the psychology department's file of student workers who might have access to the building during the time of the theft, late afternoon or early evening) for the subjects to examine. Each subject's gaze was directed toward each suspect in the lineup for 8 s, while the child's facial expressions were being recorded by a videocamera hidden behind a concealed one-way mirror. The identical procedure was followed for those subjects in the "no theft" condition, except that they were asked to play a memory game to see if they could identify the RA (the one who had taken the money box) from a live or photo lineup. Confidence ratings were obtained for all subjects. Parents and a RA independently rated the child's level of anxiety during his or her interaction with the stranger and during the lineup (live or photo) identification period.

Results and Discussion

Manipulation checks of the stress conditions revealed that there was good interrater agreement between parent and RA ratings (9-point Likert scale) of the children's anxiety ($r = .81$, $p < .05$), so we combined scores for one mean anxiety rating per child. Subjects showed, as anticipated, the most anxiety during the theft

Table 5

EFFECTS OF EVENT STRESS, TYPE OF LINEUP PRESENTATION, AND
TARGET PRESENCE IN A LINEUP ON EYEWITNESS MEMORY

| | Type of lineup presentation | | | |
| | Live | | Photograph | |
Event stress	Target present	Target absent	Target present	Target absent
High (theft)	(%)	(%)	(%)	(%)
correct response	33 (4)	67 (8)	75 (9)	42 (5)
false ID	8 (1)	33 (4)	17 (2)	58 (7)
false non-ID	58 (7)		8 (1)	
Low (non-theft)				
correct response	75 (9)	50 (6)	83 (10)	33 (4)
false ID	8 (1)	50 (6)	17 (2)	67 (8)
false non-ID	17 (2)		0 (0)	

Note. Frequencies appear in parentheses.

condition (7.8) versus nontheft (3.6) and during the live lineup (6.9) versus photo lineup identification (4.16). These differences were statistically significant ($ps < .01$).

The recognition findings seen in Table 5 show that the best correct identification performance (83%) was by subjects in the nontheft condition who viewed photo lineups with the target-present. The lowest number of correct identifications (33%) occurred for subjects in the high event-stress (theft) condition and who viewed a live, target-present lineup. A log-linear analysis yielded only one reliable main effect: Target-present lineups generated higher levels of recognition accuracy versus target-absent lineups. The most striking finding in this study was a 2-way interaction ($p < .01$) of Event-Stress (theft vs. no theft) × Type of Lineup (live vs. photo). This interaction revealed that only when the witnessed event was serious and anxiety provoking (i.e., the theft condition), did the presence of a live lineup impair eyewitness performance.

The level of false nonidentification, (i.e., incorrectly saying that the thief was not in the lineup) was quite high (58%) for subjects who had experienced the theft and then viewed a live, target-present lineup. The other experimental conditions yielded significantly ($ps < .01$) less false nonidentifications, ranging from 0–17%. Several parents (4 out of a possible 7) of children from this one group that had so many false nonidentifications, said in follow-up conversations that their children had been afraid to identify the thief whom they did recognize in the live lineup. They said that their children were afraid something bad might happen, or that someone would get into trouble. No other parents from any other conditions suggested that their children had reported doing such a thing, withholding a positive identification when the target was in fact recognized. It is encouraging to see that, if what these parents are reporting is true (we have no reason to suspect otherwise), their children made an error of omission—withholding a positive identification—that is viewed in our society or system of criminal justice, as much less serious than the alternative mistake, falsely accusing an innocent suspect.

What is also suggested here is that the poor eyewitness performance for this group of children, 58% incorrect nonidentifications, was not a failure of memory, but rather the result of powerful social factors which can inhibit or impair eyewitness accuracy. Evidence of this type underscores the necessity for studying children's eyewitness identification and testimony with designs that do not remove children from the social and motivational contexts they are likely to experience in real life. These results may have some relevance for discussions regarding "shield laws," the practice in some states where child witnesses in sexual abuse cases, for example, are shielded from the defendant in a physical sense by the use of something like a screen placed in front of the defendant, which allows the child to testify without having to experience the presumed stress of directly confronting the suspected child abuser. One may note that this procedure has been ruled unconstitutional (it violates the defendant's right to confront his or her accusers) in the recent *Coy v. Iowa* (1988) Supreme Court case. However, in a more recent ruling, *Maryland v. Craig* (1990), the testimony of children by means of one-way, closed-circuit television was judged admissable under certain circumstances. Our findings with the live lineup identifications would suggest that increasing confrontational stress will impair eyewitness performance, at least with young children.

Event-anxiety was negatively correlated with subjects age ($r = -.38, p < .05$), indicating that the younger children were perceived as displaying greater amounts of anxiety during the time the confederate was alone in the room with them. Lastly, subject confidence in his or her identification was not reliably related to age, but was to correct identification ($r = .26, p < .05$).

STUDY 5: FIRE ALARM AND SUGGESTIBILITY

Method

The last study to be presented looked at, in addition to event-stress, the effects of misleading information on eyewitness performance, a topic of considerable interest within eyewitness research (e.g., Ceci, Toglia, & Ross, 1987). A total of 64 children (6–9-year-olds, $M = 7.3$ years) came to a room located on the top (4th) floor of the Department of Psychology building for a "study of children's physical characteristics and skills." A 2 × 2 factorial design with two levels of Event-Stress (fire alarm vs. no fire alarm) and two levels of Type-of Question (misleading vs. neutral) was used. The children progressed through seven phases in the study:

1. Measures of body weight, blood pressure, and pulse were taken.
2. A card-sorting task was administered and all subjects received a monetary reward, 25 cents, for superior performance, "being in the top half of their age group."
3. Subjects were asked a few personal questions regarding such things as their favorite food and TV show.
4. Ten seconds before a 20-year-old female confederate (the target) entered the room, a fire alarm (smoke detector) went on for the subjects in the fire alarm condition, while the no-fire-alarm subjects had a radio turned on at the same time. Blood pressure and pulse recordings were taken for a second time during this period, thus providing physiological measures of the children's arousal in the two groups.
5. For approximately 1 min the confederate acted out a rehearsed script. She explained why she entered the room (i.e., for the fire alarm condition—she is worried about a fire and wants to see if others in the building smell smoke; in the no-fire-alarm condition—she wants to look outside the window to see if a delivery truck is moving equipment into the building), goes to the window, looks out and makes several comments, starts to leave but drops something on the floor, and finally departs, indicating where she is going. Ten seconds after the confederate leaves, the fire alarm and the radio were turned off. The researcher comments about a false alarm, "There have been several in the past few weeks," when the fire alarm stops.
6. A second card-sorting task was given with each child receiving a 25-cent reward.
7. And finally, a set of memory tests were administered. The children's parents had prior knowledge of the procedures and were in the testing room with their child at all times.

The subjects were asked to give a free narrative of what took place when the confederate entered the room, including information about what she did and what she looked like. These narratives were recorded on audiotape for later analyses. Next, 10 objective (yes/no) questions (e.g., "Did the girl knock on the door before coming in?", "Did the girl wear glasses on her face?", "Was the girl carrying a cup in her hands?", "Did the girl say why she came into the room?") with five critical items concerning the 1-min period when the confederate was in the room were asked. Half of the fire alarm and no-fire-alarm subjects received misleading information for the critical items, e.g., "Did the girl wearing a yellow sweater have brown hair" (vs. "Did the girl have brown hair?"), "While you were doing the card-sorting, did the girl give anything to your mommy or daddy?" (vs. "Did the girl give anything to your mommy or daddy?"), "After she saw people running out of the building, did the girl see a firetruck outside the window?"

(vs. "Did the girl see a firetruck outside the window?"), "Was the girl angry when she dropped her purse on the floor?" (vs. "Was the girl angry when she dropped something on the floor?"). The other half of the subjects received the neutral wording for the critical questions as stated in parentheses.

After this the children were given a filler task of drawing a picture of their home with as many people and things as they wanted. At the end of 5 min they explained their drawings and received praise by the experimenter. Next, the subjects were given a test to evaluate the influence of the misleading questions. The suggestibility test consisted of two-alternative forced-choice questions for the five critical items, e.g., "Did the girl wear a white or yellow sweater?", "When the girl was in the room, were you doing the card-sorting or having your blood pressure taken?", "Did the girl see any people running out of the building when she looked out of the window?", "Did the girl drop her purse or keys on the floor?" Finally, 6-person photo lineups were given to the subjects to evaluate their recognition memory of the confederate's appearance. Half of the subjects saw lineups in which the confederate was present while half were given target-absent lineups. The children also provided confidence ratings for this task.

Results and Discussion

The fire alarm and no-fire-alarm subjects did not reliably differ on the first blood pressure or pulse rate recordings, but did for the second. The fire alarm group showed a systolic and diastolic increase of 11.2 and 7 points, respectively, compared to a 1.8 and 3 point rise for the no-fire-alarm subjects ($ps < .05$). The greatest difference between the two groups was seen with pulse rates. The fire alarm group increased their pulse scores by an average of 23.7 points versus a slight decrease of -0.7 for the no-fire-alarm group ($p < .001$). These findings, especially the 23-point elevation in pulse rate, provide strong evidence that the fire alarm manipulation was effective in producing high levels of arousal.

Analyses of the free recall narratives yielded nonsignificant differences between the fire alarm and no-fire-alarm subjects, although the no-fire-alarm group did make more correct statements and fewer incorrect ones. On the 10 objective questions regarding the period when the confederate was in the room, the no-fire-alarm group was superior in recall to the fire alarm group, 82.5% versus 72.5% correct ($p < .04$).

An analysis of variance performed on the suggestibility data (accuracy on the five critical questions) revealed a significant ($p < .01$) interaction between Type-of-Question and Event-Stress. When subjects were in the no-fire-alarm condition (low stress), they showed a 20.9 point suggestibility effect, i.e., better eyewitness performance following neutral-worded versus misleading questions (77.5% vs. 56.6% correct recall), but the effect was even greater, 32.2 points

Table 6

PERCENT CORRECT RECALL AS A FUNCTION OF QUESTION BIAS AND
AROUSAL LEVEL

	Arousal condition	
Question bias	Fire alarm	No fire alarm
	(%)	(%)
Misleading	36.6	56.6
Neutral	68.8	77.5

(68.8% vs. 36.6% correct recall) when subjects experienced the fire alarm (high stress) condition. Both main effects, Event-Stress and Type-of-Question, were significant with recall being superior for the no-fire-alarm versus fire alarm condition (67.1% vs. 52.7% correct, $p < .05$) and the neutral-worded versus misleading questions (73.2% vs. 46.6% correct, $p < .01$). In looking at the data presented in Table 6, it is clear that for our subjects the experience of high stress in the fire alarm condition coupled with a series of misleading questions greatly reduced their eyewitness accuracy. In fact their level of recall, 36.6% correct, is significantly ($p < .04$) below what would be expected on the basis of chance alone, 50% for a yes/no decision.

The results of the photo recognition can be seen in Table 7. As has been consistently found throughout this research, the subjects were more accurate when shown target-present versus target-absent lineups (61.5% vs. 48% correct identification, $p < .05$). The effect of Event-Stress was also significant with subjects in the no-fire-alarm condition doing better than those in the fire alarm condition (65% vs. 44% correct identification, $p < .01$). There was a small but reliable confidence-accuracy relationship ($r = .23$, $p < .05$). Additional analyses failed to yield any significant effect of gender or age, although older children typically gave more detail on the free recall task.

A recent paper (Ochsner & Zaragoza, 1988) presented at the 1988 meeting of the American Psychology and Law Society reported that first graders who witnessed a theft in groups of three were less suggestible than children who viewed a neutral (and presumably less stressful) event, and were more accurate on some

Table 7

PHOTO RECOGNITION ACCURACY AS A FUNCTION OF AROUSAL LEVEL
AND LINEUP CONDITION

	Arousal condition	
Lineup condition	Fire alarm	No fire alarm
	(%)	(%)
Target present	52	71
Target absent	36	60

recall tasks. Unfortunately, methodological difficulties with this interesting study (primarily a confounding of the theft manipulation and the motivation-relevant behavior of the experimenter following the theft versus the neutral event), as well as the presence of group witnessing and the absence of recognition tests and different age groups, make comparisons with the present investigation difficult, and thus the significance of this data for our findings remains unclear.

CONCLUSION

The overall picture regarding arousal effects from this research based on observations of close to 400 children in which several measures of stress or arousal were used (parent, experimenter, and teacher ratings; behavioral indices of arousal the POSA scores from videotapes analyses; and physiological recordings, pulse and blood pressure) in five different settings (three naturalistic, two laboratory simulations) is that high arousal levels during event witnessing can, at times (like in the adult literature—for recent evidence see Christianson, Nilsson, Mjorndal, Perris, Tjellden, 1987; Christianson & Nilsson, 1984; Peters, 1988b) impair the eyewitness performance of children. The last experiment presented in this chapter raises the possibility that highly aroused children may also be more susceptible to misleading postevent information.

One group of researchers (Goodman, Aman, & Hirschman, 1987; Goodman, Rudy, Bottoms, & Aman, in press), have generally failed to find any reduction in eyewitness accuracy for their high arousal subjects, children who received inoculations and venipuncture. The one exception (from their immunization study) is where recognition accuracy with photo lineups is better for the low stress as compared to high stress subjects (62% vs. 40% correct identification), a finding consistent with the recognition results presented in this chapter. Unfortunately this research, done in real-world settings where methodological considerations must often be compromised, is plagued with a number of problems. These include small samples (e.g., $n < 10$ for high stress groups), resulting in low research power, making it more likely that the null hypothesis will not be rejected; potential health differences between high and low stress groups (e.g., children needing growth hormone treatment or have been exposed to hepatitis versus normal-health subjects); the use of single ratings or measures of anxiety/stress; questionable control groups (e.g., calling the rubbing of a decal of a syringe on a child's arm- "low" stress); and uncertainty about what the anxiety measure actually reflects (a dispositional/trait characteristic, or situational, event-produced arousal?). The utility of this work remains limited until these problems are overcome.

It should be noted that in our studies, sometimes arousal effects did not materialize and it is important to discover the reasons why. What are the variables that interact with or moderate the impact of stress on the eyewitness performance of children? Christianson, et al. (1986) have data that suggest that emotional arousal may mediate memory deficits only when the source of arousal is related to the to-be-remembered material. High arousal per se may be ineffective. I would hasten to add that we should not only study arousal when it occurs at the time of witnessing, but also later during times of suspect identification and pretrial and trial testimony. If the child witness experiences high levels of stress relating to the confrontational aspects of a criminal case, then it is important to discover exactly what impact this will have on the child's performance as a reliable witness. The implication from the live lineup findings reported here (Study 4), if they can be generalized, is that child witness-defendant confrontations can have a substantial negative effect on the child's ability or willingness to be accurate.

One fact is very apparent from our data. Heightened arousal never increased the recognition or recall accuracy of our subjects. Based on these findings, the unconditional belief, apparently held by a large number of trial judges and prosecutors, as well as many potential jurors, that high arousal facilitates the eyewitness accuracy of children, does not appear to rest on solid empirical ground.

References

Brigham, J. C. (1981, November). The accuracy of eyewitness evidence: How do attorneys see it? *The Florida Bar Journal, 55,* 714–721.

Brigham, J. C., & Wolfskeil, M. P. (1983). Opinions of attorneys and law enforcement personnel on the accuracy of eyewitness identifications. *Law and Human Behavior, 7,* 337–349.

Ceci, S. J., Toglia, M., & Ross, D. (1987). *Children's eyewitness memory.* New York: Springer-Verlag.

Christianson, S., & Nilsson, L. (1984). Functional amnesia as induced by a psychological trauma. *Memory & Cognition, 12,* 142–155.

Christianson, S., Nilsson, L., Mjorndal, T., Perris, C., & Tjellden, G. (1986). Psychological versus physiological determinants of emotional arousal and its relationship to laboratory induced amnesia. *Scandinavian Journal of Psychology, 27,* 300–310.

Coy v. Iowa, 108 S.Ct. 2798 (1988).

Deffenbacher, K. (1983). The influence of arousal on reliability of testimony. In B. R. Clifford & S. Lloyd-Bostock (Eds)., *Evaluating witness evidence* (pp. 235–251). Chichester, England: Wiley.

Deffenbacher, K., & Loftus, E. F. (1982). Do jurors share a common understanding concerning eyewitness behavior? *Law and Human Behavior, 6,* 15–30.

Dent, H. R., & Stephenson, G. M. (1979). Identification evidence: Experimental investigations of factors affecting the reliability of juvenile and adult witnesses. In Farrington, Hawkins, & Lloyd-Bostock (Eds)., *Psychology, law and legal processes.* Atlantic Highlands, NJ: Humanities Press.

Glennon, B., & Weisz, J. R. (1978). An observational approach to the assessment of anxiety in young children. *Journal of Consulting and Clinical Psychology, 46,* 1246–1257.

Goodman, G. S., Aman, C., & Hirschman, F. (1987). Child sexual and physical abuse: Children's testimony. In S. J. Ceci, M. P. Toglia, & D. F. Ross (Eds.), *Children's eyewitness memory* (pp.1–23). New York: Springer-Verlag.

Goodman, G. S., Rudy, L., Bottoms, B. L., & Aman, C. (in press). Children's concerns and memory: Ecological issues in the study of children's eyewitness testimony. In R. Fivush & J. Hudson (Eds.), *What young children remember and why*. Boston: Cambridge University Press.

Goodman, G. S., Saywitz, K., Aman, C., & Powders, M. (1988, March). *How suggestible are children? A new view of the child victim/witness in sexual assault cases*. Paper presented at the biannual meeting of the American Psychology and Law Society, Miami.

Hagen, S. (1987). The effects of arousal on children's memories in a natural setting. Unpublished master's thesis, University of North Dakota, Grand Forks, ND.

Hastie, R. (1980). *From eyewitness testimony to beyond reasonable doubt*. Unpublished manuscript, Harvard University.

Levine, F. J., & Tapp, J. L. (1973). The psychology of criminal identification: The gap from Wade to Kirby. *University of Pennsylvania Law Review, 121,* 1079–1131.

Manson v. Braithwaite, 97 S. Ct. 2243 (1977).

Maryland v. Craig, 110 S. Ct. 3157 (1990).

Neil v. Biggers, 409 U.S. 188, 93 S. Ct. 375, 34 L. Ed. 401 (1972).

Ochsner, J. C., & Zaragoza, M. (1988, March). *Children's eyewitness testimony: Accuracy and suggestibility of a memory for a real event*. Paper presented at the biannual meeting of the American Psychology and Law Society, Miami.

Peters, D. P. (1987). The impact of naturally occurring stress on childrens' memory. In S. J. Ceci, M. P. Toglia, & D. F. Ross (Eds.), *Children's eyewitness memory* (pp.122–141). New York: Springer-Verlag.

Peters, D. P. (1988a, March). The effects of event-stress during lineup identifications on eyewitness accuracy in children. In D. Peters (Chair), *The child witness today: Research and international perspectives*. Symposium conducted at the meeting of the American Psychology and Law Society, Miami.

Peters, D. P. (1988b). Eyewitness memory and arousal in a natural setting. In M. M. Gruneberg, P. E. Morris, & R. N. Sykes (Eds.), *Practical aspects of memory: Current research and issues. Vol. 1: Memory in everyday life* (pp.89–94). Chichester: Wiley.

Peters, D. P. (1989, April). *Stress and arousal on the child eyewitness*. Paper presented at the Children's Ability to Remember Witnessed Events: Theoretical and Applied Perspectives, C. Brainerd, Chairman. Society for Research in Child Development, Kansas City.

Peters, D. P., & Hagen, S. (1986, May). *A Stranger at daycare: Preschoolers' memory of physical contact, faces, and voices*. Paper presented at the meeting of the Midwestern Psychological Association, Chicago.

Wells, G. L., & Murray, D. M. (1983). What can psychology say about the *Neil v. Biggers* criteria for judging eyewitness accuracy? *Journal of Applied Psychology, 68,* 347–362.

Yerkes, R. M., & Dodson, J. D. (1908). The relation of strength of stimulus to rapidity of habit formation. *Journal of Comparative Neurology and Psychology, 18,* 459–482.

COMMENTARY: ON STRESS AND ACCURACY IN RESEARCH ON CHILDREN'S TESTIMONY

GAIL S. GOODMAN

Understanding the effects of stress on memory has important implications for justice and psychological theory. If stress is detrimental to memory, people who experience or witness violent crime may have difficulty accurately reporting events. If stress is beneficial to memory, reports of particular clarity might result. These two possibilities are often debated in courts of law and motivate much of the relevant psycholegal research. In this commentary I will argue that dichotomous thinking of this sort is overly simplistic, and that it is time to move on to more sophisticated approaches— for example, those linked with current emotion theory. Before doing so, I will provide a brief introduction and then comment on Peters' research.[1]

In 1984, when I first investigated children's testimony for stressful events, I could not find a single scientific study (published or unpublished) on this topic. Relevant case studies examining children's memory for traumatic events (Terr, 1981) and relevant scientific research on adults existed, but the findings were mixed. As Yuille and Cutshall (1986) point out, Deffenbacher's (1983) often-cited review reveals that detrimental effects of arousal on memory were associated mainly with artificial studies, while beneficial effects were associated with studies using real-life events.

My students and I now have carried out a variety of studies on children's memory for stressful events (e.g., Goodman, Aman, & Hirschman, 1987; Goodman, Bottoms, Schwartz-Kenney, & Rudy, 1991; Goodman, Reed, & Hepps, 1985; Goodman, Hirschman, Hepps, & Rudy, 1991). Others have pursued similar questions (e.g., Merten, 1987; Ochsner & Zaragoza, 1988; Peters, this volume; Warren-Leubecker & Springfield, 1987). Some of our findings conflict. For example, Ochsner and Zaragoza (1988) and Goodman et al. (in press) find that higher stress is associated with increased recall and reduced suggestibility. Peters

---

[1] Although I will use the terms *stress* and *arousal* interchangeably here, it should be noted that stress, anxiety, arousal, and fear actually may refer to a variety of emotional states with somewhat different mental, physiological, and behavioral manifestations.

(1987; this volume) reports several detrimental effects of stress on memory. Goodman, Bottoms, Schwartz-Kenney, and Rudy (1991) found neither detrimental or beneficial effects of stress on children's memory. Although our findings disagree, we do have one thing in common: We all have faced a number of thorny methodological and conceptual issues over the years.

METHODOLOGICAL ISSUES

Although Peters' research is impressive in the number of children and situations studied, a close examination reveals difficulties. Some of these difficulties are inherent in research on stress and memory, due in large part to ethical constraints. Some are more specific to Peters' research. Some of the latter difficulties may be resolved by Peters, here or elsewhere, by the time the present commentary goes to press. In any case, my goal in this critique is to point out some pitfalls that future researchers may want to avoid, using Peters' work as an example.

The study in which 3- to 8-year-olds visited the dentist represents Peters' earliest research on stress and memory and is perhaps the most problematic. After a delay, a research assistant (RA) came to the children's home to administer memory tests about the dentist visit. Following a second delay, another RA visited the children to administer memory tests concerning the first RA. Peters reports that stress was detrimental to correct identification. Is this conclusion valid? One problem is that age and stress levels were positively related ($p < .05$, see Peters, 1987). Because younger children typically perform relatively poorly on identification tests and the younger children were more stressed, age may account for Peters' findings. Presenting simple correlations without controlling for age is insufficient (see Peters, 1987). As Peters rightly concluded, "the data here are somewhat equivocal with respect to the issue of stress and eyewitness memory" (1987, p. 131).

Second, differences in identification of the dentist and RA might result from differences in task difficulty. Photo-identification tasks can be made easy or hard depending on the distractor pictures chosen. The lineups should be equated in difficulty (not just in functional size; see Peters, 1987), or better, the same confederate and lineup should be used across stress conditions. Finally, although an attempt was made to equate exposure time for all of the children, the amount of time spent looking at the dentist and his assistant was probably limited. Because children may have closed their eyes, stared at ceiling lights and dental instruments, and generally looked away from the dentist when the dentists hands were in the children's mouths, actual exposure time to the dentist and the dental assistant may have been less than to the RA.

In sum, we can have little confidence of detrimental effects of stress on memory based on this study. Moreover, it is unclear that the children were actually stressed.

Only one of 71 received a filling. Most simply had a check-up or cleaning (see Peters, 1987). Finally, Peters uses a 9-point scale, only one point of which indicates lack of anxiety. Such scales pull for ratings of anxiety even when little exists.

For Study 2, a confederate engaged in a brief interaction (including rubbing the heads of half of the children), with 3- to 6-year-olds at their preschool. The children were later questioned. Peters reports that the more anxious children were less accurate in identifying the confederate. Again, possible age effects are uncontrolled: Children were divided into high and low stress groups with no attention paid to the likelihood that the more stressed children were also younger. Given this possible confounding, it is difficult to conclude anything about the relation between stress and memory. If the relation is still found when age is statistically controlled, the result is still open to question. Dividing children into more or less stressed groups carries with it the typical burden carried by correlational studies. A third factor (e.g., intelligence) could account for the findings. We faced the same problem in our work in which beneficial effects of stress on memory were uncovered (Goodman, Hirschman, Hepps, & Rudy, 1991). It is a relatively common problem in this area of research.

In Study 3, Peters attempts a partial replication of my research on children's memory for immunizations. As nonstressed controls, groups of children heard a lecture by a nurse about immunizations. Stress did not affect the children's ability to describe or identify the nurse. Children who were immunized had more difficulty identifying the room, however. But the rooms were not the same for immunization and control children. Again, the room lineups may have differed in difficulty, with the lineup for the lecture hall easier than the lineup for the immunization clinic, or one room may simply have been more memorable than the other. Once again, we learn little about the effects of stress from this study.

Study 4 is the most interesting. Children viewed either a man stealing some money or an RA retrieving some money; they were then either tested with live or photo lineups. The study is a partial replication of Dent's (1977) groundbreaking research, but with several additional features added, such as stress at the time of the event. Peters finds that children in the theft-and-live lineup condition were less accurate in that they more often refused to make an identification. These findings replicate Dent's, except that children in her study made more nonidentification errors even when the initial event was nonstressful.

In discussing Study 4, Peters makes the reasonable point that it is important to test children in the motivational and social context real witnesses find themselves in. These contexts vary considerably, however. Some situations involve little intimidation, some a considerable amount; some involved repeated interviewing of children, some do not; and so forth. In any case, Study 4 has important implications for how children may respond to face-to-face confrontation in court, at depositions, and in defendant-present interviews. The findings imply that children may be easily intimidated into silence and that special care is needed to encourage their potentially valuable testimony. In my opinion, it is here that Peter's work shines the brightest, methodologically and in terms of application.

Finally, what of Study 5, in which a fire alarm or radio was turned on while a woman entered the room, looked out the window, dropped something, said various things, and left? In the fire alarm condition, the woman entered to see if others smelled smoke; in the no-fire-alarm condition, the woman entered to see whether a delivery truck was moving furniture into a building. The children's memory, including their suggestibility, was later assessed. As Ochsner and Zaragoza (1988) point out, it may be possible to obtain any pattern of results depending upon the questions asked. For example, one misleading suggestion used by Peters is that when the woman looked out the window, she saw people running out of the building. Given an active fire alarm, people would be expected to evacuate, but they would not be expected to do so when furniture was being moved into a building. Thus, the suggestion may have been more acceptable to fire-alarm children regardless of stress. Moreover, for both the objective and misleading questions, Peters presents proportion correct responses. What if the children said "I don't know" or gave some other answer that was not really incorrect? Especially for assessing children's suggestibility, presentation of the proportion of commission errors (i.e., errors of actually accepting the suggestion) is important. It is possible that Study 5 contributes valuable information, but one cannot tell from the present write-up.

Peters' Critique of My Research

Peters makes several avoidable errors in describing my own studies, and these require correction. Goodman, Saywitz, Aman, and Powders (1988) did not contend that children never or rarely make errors when asked about personally meaningful events involving their bodies. In fact, Goodman et al. (1908) reported that children made errors about the touching of their bodies, but noted that many more omission than commission errors were made (see also Goodman & Clarke-Stewart, this volume; Saywitz, Goodman, Nicholas, & Moan, 1989). Peters replicates this pattern of results. However, it is true that in a number of my studies, children at least by the age of 4 to 5 years have been surprisingly accurate in resisting misleading "abuse" questions such as "He took your clothes off, didn't he?", when in fact the children's clothes had remained on (see Goodman & Clarke-Stewart, this volume). In a recent study (Goodman & Schwartz-Kenney, in press; Tobey, 1991), we have again found high resistance to abuse suggestions when 4-year-olds were led to believe that an actual police investigation was ongoing (although other errors were evident). These new results are relevant not only to Peters' critique of my research but also to that provided by Raskin and Esplin (this volume).

Second, regarding the procedures in Goodman et al.'s inoculation studies, the research is now published, enabling readers to evaluate them on their own. I am confident that readers will realize that all research on stress and children's memory has important strengths and limitations, but that despite the latter, such research is well worth conducting.

CONCEPTUAL ISSUES

Because of the above mentioned and other methodological problems, it is little wonder that discrepancies exist in the literature on stress and children's memory. Nevertheless, it is worth considering whether the discrepancies can be resolved on a conceptual rather than a purely methodological level. One possible resolution requires abandonment of arousal as the main theoretical construct and adoption of a discrete-emotions approach (e.g., Izard, 1978). By considering that discrete emotions (fear, anger, joy) guide attentional processes based on emotion-related goals, a resolution may be possible (see Goodman, Hirschman, Hepps, & Rudy, 1991). This orientation, which fits better with current emotion theory, would lead to the prediction that stress can have detrimental or beneficial effects on memory depending upon the information tested. In general, we need more attention to proposed mechanisms rather than continued adherence to value concepts like arousal and pseudo-explanations such as the well-worn Yerkes-Dodson Law. (This law is a valuable and debatable empirical generalization. In itself, it does not explain anything.)

CONCLUSION

I find myself sympathetic to Peters' research program and to the unavoidable weaknesses in his paper (weaknesses that many studies on stress and memory share, such as inevitable differences in stimuli across high and low stress groups), but I am distressed by the avoidable weaknesses. If, as Peters claims, conclusions are unclear from my work and that of Ochsner and Zaragoza (1988), better studies than his also are needed to resolve the problems.

References

Bulkley, J. A. (1988). After *Coy v. Iowa*: The status of videotaping, closed-circuit television and other methods of taking a child victim's testimony outside the defendant's presence. *Children and the law*. Washington, DC: American Bar Association.

Deffenbacher, K. (1983). The influence of arousal on reliability of testimony. In S. M. A. Lloyd-Bostock & B. R. Clifford (Eds)., *Evaluating eyewitness evidence* (pp. 235–251). New York: Wiley.

Dent, H. R. (1977). Stress as a factor influencing person recognition in identification parades. *Bulletin of the British Psychological Society, 30,* 339–340.

Goodman, G. S., Aman, C., & Hirschman, J. (1987). Child sexual and physical abuse: Children's testimony. In S. Ceci, M. Toglia, & D. Ross (Eds.), *Children's eyewitness memory* (pp. 1–23). New York: Springer-Verlag.

Goodman, G. S., Bottoms, B. L., Schwartz-Kenney, B., & Rudy, L. (1991). Children's memory for a stressful event: Improving children's reports. *Journal of Narrative and Life History, 1,* 69–99.

Goodman, G. S., Hirschman, J., Hepps, D., & Rudy, L. (1991). *Children's memory for a stressful event.* Merrill-Palmer Quarterly, 37, 109–158.

Goodman, G. S., Reed, R. S., & Hepps, D. (1985, August). The child victim's testimony. In M. Toglia (Chair), *Current trends in evaluating children's memory for witnessed events.* Symposium presented at the meeting of the American Psychological Association, Los Angeles, CA.

Goodman, G. S., Rudy, L., Bottoms, B. L., & Aman, C. (1990). Children's memory and children's concerns: Issues of ecological validity in the study of children's eyewitness testimony. In R. Fivush & J. Hudson (Eds.), *Knowing and remembering in young children* (pp. 249–284). NY: Cambridge University Press.

Goodman, G. S., & Schwartz-Kenney, B. (in press). Why knowing a child's age is not enough: Effects of cognitive, social, and emotional factors on children's testimony. In R. Flin & H. Dent (Eds.), *Children as witnesses.* London, Wiley.

Goodman, G. S., Saywitz, K., Aman, C., & Powders, M. (1988, March). A new view of children's suggestibility. Presented in D. Peters (Chair), *Children's testimony.* Symposium, American Psychology and Law Association Meetings, Miami Beach, Florida.

Izard, C. E. (1978). Emotions as motivations. An evolutionary-developmental perspective. In R. A. Dienstbier (Ed.), *Nebraska Symposium on Motivation,* (pp. 163–200). Lincoln, NE: University of Nebraska Press.

Merten, P. G. (1987). *Immunization study.* Unpublished manuscript.

Oschsner, J. E., & Zaragoza, M. S. (1988, March). *The accuracy and suggestibility of children's memory for neutral and criminal eyewitness events.* Paper presented at the American Psychology and Law Meetings, Miami, FL.

Peters, D. P. (1987). The impact of naturally occurring stress on children's memory. In S. J. Ceci, M. P. Toglia, & D. F. Ross (Eds.), *Children's eyewitness memory* (pp. 122–141). New York: Springer-Verlag.

Saywitz, K. J., & Goodman, G. S., Nicholas, E., & Moan, S. (1989, April). Children's testimony for a genital examination: Implications for children's testimony in child sexual abuse cases. In G. S. Goodman (Chair), *Do children provide accurate eyewitness reports?* Symposium conducted at the meeting of the Society for Research in Child Development, Kansas City, MO.

Terr, L. (1981). Psychotrauma in children: Observations following the Chanchilla school bus kidnapping. *American Journal of Psychiatry, 138,* 14–19.

Tobey, A. (1991). *Children's eyewitness testimony: Effects of participation and forensic realism.* Unpublished Masters Thesis, State University of New York at Buffalo, Buffalo, NY.

Yuille, J. C., & Cutshall, J. (1986). A case study of eyewitness memory of a crime. *Journal of Applied Psychology, 71,* 291–301.

Warren-Leubecker, A., & Springfield, M. R. (1987, April). *Flashbulb memory revisited: Children recall the space shuttle accident.* Paper presented at the Society for Research in Child Development, Baltimore, MD.

COMMENTARY: THE INFLUENCE OF STRESS AND AROUSAL ON THE CHILD WITNESS

AMYE WARREN-LEUBECKER

The studies reported by Peters in this chapter represent a significant advance in our understanding of the effects of stress on children's eyewitness performance. In general, they suggest that stress impairs rather than facilitates such performance, in contrast to the widely-held beliefs of many judges, attorneys, and potential jurors. Peters and others working in this important area should be applauded for cleverly managing to preserve sound methodology while simultaneously using natural contexts and remaining within tight ethical constraints. My excitement about the results of all the studies in this area thus far is tempered, however, by several nagging questions that have yet to be addressed. The remainder of my commentary thus will pose these questions as a challenge for future research.

First, how high is the arousal (or how low the arousal) in these studies? The lack of a clear definition of stress or arousal and a concommitant inability to manipulate and measure it confidently have constantly plagued those who research arousal and eyewitness reports from adults. This poses no lesser problem for child witness research. The famous Yerkes-Dodson inverted U function would lead us to predict that the high arousal in these studies is indeed toward the extreme high endpoint, in that it often led to decrements in performance, but such reasoning is circular. Therefore, we need to design studies in which at least three levels of arousal—high, moderate, and low—are observed or produced. The results of such studies might be more easily reconciled with those of "flashbulb" memories, where higher arousal is consistently associated with better event gist recall (e.g., Bohannon, 1988; Christianson & Loftus, 1987). Indeed, in my own study of children's memories of the space shuttle accident, those with greater affective reactions remembered more, regardless of other factors (e.g., age, rehearsal, etc.; Warren-Leubecker, Bradley, & Hinton, 1988). Perhaps the arousal engendered by such surprising news is only in the "moderate" range in comparison to that produced by a personal trauma. While I am only speculating here, these are empirical questions.

Second, how do children compare with adults both in arousal/stress and eyewitness performance? Are children more or less stressed than adults by witnessing "robberies" or hearing fire alarms? To my knowledge, no extant study of arousal and eyewitness reports has included both adult and child subjects. While researchers in this area might protest that devising tasks that are equally valid for subjects over such a large age range is impossibly difficult, I would counter that in reality, both children and adults are witnessing and falling victim to similar crimes. These events are not necessarily "child-adapted," meaning, presented on an optimal level for children's understanding. Although using the same events for adult and child witnesses might lead to differences in memory/reports due to differences in initial comprehension of the event itself, I would argue that since such differences certainly exist in the real world, they should be simulated in our research.

Third, how well do levels of stress and measures of eyewitness performance generalize to those involved in various types of crimes that children might witness? Whereas Peters argues that only high stress is forensically relevant, I believe his assumption is unwarranted until more data on children's affective reactions to various types of events are collected. Further, Peters' work focuses largely on the child witnesses' abilities to visually recognize or describe physical characteristics of actors and settings (e.g., the nurse, the research assistant, the dentist's office) within events. These skills are unquestionably needed when children witness crimes perpetrated by strangers in unfamiliar settings, but different skills better measured by other means (e.g., free and prompted recall of coherent event sequences, recall of repeated events, repeated recall of single events, and possibly even estimates of event duration or time of occurrence) are likely to be necessary and therefore forensically relevant under other conditions. In a similar vein, more work entailing stress effects on memory for details defined as "central," "peripheral" or "irrelevant" (measures easily borrowed from the research on children's episodic, script memory) may prove to be beneficial.

Finally, even if all my previous questions were adequately addressed empirically, I would still be left without a coherent or cogent explanation of the findings. Why or how does stress impair or enhance children's eyewitness reports? Those researching adult eyewitnesses' reports appear to have settled on the conclusion that stress results in a decreased attentional focus and thereby less information encoded or subsequently recalled. Stress may operate similarly on children, and Peters' fire alarm study results are certainly consistent with this thesis (the stressed children paid less attention to the confederate, later answered fewer objective questions regarding the confederate correctly and ultimately proved to be more suggestible about the confederate as well).

However, other results reported by Peters do not fit as neatly with this hypothesis, nor any explanation resting solely on mnemonic factors (e.g., the children's ability to recognize the thief but failing to select him in a live lineup). A recurring theme throughout the conference and this book has been that children's eyewitness reports require numerous mnemonic and non-mnemonic skills that are in turn affected by numerous factors. Any attempt to explain the effects of stress on eyewitness reports must therefore consider these multiple skills and factors, individually and in interaction. I urge Peters and his colleagues to devote more effort to disentangling the varied contributions of social, mnemonic, and even underlying physiological factors (e.g., see the work of Gold, 1988, on glucose or adrenaline enhancing memory) to children's eyewitness performance. Despite the considerable research challenge Peters and others in this area now face, the ingenuity they have already evidenced gives rise to high hopes for their eventual success.

References

Bohannon, J. N. III (1988). Flashbulb memories for the space shuttle disaster: A tale of two theories. *Cognition, 29,* 179–196.

Christianson, S. & Loftus, E. (1987). Memory for traumatic events. *Applied Cognitive Psychology, 1,* 225–239.

Gold, P. E. (1988). Plasma glucose regulation of memory storage processes. In C. D. Woody, D. L. Alkon, & J. L. McGaugh (Eds.), *Cellular mechanisms of conditioning and behavioral plasticity* (pp 329–341). New York: Plenum.

Warren-Leubecker, A., Bradley, C., & Hinton, I. (1988, March). *Scripts and the development of flashbulb memories.* Paper presented at the conference on Human Development, Charleston, SC.

COMMENTARY: RESPONSE TO GOODMAN

DOUGLAS P. PETERS

INTRODUCTION

When one tries to condense the findings of five complex studies into a limit of 17 manuscript pages, the resulting loss of detail can create some confusion for the reader. The commentary of Gail S. Goodman seems to be a case in point. However, not only does it represent some misunderstanding, but it is misleading and at times a misrepresentation of my research, as well as her own. What follows is a refutation of the major points of criticism raised by Goodman.

Reviewing Studies

Study 1
It is asserted that age could account for the stress effects observed, but given the fact that this was a within-subject manipulation where the same subjects were tested over the two stress conditions, acting as their own controls, the internal logic of this design would preclude such an interpretation. Furthermore, if you exclude the youngest group of children, ages 3–4 (28% of the sample) the stress effects are still significant. Also, Goodman's statement about younger children typically performing poorer on identification/recognition tasks is misleading because this age effect is most often reported in laboratory (not simulation) studies with children younger than 12 years being compared to adolescents and adults (see Chance & Goldestein, 1984). Interestingly, Goodman's own data for the venipuncture study are contrary to the above statement regarding age effects, i.e., "Age did not correlate with correct or incorrect free recall, nor with the ability to make a correct or false photo identification" (Goodman, Aman, & Hirschman, 1987, p. 15), and no significant age effects were seen in three out of four analyses of photo identification for their inoculation study.

The concern about differences in task difficulty when our subjects viewed lineups of dentists versus research assistants (RA) is reasonable but, in actuality, it is not a factor. Subsequent testing with mock-witness controls (children who were exposed to pictures of the targets and then later given identification tests with the respective lineups) produced no evidence to suggest that some lineups were significantly more difficult than others. In discussing lineup construction, one wonders why Goodman et al. (1987) did not employ target-absent lineups for the photo identification tasks? The use of both target-present and target-absent lineups is the standard procedure for modern eyewitness researchers. The use of only one type of lineup severely limits the forensic value of the research (Wells, 1984).

Goodman suggests that the stress effects on recognition could be due to the reduced amount of time the children spent looking at the dentist versus the RA. She offers several reasons why this might be possible (all related to looking away from the target), but I find this less than convincing because one could argue that with the dentist's face being much closer to the child's face during the examination period as compared to the situation for the RA visiting the child's home, the opportunity to view was greater in the case of the dentist, and therefore, the stress effects observed (poorer dentist recognition) were even more impressive because they overrode the advantage of opportunity to view. Given that children are taught today to be wary of strangers, one might also suggest that the children looked less directly at the RA, a stranger visiting their home, than at the dentist, a person endorsed by their parents.

Finally, is Goodman really suggesting that young children visiting a dentist for the first (86%) or second time (14%) will not experience any anxiety? She seems to be saying that the dental procedure involved with a check-up or teeth cleaning is stress-free, e.g., "it is unclear that the children were actually stressed." All of the verbal statements made by the dentists, hygienists, and parents revealed that the children were experiencing some amount of stress or anxiety while in the dental office, and the independent ratings of anxiety reflected this with scores typically around 5 (moderately anxious). Too suggest otherwise is illogical and behaviorally unfounded. In contrast, a close look at the stress ratings for the children in Goodman et al. (1987) does raise some questions about the level of "stress" being experienced by these subjects. Using a 6-point scale where 1 indicated "extremely happy or relaxed" and 6 indicated "extremely frightened or upset," Goodman and her colleagues obtained mean stress ratings of 3.7 for the subjects in the inoculation study and the experimental (high stress) group in the venipuncture study. Considering that a score of 3.5 represents the neutral, midpoint on the scale, one can hardly be impressed by a stress rating of 3.7.

Study 2

Goodman suggests again, despite contrary findings in her own stress studies that age effects could account for the poorer eyewitness performance of the high stress subjects. This possibility can be ruled out because age did not reliably correlate with identification accuracy, nor did the stress groups significantly differ in terms of age.

Study 3

The criticism here is that the room the immunization group had to identify in a lineup was perhaps less memorable than the one the nonimmunization group saw, or that the lineups differed in difficulty for the two groups. Although possible, these confounds can be excluded from consideration because pretesting with mock-witness controls (children who were exposed to pictures of the rooms and then later given identification tests) produced no evidence to suggest that one room was significantly more difficult to remember than the other, or that recognition performance was differentially affected by the lineups used for the immunization versus nonimmunization groups.

Study 4

In singling out only the stress variable, Goodman glosses over several very significant design elements that differentiate my study from that of Dent and Stephenson (1979). Some of the more significant design elements included in my study but not in Dent and Stephenson's were the use of target-absent lineups, the staging of a simulated crime (they had their children witness a workman inspecting doors and windows or an adult telling jokes and tossing sweets to them), manipulation checks for stress levels, and independent ratings of anxiety (they employed no rating scheme or stress measures).

Study 5

If, as Goodman suggests, the fire-alarm subjects were more receptive to accepting certain types of misleading suggestion, e.g., people running out of the building, than the no-fire-alarm subjects, then we would expect to see the least accurate recall (i.e., a larger suggestibility effect) for those questions associated with this potential bias. However, an examination of the data for the fire-alarm group reveals no significant differences in recall performance for the five critical items on the suggestibility test. Thus, the suggestibility effect of saying that people were running out of the building was no more potent than any other of the misleading questions for the fire-alarm subjects.

The issue of commission errors that Goodman raises is important. In looking at the children's responses to the 10 objective questions (answered "yes" or "no") that could not be scored as correct, a significant difference in giving the incorrect answer is seen between the fire alarm and no-fire alarm subjects, 25.5% ($n = 82$) vs. 15% ($n = 48$), respectively, while there was no reliable difference in the "I don't know" type of answer, 2% ($n = 8$). A similar pattern emerges when the suggestibility data in Table 6 is analyzed. For those subjects given the misleading information, 57.5% ($n = 46$) and 39% ($n = 31$) of the answers on the suggestibility test were incorrect (i.e., the biased alternative choice was selected) in the fire alarm and no-fire-alarm groups, respectively. This was a significant difference. The number of incorrect answers significantly decreased for the subjects who received the neutral-worded questions, 25% ($n = 20$) and 17.5% ($n = 14$) for the fire-alarm and no-fire-alarm subjects, respectively. The "I don't know" response was given equally often, 5%–6%, for subjects in all four conditions.

Conceptual Issues

It is unclear to me how an application of a discrete-emotions orientation (Izard, 1978) will resolve conflicts between the current findings and those of Goodman regarding stress. Goodman argues that depending upon the information tested, this conceptual framework can predict positive or negative effects of stress. (The criticized Yerkes-Dodson law also allows for bidirectional effects of stress or arousal.) However, in looking at our respective eyewitness work with children, the types of information being examined appear quite similar, and Goodman does not present any evidence to show otherwise. From this, I would have to conclude that our differences are more methodological than conceptual in nature.

Further Comments

In my evaluation of the results of Study 2 (stranger visits a nursery school) I should have said that Goodman and her colleagues have asserted that children rarely (as opposed to "do not") err when asked about personally significant events, especially those involving their bodies. In her presentation at the Cornell conference (June, 1989) and also in Goodman, Saywitz, Aman, and Powers (1988) she used the data from 7-year-olds, in which they made only "one" commission error out of 252 opportunities on memory tests, to make her case that children almost always never get it wrong regarding body-events. In summarizing her stress research Goodman reports, "Interestingly, across the studies, children never made up false stories of abuse even when asked questions that might foster such reports" (Goodman et al., 1987, p. 18). The point I was making in my discussion of Study 2 is that my findings of 56% false negatives for the Touched subjects and 21% false positives for the Not-Touched subjects regarding questions about prior physical contact are inconsistent with the extreme view of children's memory expressed by Goodman et al., 1987.

   Goodman would have us accept her belief that young children are highly accurate in resisting misleading abuse questions because they correctly deny such leading questions as "He took your clothes off, didn't he?". However, a study conducted by Goodman herself (Goodman, Wilson, Hazan, & Reed, 1989), which was overlooked in her commentary, seriously questions the validity of this belief. In her study 33% of the children examined agreed with an interviewer's suggestion that they had been hugged or kissed by a strange male four years earlier, when in reality they had not. These statements by the children could in some circumstances provoke allegations of abuse. Furthermore, as Ceci, DeSimone, Putnick, and Nightingale (in press) point out, Goodman's often-cited suggestibility research with children is problematic because there is typically no motivation for the children to lie. There is no reason for her subjects to withhold or distort what they experienced. To do otherwise, for example, say they took their clothes off or were sexually touched when they were not, could result in considerable personal embarrassment for them. In this context Goodman's work appears biased toward discovering truthfulness among young children by employing motives that implicitly favor truthful outcomes.

Recent studies have shown that many children will in fact lie when there is sufficient motivation to do so (e.g., to sustain a secret game, Warren-Leubecker & Tate, 1990; to obtain candy, Ceci et al. in press; when afraid of reprisal, Bussy, 1990; Peters, 1990; to keep a secret, Peters, 1991). If it could be replicated and extended to a larger sample, the Ceci et al. (in press) finding where preschoolers lied about being kissed while naked in a bathtub would be the most compelling evidence to date that children can be misled into making false reports about bodily events that are potentially relevant to sexual abuse accusations.

One final point should be made. Recent research with adults that I cited in my paper, as well as older studies mentioned by Deffenbacher (1983) in his review of eyewitness memory and stress, contradict Goodman's stress findings with children. In describing Goodman's venipuncture and inoculation studies in his 1990 edition of *The Development of Memory in Children*, Robert Kail concludes, "Contrary to the typical finding with adults, stress does not seem to impair memory" (p. 195). The fact that Goodman's research is at odds with much of the adult literature on stress needs to be addressed. If Goodman really wants us to believe that high levels of stress facilitate children's recollections, then, as this rebuttal has indicated, considerably better studies than hers are going to be necessary to prove this point. She is also going to have to recognize that there are now at least three additional, independent studies of young children (Vandermass, 1991; Ornstein, Gordon, & Lorus, in press; Leippe, Romanczyk, & Manion, in press) possessing data consistent with the overall results of the five studies I have described in this chapter; that is, if event-stress or anxiety does have an effect on children's memory (it may not always), the impact is negative not positive. On the basis of the accumulating evidence, Goodman must face the reality that her position regarding children's memory and stress may be more wishful thinking than empirical fact.

References

Bussy, K. (1990, March). *Children's lies: A developmental analysis.* Paper presented at the biennial meeting of the American Psychology and Law Society. Williamsburg, VA.

Ceci, S. J., DeSimone, M., Putnick, M., & Nightingale, N. (in press). Age differences in suggestibility. In D. Cicchetti (Ed.), *Child witness, child abuse, and public policy.* Norwood, NJ: Ablex.

Chance, J. E., & Goldstein, A. G. (1984). Face-recognition memory: Implications for children's eyewitness testimony. *Journal of Social Issues, 40,* 69–85.

Coy v. Iowa, 108 S. Ct. 2798 (1988).

Dent, H. R., & Stephenson, G. M. (1979). Identification evidence: Experimental investigations of factors affecting the reliability of juvenile and adult witnesses. In Farrington, D. P., Hawkins, K. & Lloyd-Bostock, S. M. (Eds.), *Psychology, law and legal processes,* (pp. 195–206). Atlantic Highlands, NJ: Humanities Press.

Deffenbacher, K. (1983). The influence of arousal on reliability of testimony. In S. M. A. Lloyd-Bostock & B. R. Clifford (Eds.), *Evaluating eyewitness evidence* (pp. 235–251). New York: Wiley.

Goodman, G. S., Aman, C., & Hirschman, J. (1987). Child sexual and physical abuse: Children's testimony. In S. J. Ceci, M. P. Toglia, & D. F. Ross (Eds.), *Children's eyewitness memory* (pp. 1–23). New York: Springer-Verlag.

Goodman, G. S., Saywitz, K., Aman, C., & Powers, M. (1988, March). *A new view of children's suggestibility.* Presented in D. Peters (Chair), Children's Testimony, Symposium, American Psychology and Law Society Meeting, Miami.

Goodman, G. S., Wilson, M. E., Hazan, C., & Reed, R. S. (1989, April). *Children's testimony nearly four years after the event.* Paper presented at the annual meeting of the Eastern Psychological Association, Boston, MA.

Izard C. E. (1978). Emotions as motivations: An evolutionary-developmental perspective. In R. A. Dienstbier (Ed.), *Nebraska symposium on motivation,* (pp. 163–200). Lincoln, NE: University of Nebraska Press.

Kail, R. (1990). *Development of memory in children* (3rd ed.). New York: W. H. Freeman.

Leippe, M. R., Romanczyk, A., & Manlon, A. P. (in press). Eyewitness memory for touching experiences: Accuracy and communication style differences between child and adult witnesses. *Journal of Applied Psychology.*

Ornstein, P. A., Gordon, B. N., & Larus, D.M. (in press). Children's memory for a personally experienced event: Implications for testimony. *Applied Cognitive Psychology.*

Peters, D. P. (1990, March). *Confrontational stress and lying.* Paper presented at the biennial meeting of the American Psychology and Law Society, Williamsburg, VA.

Peters, D. P. (1991, April). *Confrontational stress and children's testimony.* Paper presented at the biennial meeting of the Society for Research in Child Development, Seattle, WA.

Vandermaas, M. (1991, April). *Does anxiety affect children's event reports?* Paper presented at the biennial meeting of the Society for Research in Child Development, Seattle, WA.

Warren-Leubecker, A., & Tate, C. (1990, March). *Can children lie convincingly?* Paper presented at the biennial meeting of the American Psychology and Law Society, Williamsburg, VA.

CHAPTER 6

SUGGESTIBILITY IN CHILDREN'S TESTIMONY:
IMPLICATIONS FOR SEXUAL ABUSE INVESTIGATIONS

GAIL S. GOODMAN and ALISON CLARKE-STEWART

When an adult is suspected of sexually abusing a child, in most states a report is made to county child abuse registries and then referred to a social worker and police for investigation. A key part of these investigations is an interview with the child who is the alleged victim. The belief that children are susceptible to suggestions made by adult interrogators has raised apprehension about the accuracy of information obtained from children during such interviews. Similar concerns have been voiced about the credibility of children who testify in court after extensive "preparation" by authorities. Some fear that the use of leading questioning by legal and mental health professionals is resulting in false allegations of abuse and consequently prosecution and conviction of innocent adults. Others claim that children do not report abuse readily and that leading questioning may be necessary to facilitate children's disclosures.

Despite strong claims by both sides, ecologically valid and scientifically sound research to determine whether, when, and to what extent children's testimony in such cases is accurate or is influenced by suggestive questioning has been virtually nonexistent. Instead, most research on children as eyewitnesses has relied on situations that are very different from the personal involvement and potential trauma of sexual abuse. Researchers have used brief stories, films, videotapes, or slides to simulate a witnessed event. A few have used actual staged events, but these events—for example, argument between two adults over the scheduling of a room, or man tending plants—are also qualitatively different from incidents of child abuse. The children are typically bystanders to the events, there is no bodily contact between the child and adult, and it is seldom even known whether the events hold much interest for the children. Of even more importance in relation to this chapter, the questions the children are asked often focus on peripheral details of the incident, like what the confederate was wearing, rather than on the main actions that occurred or, more to the point, whether sexual acts were committed.

The studies described in this chapter represent two independent efforts to explore more directly issues of children's suggestibility in relation to sexual abuse cases. To design research that approaches the issues of sexual abuse and suggestibility in an ecologically valid and ethical manner is a challenge. We could not, for the sake of our research, actively abuse or threaten children. We could not observe actual sexual abuse occurring naturalistically and then document children's recounting of their experiences. We could not pose as social workers or police about to remove children from their homes. In considering the experiments we describe, we acknowledge that sexual abuse of young children and subsequent social service and police investigations are unique events; they have no perfect analogies in the lab. The results of our studies, therefore, are inevitably limited in their applicability.

It should also be kept in mind, however, that our studies are not so much concerned with simulating abusive events as they are with testing the claim that nonabused children can be led by adult interviewers to make false reports of abuse when nothing sexual or traumatic happened. Our strategy was to expose children to nonabusive events and then to interview the children in ways that mimic important features of child abuse investigations. Studies of this sort mainly address concerns that children's suggestibility leads to false reports rather than concerns about abused children's reports. By doing so, our findings help identify issues that professionals should consider in questioning young children about abuse.

There are a number of reasons to study children's suggestibility in relation to sexual abuse invetigations. First, surprisingly high prevalence rates of this crime (e.g., Finkelhor, 1984), dramatic increases in its reporting (American Humane Association, 1988), and important changes in laws governing these cases (e.g., Bulkley, 1982; McGough & Hornsby, 1987; Myers, 1987) are bringing considerable attention to this topic. Second, unlike many other crimes, sexual abuse of children often leaves no physical evidence and excludes other witnesses and thus pits a child's word against that of the accused. The possibility that interviews might contaminate children's reports through suggestion is therefore of special concern. Third, a number of highly sensational cases, particularly preschool cases, has aroused public attention about investigations of this crime. Fourth, at least in America where child witness laws have been liberalized, there is the perception, if not the reality, that increasing numbers of children are testifying in court about sexual abuse (e.g., Whitcomb, Shapiro, & Stellwagen, 1985). And finally, in sexual abuse cases the stakes are extremely high: Failure to detect actual abuse may expose the child as well as other children to continued victimization; elicitation of a false report may lead to the arrest, prosecution, and imprisonment of an innocent adult. The first set of studies described in this chapter, carried out by Goodman and associates, concern whether children can be led by suggestive questioning to falsely report that certain potentially sexual acts (e.g., having one's clothes removed) had occurred, when, in fact, they had not.

STUDY 1: PARTICIPATING VERSUS WATCHING

Rudy and Goodman (see Goodman, Rudy, Bottoms, & Aman, 1990; Rudy, 1986) investigated whether children were influenced by suggestive questioning when they were either bystanders to or participants in a neutral event. In a delapidated research trailer equipped with a one-way mirror and a few chairs, thirty-six 4- and 7-year-old children, in same-age, same-sex pairs, were introduced to a male confederate who had been waiting for them inside. One of the children was randomly selected to play with the confederate while the other child watched. In the course of the games, the confederate touched the child, dressed the child in a clown costume that fit over the child's clothes, lifted the child onto a table and took his or her photograph in several poses, and played a game invented for the experiment called "Funny Things That Clowns Do," which involved actions such as the child tickling the confederate. The bystander was frequently told to watch carefully and was complimented for paying attention.

Ten to 12 days later, the children were interviewed. Each was asked to tell the interviewer every thing about what happened in the trailer and then to answer specific questions about the appearance of the confederate, the activities played in the trailer, the appearance of the inside of the trailer, and the timing of the event. Some of the questions were misleading, in that they suggested that actions that had not occurred had occurred. Some concerned actions that might lead to an accusation of child abuse, such as "He took your clothes off, didn't he?" Many of the questions were asked in relation to the child himself or herself and also in relation to the other child ("Did he kiss you?" and "Did he kiss the other child?").

In response to the initial question ("I need you to tell me exactly what happened"), the children recalled little incorrect or ambiguous information. On average, they provided less than one incorrect or ambiguous item of information. The younger children recalled less than the older children, but what they did recall was typically correct. In response to the specific questions, the older children were also more accurate than the younger children, and they were better able to resist misleading suggestions about the confederate and his actions.

In general, the children were very accurate in answering questions about potentially abusive actions. The 7-year-olds answered 93% of them correctly, and the 4-year-old answered 83% correctly. Out of 252 opportunities, the 7-year-olds made only one commission error, the 4-year-olds only 13. The more common error was to omit actions that did occur (16 errors for 7-year-olds, 22 for 4-year-olds).

Virtually all of the omission errors were in response to a specific subset of questions—those concerning touching. These questions were intentionally vague in that they did not indicate what parts of the body might have been touched. It seemed to be unclear to children what constituted a touch: Was it a touch when the man helped the child put on the costume? Is a tickle a touch? Is it a touch to tweak someone's nose, as they did in the Funny-Things-Clowns-Do game? The children tended to add qualifiers to their answers to the touch questions, such as "I don't think so" or "Only to get the clown costume on," indicating that they felt the questions about touching were unclear. One child recounted to us that there is good touch and bad touch, but that there had been no bad touch in the trailer.

In response to the misleading abuse questions, no participant children and only one 4-year-old bystander made a commission error. Participants were more resistant than bystanders to suggestions, in general, but the participants' and bystanders' resistance to suggestion did not vary for the abuse questions: Both groups were highly resistant to these suggestions. A measure of individual differences among the children also was examined. Parents completed Achenbach and Edelbrock's (1983) Child Behavioral Checklist, a standardized measure of behavioral disturbance. Overall scores on this checklist were unrelated to the children's performance.

In summary, children evidenced considerable accuracy in answering specific abuse questions and even in resisting strongly worded suggestions about actions associated with abuse; they often responded to these questions with embarrassment or amazement. These findings counter the view held by many that children are highly suggestible when asked questions about abusive actions.

STUDY 2: USE OF ANATOMICALLY DETAILED DOLLS

Goodman and Aman (1987, 1990) investigated children's use of dolls to reenact an event. Eighty children (3- and 5-year-olds) played games, like tea party, with a male confederate. One week later they were interviewed. First they were asked to name the body parts of the dolls. Then they were encouraged to show and tell what had happened with the confederate. Finally, they answered a set of specific and misleading questions about the confederate's appearance and actions. Again, a subset of the questions related to potentially abusive acts, for example, "Did he touch your private parts?" and "Did he keep his clothes on?" Within each age group, one-fourth of the children were interviewed with anatomically detailed dolls, one fourth with regular dolls, one fourth with dolls present but out of reach, and one fourth with no dolls.

When the children's free recall/reenactment was analyzed so that both correct verbal responses and gestures were scored, the 5-year-olds recalled more correct information in the regular doll condition than in the no-doll condition. The 3-year-olds' recall was not significantly affected by the presence or absence of dolls. When the children's responses were scored in terms of a checklist of the games played, the 5-year-olds recalled or reenacted more correct information than did the 3-year-olds. On both recall measures, the age and doll groups did not differ in the amount of incorrect information recalled.

On the specific questions overall, the doll condition did not affect the 5- or 3-year-olds' accuracy. On the misleading questions overall, the 5-year-olds were again more accurate than the 3-year-olds, but the doll condition did not influence either age group's performance.

Again, we were particularly interested in the children's responses to abuse questions. The 3- and 5-year-olds differed reliably in the proportion of commission errors made to specific as well as misleading questions related to abuse, with 3-year-olds committing significantly more errors. Moreover, younger 3-year-olds ($M = .36$) made significantly more errors than older 3-year-olds ($M = .14$), on the misleading questions ($F (1, 57) = 12.50, p < .001$). Whether or not the children were interviewed with anatomically detailed dolls, regular dolls, or no dolls did not, however, influence incorrect responses to the specific or misleading abuse questions.

Most of the commission errors made by the children would not be likely to lead to a prosecution of child abuse, with one exception. Several 3-year-olds and a few 5-year-olds answered affirmatively to the questions about their private parts (e.g., "Did he touch your private parts?"). We therefore began asking the children where their private parts were. The children pointed to their ears, to their arms, and to other not-so-private places. Thus we were using a term that the children did not understand. It should also be noted that when the children made commission errors to the abuse questions, these errors generally consisted of nods of the head without elaboration or detail. A variety of life history and individual difference measures (e.g., exposure to nudity, family stability, and behavioral disturbance) bore no relation to the children's performance.

STUDY 3: IMPROVING YOUNG CHILDREN'S REPORTS

Because some 3- and 4-year-olds made errors in response to leading and misleading abuse questions, Goodman, Bottoms, Schwartz-Kenney and Rudy (1991) sought to reduce these errors by lessening the intimidation of the interviewer. Seventy-two healthy 3- to 7-year-olds were interviewed about having received inoculations by a nurse at a medical clinic. The inoculations were required for school attendance or general health. Half of the children were interviewed by a "nice" interviewer. These children were given support and encouragement during the interview and complimented for their performance, regardless of their accuracy. The interviewer smiled frequently, and the chilren received cookies and juice. In a more intimidating comparison condition, the interviewer was more distant and did not comment positively on the children's performance. All the children were asked a set of specific and misleading questions, including a subset of abuse questions (e.g., "She touched your bottom, didn't she?" "How many times did she kiss you?").

How positive the interviewer was did not affect the older children's error rate to the abuse questions. The 3- to 4-year-olds, however, made twice as many errors to the abuse questions in the neutral condition as in the nice condition. In fact, in the nice condition, the younger and older children's performance was nearly identical; the use of reinforcement significantly improved the younger children's performance. When encouraged and supported, these younger children generally knew that they had not been hit or kissed and that their clothes had not been removed or their bottoms touched. They were better able to resist adults' suggestions about such actions when they were made comfortable enough to do so.

STUDY 4: EFFECTS OF LONG DELAYS

In actual cases, years often pass before abuse is reported. It might be easier to obtain false reports of abuse when children are questioned about an event from their distant past. Goodman, Wilson, Hazan, and Reed (1989) examined children's suggestibility four years after an event. Fifteen 7- and 10-year-old participants from an earlier study (see Goodman & Reed, 1986) were reinterviewed about their interactions with an unfamiliar male confederate. In addition to asking abuse-related questions (e.g., "Did he do anything that made you feel uncomfortable?" "He gave you a hug and kissed you, didn't he?"), implicating comments and questions were included in an attempt to create an atmosphere of accusation (e.g., "You'll feel better once you've told"; "Are you afraid to tell?").

In free recall, few children evidenced memory of the original experience. They made a variety of errors in attempting to recall the event and answer questions. The children did not, however, provide false reports of abuse. All of the children knew their clothes had remained on, they had not been touched in a bad way, they had not been spanked, and they had not been instructed to keep a secret. Some of the children's errors, however, might lead to suspicion of abuse. For example, one child falsely affirmed that she had been given a bath, five children agreed to having been both hugged and kissed, and two children said "yes" when asked if their picture had been taken in the bathtub. Nevertheless, the children were more resistant to abuse-related than to nonabuse-related suggestions. In sum, after long delays children were not easily led into false reports of abuse—even under conditions of an implicating interview—but caution the fact that many children remembered events that had not occurred underscores the need for in interpreting the statements they made would be important in an actual abuse investigation.

STUDY 5: CHILDREN'S REPORTS OF GENITAL CONTACT

The studies described so far address the claim that nonabused children can be easily led into giving false reports of abuse through questioning alone. At least by the age of 4 or 5 years, most children tested were resistant to abuse suggestions. It could be argued, however, that the events they experienced would not be easily confused with abusive actions. Saywitz, Goodman, Nicholas, and Moan (1989) examined children's suggestibility about an event in which the children were undressed, their naked bodies touched, and for half of the children their genital and anal areas examined. The event was a medical checkup conducted by a pediatrician at a hospital, a checkup that typically includes a genital and anal component. Seventy-two healthy 5- and 7-year-old girls participated. All of the children experienced a standard medical checkup, but for half this included an external genital/anal examination, and for the other half it included a test for scoliosis instead. Either one week or one month later, the children were asked to recall what happened, to reenact the checkup with anatomically detailed dolls, and to answer specific and misleading questions.

The majority of the children who experienced genital and anal touching failed to report it in open-ended interviews. They disclosed the experience only when asked specific questions—questions that would be considered leading in an actual investigation. Out of 36 girls in the genital/anal condition, 28 failed to mention genital touching in free recall, and 30 failed to demonstrate it with anatomically detailed dolls. However, when asked a yes or no question about whether they were touched in the genitals (i.e., the interviewer pointed to the vaginal area of an anatomically detailed doll and asked, "Did the doctor touch you here?"), all but five finally disclosed the experience. (the same trend held for the children's reports of anal touching.) For the 36 girls in the scoliosis condition, only three children produced a commission error in response to the specific question about genital/anal touching, and none produced errors of this sort in free recall or doll demonstration. Two of the three children who erred could not provide any detail when probed further, whereas the third child falsely claimed that the doctor had placed a stick in her rectum.

These results highlight the dilemma faced by professionals who interview children in sexual abuse cases. The findings suggest that children may not disclose genital contact unless specifically asked, but that asking may increase the chance of obtaining a false report. However, in the present study, when all of the chances to reveal genital/anal contact were considered, children failed to disclose it 64% of the time, whereas the chance of obtaining a false report of genital/anal touching was only 1%, even when leading questions were asked.

STUDY 6: HOW CHILDREN INTERPRET ACTIONS

In an on-going series of studies conducted by Clarke-Stewart, Thompson, Lepore and Associates (1989, 1991) the focus was not on children's accuracy in recalling whether or not certain actions occurred, but on their interpretation of actions. The basis for this research strategy was the belief that part of what transpires in sexual abuse cases depends on the interpretations that children and investigators make of incidents as being either sexually abusive or innocent.

In a research room at the university, children saw and interacted with a confederate, who followed one of two scripts. Posing as a janitor, the confederate cleaned up the research room, and then he either cleaned and arranged some toys, including a doll of the same sex as the child, or he played with the toys in a somewhat rough and suggestive manner. In both scenarios, he invited the child to join in his activities ("Would you hold the doll while I straighten its legs?"). The two scenarios were balanced with respect to the confederate's specific actions, but those actions had different meanings depending on whether the confederate was cleaning or playing.

When he was cleaning, the confederate said such things as: "This doll is dirty. I'd better clean it" as he sprayed and wiped the doll's face. "I'd better see if it's dirty here, too," as he looked under its clothes. When he was playing, the confederate, performing roughly the same actions, said: "I like to play with dolls. I like to spray them in the face with water. I like to look under their clothes." In some cases, after the confederate had played with the toys, he also asked the child not to tell what he had done.

An hour or so later, an interviewer (the janitor's "boss") came into the playroom and interrogated the child in one of three ways. She was neutral and nonsuggestive, asking open ended questions. Or she was "incriminating," accusing the janitor of playing with the toys instead of doing his job. At first, she made a gentle suggestion: "Did you see the cleaning man when he was in here? I need to know what he has been doing. You know his job is to clean the room and the toys. But he sometimes stops working and plays with the toys. He's not supposed to do that. Would you tell me what the janitor did with the toys when he was in here?" Then, her suggestions became stronger and more accusatory:

"This doll didn't need to be cleaned. Did you see any dirt on it? Why would the janitor clean a doll that wasn't dirty? Do you suppose he might just have wanted to play with it? Maybe he pretended to clean it but really he was playing?" And finally, if the child continued to insist that the janitor was just cleaning: "I happen to know that the janitor is not a good worker. I don't believe he was just cleaning the toys. So come on and tell me the truth. The janitor was playing, right?" The third style of interrogation was "exculpating," as the interviewer made the claim in progressively stronger suggestions, which paralleled the incriminating arguments, that the janitor was only cleaning the toys and not playing with them.

At the end of the interrogation, the interviewer asked the child an open-ended, free-report question: "Now just to be sure I have the story straight because I have to make a report, why don't you tell me again what the janitor did to these toys?" Then she asked 17 standard, factual questions (e.g., "Did the janitor wipe the doll's face? Did he kiss the doll?) and finally, she asked the child six fixed-choice, interpretive questions (e.g., "So what do you really think, was the janitor cleaning the toys or playing with them? Was he doing his job or was he being bad?).

After this first interrogation, a second interviewer followed up with another interrogation, which was either in line with the first or opposite it, and then, finally, at the end of the entire session, the child's parent asked the child about what the janitor had done. A week after the session, a follow-up questionnaire was mailed to the parent to investigate more long-term effects of the manipulation.

One hundred 5- and 6-year-old children were randomly assigned to the conditions in this ongoing study. Of particular interest are the children whose interrogations were inconsistent with what they had actually seen, the children who saw the confederate clean and then heard an incriminating interrogation, and the children who saw the confederate play and then heard an exculpating interrogation. Children who heard interrogations consistent with what they had witnessed, or who heard the neutral interrogation, provided necessary baselines for assessing children's testimony in this situation. We were also interested in finding out whether there were predictable individual differences among children in their reactions to the suggestive interrogations and in their willingness to keep the janitor's secret. Therefore, we embedded the confederate scenario and the interrogations in a series of tasks to assess the children's memory abilities, psychological adjustment, susceptibility to suggestive questions, social desirability, compliance with adult requests, social competence, moral development, and child-rearing experiences.

Consistent with other research, when the children in this study were given no leading suggestions or no persuasive interrogation, or when the interrogation they received was consistent with what they had observed, their answers to the interviewer's questions were limited, but accurate. On the 17 standard factual questions, on the average, the children answered 14 questions correctly, and on the final, interpretive questions, they answered at least 5 of the 6 questions correctly. They continued to answer the questions accurately a week later on the follow-up questionnaire.

When children heard an interrogation that was inconsistent with what they had observed, however, it was a different story. Even after the first gentle suggestion, one-quarter of the children answered the interviewer's questions about what the janitor had done inaccurately, following the interrogator's suggestion. By the end of the interrogator's strong suggestions, only one-quarter of the children were still reporting accurately what the janitor had done; two-thirds had switched from what they had seen to what the interrogator had said; the other few children were maintaining that the janitor had both cleaned and played. On the six final interpretive questions at the end of this interrogation, 90% of the children who heard an interrogation that was inconsistent with the scenario they had witnessed answered at least four of the questions in line with the interrogation rather than the scenario; only one child answered all six questions accurately.

When the second interrogation was of the same type as the first, moreover, the suggestion planted in the first interrogation carried over to the second. When the second interviewer first asked what the janitor had done, only one-sixth of the children gave accurate responses, and, by the end of the second interrogation, only one child who heard an interrogation that was inconsistent with the confederate scenario gave fewer than 6 out of 6 responses to the interpretive questions in line with the interrogation. Nor did the children change their stories when questioned by their parents at the end of the session: All the children answered the questions posed by their parents consistently in line with the interrogators' interpretation of the confederate's activities, and one week later, on the follow-up questionnaire, the children generally retained these interpretations.

When the second interrogation was contradictory to the first, most children tended to change their interpretations in line with the second interrogation, but their reports were not as uniform as those of children who heard the same biased interrogation twice. A week later, their version of what had happened was a combination of cleaning and playing.

Although the biased interrogations strongly affected children's responses to the *interpretive* questions about what the confederate had done, their effect on children's recollection of the "*facts*" of the confederate's behavior was more subtle. Overall, the children who heard a biased interpretation inconsistent with what they had observed answered as many of the 17 standard factual questions correctly as the children who heard a neutral or a consistent interpretation. A handful of children (about one fifth of the sample), however, consistently made errors that were in the direction suggested by the biased interpretation. Although no suggestions had been given regarding these particular details of the confederate's behavior, these children, who had seen the janitor playing with the toys and then heard interrogations suggesting that he cleaned the toys, answered affirmatively (and inaccurately) that the janitor had wiped the doll's face, said the doll's clothes were dirty, cleaned the doll's shoes, straightened the doll's cap, tied the doll's bow, and dusted under the table.

Further evidence of individual differences in suggestibility was seen in children's readiness to accept the interrogators' biased interpretations. Although all children who heard interrogations that were inconsistent with what they had observed eventually converted to the interrogators' view, some did so more rapidly. When correlations were calculated between how readily the children accepted the interrogators'' interpretation and their scores on the measures of individual differences, these more suggestible children were found to be more suggestible in other contexts as well, more compliant in games with the experimenter, and less knowledgeable about what it means to tell a lie; their parents were less likely to value self-direction for the children and were not as strict about lying. More surprising, perhaps, these more suggestible children also had better verbal memories than the children who did not go along with the interrogators' suggestions as readily.

When the confederate asked the child to keep his play activities a ''secret,'' only 7 out of 18 children admitted that he played; 3 were noncommittal, and 8 said he cleaned. These children kept up their defense of the confederate throughout the open-ended questions and, if they received a neutral interrogation, they maintained the confederate's innocence even in the final questions posed by the interrogators and by their parents. (If they received a biased interrogation, all the children went along with the interrogators' suggestions, even if the janitor had asked them to keep his secret.) These children who protected the confederate were more likely to be boys, with no preschool experience and less knowledge about lying and secrets; they were less socially mature, competent, and confident, more psychologically maladjusted and negative about themselves, more anxious and withdrawn, and lower in moral reasoning; they scored higher on social desirability; and their parents placed less value on the children's independence and self-direction.

In sum, the children's interpretation of a somewhat ambiguous event was easily manipulated by an opinionated adult interviewer. In considering the implications of this research to sexual abuse investigations, however, the most important caveat to keep in mind is that the study did not involve allegations of sexual abuse but rather whether a janitor cleaned or played. Children may be more resistant to manipulation when the suggestions are about abusive acts, especially against the child himself or herself.

CONCLUSION

These studies suggest that obtaining accurate testimony about sexual abuse from young children is a complex task. Part of the complexity rests in the fact that there are dangers as well as benefits in the use of leading questioning with children. The benefits appear in the finding in the studies by Goodman and associates that leading questions were often necessary to elicit information from children about actual events they had experienced (genital touching). Benefits might also be inferred from the finding in the studies by Clarke-Stewart and associates that children were more likely to disclose the janitor's "secret" when the interviewer made strong and persistent suggestions.

The dangers of suggestive questioning lie in children's adding erroneous information to their accounts of what has occurred. The children in the studies by Goodman and associates where generally accurate in reporting specific and personal things that had happened to them. If these results can be generalized to investigations of abuse, they suggest that normal children are unlikely to make up details of sexual acts when nothing abusive happened. They suggest that children will not easily yield to an interviewer's suggestion that something sexual occurred when in fact it did not, especially if nonintimidating interviewers ask questions children can comprehend. However, leading questions in these studies also resulted in a small number of children making errors that could be misinterpreted as suggesting that abuse had occurred.

A small number of children also made error in reporting the details of what they had seen in the studies by Clarke-Stewart and associates. These errors were in line with suggestive questioning by a biased interviewer. In addition, in the Clarke-Stewart studies, even those children who reported the facts accurately were swayed in their overall interpretation of events. If these findings can be generalized to abuse investigations, they suggest that young children might be led to mislabel or misinterpret acts when something nonabusive occurred that could be confused with abuse. Children do not make up facts often, both studies agree, but Clarke-Stewart's findings indicate that children can be led by a persistent interrogator to change their descriptions of what they have seen or what has been done if the event is somewhat ambiguous to start.

Extrapolating from both sets of studies, we can conclude that children are especially likely to accept an interviewer's suggestions when they are younger, when they are interrogated after a long delay, when they feel intimidated by the interviewer, when the interviewer's suggestions are strongly stated and frequently repeated, and when more than one interviewer makes the same strong suggestions. Whether children would misconstrue events to the point that an allegation of abuse would result, is, based on our research, still debatable.

It should be noted that the studies described in this chapter all address children's testimony about one-time events experienced with unfamiliar people. In none of the studies did we examine children's memories about habitual events or the actions of familiar people. Strangers rather than parents provided the suggestions, even though parents are often the first adults to question children when abuse is suspected. The studies did not include the numerous interviews, examinations, and cross-examinations children often experience in actual cases. We did not imply to the children that our confederates were criminals, and we did not pose as legal authorities.

Our studies also do not directly answer the question, "Do children lie about sexual abuse?", and we believe there is no simple answer to this question. Even pinning down an acceptable definition of what constitutes a lie is problematic (e.g., is intentional deceit required or simply a misstatement of facts?). Children in our studies had motivation to lie, but the motivation derived mainly from social influence (e.g., social pressure to conform to suggestion) rather than other possible sources (e.g., the desire to protect or punish a parent). However, in many cases of sexual abuse—for example, when the alleged victims are young and the defendant a nonparent, as in most preschool cases—suggestibility and not intentional lying is the central issue. Thus our studies address what has historically been and what continues to be a crucial issue in forensic investigations of the sexual assault of children. In further research it would be valuable to continue the effort to simulate the complex circumstances surrounding child abuse testimony, by creating or finding situations that are repeated, and personally involving; by imposing frequent and varied interrogations by different authorities; by varying the incentives for children to give accurate testimony; and by looking for individual differences among children that predict heightened suggestibility and vulnerability.

References

Achenbach, T. M., & Edelbrock, C. (1983). *Manual for the Child Behavior Checklist and the Revised Child Behavior Profile*. Burlington: University of Vermont.

American Humane Association (1988). *Highlights of official child neglect and abuse reporting, 1986*. Denver: American Humane Association.

Bulkley, J. (1982). *Recommendations for improving legal intervention in intrafamily child sexual abuse cases*. Washington, DC: American Bar Association.

Clarke-Stewart, A., Thompson, W. C., & Lepore, S. (1989, April). Manipulating children's interpretations through interrogation. In G. S. Goodman (Chair), *Can children provide accurate eyewitness reports?* Symposium conducted at the biennial meeting of the Society for Research in Child Development, Kansas City, MO.

Finkelhor, D. (1984). *Child Sexual assault*. New York: Free Press.

Goodman, G. S., & Aman, C. (1987, April). Children's use of anatomically detailed dolls to recount an event. In M. Stewart (Chair), *Anatomically detailed dolls: Developmental, clinical, and legal implications*. Symposium conducted at the meeting of the Society for Research in Child Development, Baltimore, MD.

Goodman, G. S., & Aman, C. (1990). Children's use of anatomically detailed dolls to recount an event. *Child Development, 61*, 1859–1871.

Goodman, G. S., Bottoms, B. L., Schwartz-Kenney, B., & Rudy, L. (1991). Children's memory for a stressful event: Improving children's reports. *Journal of Narrative and Life History, 1*, 69–99.

Goodman, G. S., & Reed, R. S. (1986). Age differences in children's eyewitness testimony. *Law and Human Behavior, 10*, 317–332.

Goodman, G. S., Rudy, L., Bottoms, B., & Aman, C. (1989). Children's concerns and memory: Ecological issues in the study of children's eyewitness memory. In R. Fivush & J. Hudson (Eds.), *What young children remember and why*. Cambridge, England: Cambridge University Press.

Goodman, G. S., Rudy, L., Bottoms, B. L., & Aman, C. (1990). Children's memory and children's concerns: Issues of ecological validity in the study of children's eyewitness testimony. In R. Fivush & J. Hudson (Eds.), *What young children remember and know* (pp. 249–284). New York: Cambridge University Press.

Goodman, G. S., Wilson, M. E., Hazan, C., & Reed, R. S. (1989, March). *Children's testimony nearly four years after an event*. Paper presented at the meeting of the Eastern Psychological Association, Boston, MA.

McGough, L., & Hornsby, M. (1987). Reflections upon Louisiana's child witness video-taping statue: Utility and constitutionality in the wake of Stincer. *Louisiana Law Review, 47*, 1255–1303.

Myers, J. (1987). *Child witness law and practice*. New York: Wiley.

Rudy, L., & Goodman, G. S. (in press). Effects of participation on children's reports: Implications for children's testimony. *Developmental Psychology*.

Saywitz, K., Goodman, G. S., Nicholas, E., & Moan (1989). Children's memory for a genital examination: Implications for child sexual abuse cases. In G. S. Goodman (Chair), *Can children provide accurate eyewitness reports?* Symposium presented at the meeting of the Society for Research in Child Development, Kansas City, MO.

Thompson, W. C., Clarke-Stewart, A., Meyer, J., Pathak, M. K., & Lepore, S. (1991, August). *Children's susceptibility to suggestive interrogation*. Paper presented at the annual meeting of the American Psychological Association, San Francisco, CA.

Whitcomb, D., Shapiro, E., & Stellwagen, L. (1985). *When the victim is a child: Issues for judges and prosecutors*. Washington, DC: U.S. Department of Justice.

COMMENTARY: REHABILITATION OF THE CHILD WITNESS

MAX STELLER

Goodman and Clarke-Stewart aim at "testing the claim that nonabused children can be led by adult interviewers to make false reports of abuse when nothing sexual or traumatic happened." For that purpose they undertook a series of more or less interconnected studies including several independent variables and tried to assess their impact on the accuracy of the children's recall. They conclude that "it seems unlikely that normal children will easily yield to an interviewer's suggestion that something sexual occurred when in fact it did not, especially if interviewers ask questions that children comprehend. It seems unlikely tha normal children will make up details of sexual acts when nothing abusive happened."

Space limitations do not permit going into details of the reported studies. Instead some general problems will be addressed that are inherent to the underlying logic of the reported studies and the interpretation of their findings. These general problems will be discussed under three core issues: (a) the relevance of accuracy versus credibility assessment in sexual abuse cases, (b) whether experimental realism enhances external validity, and (c) whether children's suggestibility or the suggestion, inherent in certain interview and contextual characteristics, is the appropriate area for research.

ACCURACY VERSUS CREDIBILITY

In describing a second overarching issue in the child suggestibility debate, Ceci (Chapter 1) points out that one must distinguish distortions of memory of which the reporting child is unaware from motivationally based, deliberate fabrications. This distinction between *errors* and *lies* may seem trivial, but it is not. Goodman and Clarke-Stewart's experimental studies are clearly in the long tradition of accuracy research, which started around the beginning of this century. The authors themselves acknowledge that their findings do not contribute at all to the question of whether children may intentionally lie about sexual abuse. They state that errors induced by inappropriate questioning procedures have "historically been" and continue to be "a crucial issue in forensic investigations." This assertion is open to serious question because the primary task in cases of alleged sexual abuse is to assess the credibility of the accusation. In light of the burgeoning problems of sexual abuse as expressed in the mass media and in the scientific literature in the United States, it can be assumed that the problem of deliberate false allegations of sexual abuse might be even more virulent in the United States than in other countries that have not yet experienced the "dramatic increase" in reports about sexual abuse cited by Goodman and Clarke-Stewart. In spite of the fact that in Germany there has not been any observed increase in the number of reported sexual abuse cases during the past 20 years, credibility assessment of children's statements in such cases is a common task for psychologists who are appointed as expert witnesses by trial courts. However, assessing child witnesses' competency to give accurate descriptions about observed events is of only peripheral importance in forensic practice in Germany.

EXPERIMENTAL REALISM VERSUS EXTERNAL VALIDITY

Because many professionals, police investigators, social workers, and psychologists seem to lack adequate training and sophistication in interview techniques for cases of sexual abuse allegations, the problem of interview-induced errors may be an important consideration in evaluating the validity of children's statements in forensic practice. The term *validity* is used here to refer to the combination of credibility and accuracy, *statement validity* being the ultimate forensic issue. The specific problem of interviewer-induced errors is the object of the studies reported by Goodman and Clarke-Stewart.

Interviewers' mistakes in forensic practice, however, are not always as obviously unrealistic as exemplified by the "abuse questions" used by the interviewers in Goodman's studies. It is not at all surprising that the subjects in the first study reacted with "embarrassment or amazement" to questions that were unrealistic in content and had nothing to do with the event observed by the children prior to the interview. In forensic contexts, however, the actual problems consist of interviewers' mistakes that are less obvious than those introduced by the so-called abuse questions in these experiments. Realism of their experimental design was defined by the children's experiences that were studied. However, this does not mean that external validity was actually achieved. On the contrary, any generalizations of the findings of these experiments seem to be problematic because of the unrealistic way in which the abuse questions were formulated and introduced during the interviews. The interviews and not the medical examination are the crucial aspect of the studies when considering the question of generalizability of the findings to real-life sexual abuse investigations. The face validity of some elements of the experimental design must not be mistakenly viewed as guaranteeing external validity.

It must also be pointed out that some children in the reported studies did make commission errors (e.g., see Studies 2 and 5). In the fifth study 3 of the 36 girls in the scoliosis condition (medical examination without inspection of rectum or genitals) did make commission errors in response to questions about genital or anal touching. This means that 8% of the subjects of this condition made errors. Extrapolating this finding to forensic contexts produces an alarmingly high number of false accusations. It is reasonable to assume that the danger for analogous errors in real-life situations would be much greater than in the experimental setting.

Goodman and Clarke-Stewart seem to have ignored their own findings in concluding that "it seems unlikely that normal children will easily yield to an interviewers's suggestion that something sexual occurred when in fact it did not." The dramatic finding was that one girl not only acquiesced to suggestions by nodding like others did, but also she "falsely claimed that the doctor had placed a stick in her rectum." The fact that the majority of children did resist overtly misleading questions is not an exciting finding; this would only be the case if one would make the assumption that all children are stupid. The finding that an erroneous allegation of extreme severity could be provoked in an experimental setting with a small sample of children is of striking importance for forensic investigations.

Nobody with forensic experience would expect high frequencies of fictitious allegations of sexual abuse. In practice, the difficult detection task is to identify the false alarms, which apparently do occur to an unknown and probably low degree. According to the findings obtained by Goodman and Clarke-Stewart, they occur even under experimental conditions in which less powerful suggestive influences can be expected than under the conditions of real-life interviews conducted by parents, laypersons, and poorly trained professionals.

SUGGESTIBILITY VERSUS SUGGESTION

On the basis of the research reported by Goodman and Clarke-Stewart, I recommend that the focus of attention in research should shift from witness psychology toward statement psychology. The term *suggestibility* clearly has a connotation that is closer to "person assessment" than to assessing whether a specific statement is credible or accurate, that is, a valid description of a real occurrence. *Suggestibility* implies the concept of a personality construct. Even if a corresponding psychological trait of suggestibility does exist, general findings about the degree of suggestibility of groups of persons, such as children as compared to adults, would contribute very little to resolving specific forensic cases.

If research, however, could help to define characteristics of interview techniques and settings that include more or less suggestive cues, this could certainly have a direct impact on improving forensic practice. Using Goodman and Clarke-Stewart's chapter title, this clearly would have "implications for sexual abuse investigations." A shift of the focus from witness psychology to statement psychology would place emphasis on interview, interviewer, and contextual characteristics rather than on "individual differences among children that predict heightened suggestibility," as suggested by Goodman and Clarke-Stewart. Specifying forensically relevant methodological and contextual variables of the investigative interviews seems to be more promising than the resurrection of the debate from the beginning of the century about whether children are generally reliable witnesses.

The range of topics to be scrutinized by empirical research in statement psychology covers areas in which the operationalization of relevant variables seems to be fairly easy, for example, question types (see, Chapter 8, this volume) or the amount of stress experienced during the incident (see Chapter 5, this volume). But there are also possible influences on the content of children's statements that are so complex that their definition seems to be an area of research in its own right. An example is the complex configuration of emotional as well as material gains and losses at stake for a child who testifies in a custody dispute.

Stern's (1902) overgeneralization that erroneous statements are the rule and accurate statements are exceptions was based on witness accuracy research that used inadequate research paradigms. It was later uncritically transferred to the issue of credibility, especially credibility of children's statements. For a long period, this overgeneralization had a detrimental impact on the acceptance of children's statements in judicial proceedings. The broad conclusions of Goodman and Clarke-Stewart obscure the narrow limitations of their experimental findings and increase the risk that their readers will not sufficiently appreciate the problems in their research and their generalizations to sexual abuse investigations. The way in which Goodman and Clarke-Stewart present their conclusions creates a danger that the importance of carefully prepared and professionally conducted interviews of the child witnesses in cases of alleged sexual abuse will be underestimated. This might cause serious problems, not only for the falsely accused but for the real child victim whose testimony might be discounted or dismissed because of poor interview techniques rather than because of their actual credibility.

Future research should be directed toward enhancing our knowledge about the specific conditions under which uncontaminated statements can be obtained from children and adults. Such research could also help to avoid a constant swing of the pendulum between extreme and unrealistic positions about the potentials of children to serve as credible witnesses.

References

Stern, W. (1902). Zur psychologie der aussage. *Zeitschrift für die Gesamte Strafrecht-swissenschaft, 22,* 315–370.

COMMENTARY: ISSUES IN THE EMPIRICAL STUDY OF THE SEXUAL ABUSE OF CHILDREN

JOHN C. BRIGHAM

The experimental studies carried out by Goodman, Clarke-Stewart, and their co-workers represent ambitious attempts to gather pertinent information about children's ability to accurately describe meaningful events. As these researchers have pointed out, this research area is fraught with methodological, conceptual, and ethical difficulties. Clearly, it is impossible to recreate the dynamics of sexual abuse in the laboratory. Given the limitations that a researcher faces, what questions can be asked and what answers are, or may be, forthcoming?

From the perspective of enhanced ecological validity, it is crucial to specify the real-world analog that a researcher wishes to understand and predict, as Ceci (Chapter 1) has pointed out. There are at least five possible situations involving alleged sexual abuse that vary in the presence or absence of sexual abuse, social pressure and suggestion (intentional or unintentional) to the child, and preexisting motives of the child to report falsely. The psychological dynamics, pertinent research questions, and applicable research designs will differ depending on which situation is investigated. The five situations are as follows.

1. Sexual abuse, no suggestion, no motive to fabricate. Can (and will) children accurately report the dynamics of sexual abuse when they are free of external pressures?
2. Sexual abuse, intentional suggestion. Can children be induced to deny abuse that has occurred or to retract previous allegations of sexual abuse? Can children be induced to exaggerate or retract descriptions of abuse that did occur? These first two situations have been of greatest concern to people concerned about children's rights. Unfortunately, however, they are not amenable to direct experimental analysis, because researchers cannot create incidents of sexual abuse.
3. No sexual abuse, unintentional suggestion. This might occur when a child experiences an unusual situation, perhaps involving some bodily

contact, that does not constitute sexual abuse but could possibly be misinterpreted by the child, other children, or a concerned adult as having a sexual nature. Controversies surrounding widely publicized allegations of multiple sexual abuse of nursery school children might fall into this category (e.g., Humphrey, 1985).

4. No sexual abuse, intentional suggestion. A child, perhaps caught in the midst of an acrimonious divorce, custody, or visitation dispute, may be pressured by an important adult (e.g., a parent) to invent an incident that never occurred or reinterpret one that did.

5. No sexual abuse, no suggestion, internal motivation to fabricate. Finally, an older child might be motivated to make false accusations of sexual abuse to meet his or her own needs in the midst of family chaos.

Several commonalities crosscut these distinctions. The child will encounter multiple interviews with people having varying motivations (child care workers, law enforcement personnel, and attorneys). The initial "interview" is likely to have been a completely uncontrolled interaction with a parent or someone else close to the child (e.g., relative, teacher, or friend). The child is likely to experience high stress and arousal at several points—during and after the sexual abuse (if abuse occurred), during multiple interviews, and during legal actions.

Among all cases of alleged sexual abuse, how common is each of these scenarios? We can never know the exact prevalence of suggestion, misinterpretations, or deliberate fabrications, but some authorities have suggested that as many as 8% of reported sexual abuse cases are fictitious (Jones & McGraw, 1987). This rate may be much higher in acrimonious custody, divorce, or visitation battles; Raskin and Yuille (1989) have speculated that the rate of fictitious allegations in such situations may be as high as 50%.

To get estimates of the prevalence of these scenarios, my colleagues and I (Brigham & Spier, in press; Leippe, Brigham, Cousins, & Romanczyk, 1989) conducted statewide surveys of Florida defense attorneys, prosecuting attorneys, child protection workers, and law enforcement personnel who work with child witnesses. Most respondents (except defense attorneys) felt that a 5- to 9-year-old children's reports would be "quite accurate" 60% to 70% of the time. Defense attorneys, in contrast, felt that less than half (44%) of the reports would be quite accurate. None of the groups believed that completely fabricated reports were common. Most defense attorneys, prosecutors, and child protection workers felt that this occurred about 20% of the time, whereas most law enforcement personnel believed fabricated reports were even less common (8%).

We also asked our respondents why a child might recant an accusation of sexual abuse. All four groups believed that recantations were most often due to pressure from a parent or family member. Only 25% of the defense attorneys and roughly 5% of the others responded that recantations were often because the child knew his or her previous testimony was false.

At a conceptual level, the creative studies described by Goodman and Clarke-Stewart seem most relevant to the third scenario outlined previously—unusual events that might be subject to deliberate suggestion by adults (Goodman's studies) or to misinterpretation (Clarke-Stewart). What do those studies tell us? The results suggest that children are not easily led into false reports of sexual abuse when interviewed once by a stranger. The Clarke-Stewart and Thompson results, however, suggest that repeated "incriminating" interviews can have a strong effect on childrens' interpretations of what they have experienced. Although the apparent degree of children's susceptibility to suggestion could be increased or decreased by varying the complexity of the situation, questioning style, status of the interviewer, number of interviews, and other factors, it seems evident that children are not as infinitely malleable as some legal observers have assumed (see Goodman, 1984, for a historical review). What the studies do not tell us, as the authors themselves point out, is what happens in situations that more closely match prototypical child abuse situations (i.e., the first two real-life analogs discussed earlier): sexual violation accompanied by high stress, often a long delay between the incident and the report, possible strong and frequent suggestion, and multiple interviews beginning with an uncontrolled initial interview by a highly concerned parent.

One striking characteristic of most research in this area, in my view, is an atheoretical approach. Many researchers seem to have adopted a problem-oriented focus, beginning with a concern for the horrors of sexual abuse and working backward to a research design. Although this is a legitimate approach, more attention to theory would be valuable. What do our theories of learning, memory, persuasion, communicator credibility, and compliance tell us about responses to situations having the general characteristics associated with allegations of sexual abuse? An example might be the recent empirical controversy and theoretical debate about the effect of misleading postevent information on adults' memories (e.g., see Belli, 1989; Ceci, Ross, & Toglia, 1987; Loftus & Hoffman, 1989; Tversky & Tuchin, 1989; Zaragoza & McCloskey, 1989). Are children's memories for traumatic or confusing events, or their memory reports, impaired by postevent information to a greater or lesser degree than adults' memories are? Can certain retrieval strategies identify children's memories that have been tainted by postevent information? Might the status of the source of the misleading information source (e.g., a parent, the perpetrator, or an interviewer) be more important for children than for adults? Are there personality characteristics that are associated, on a theoretical basis, with greater memory accuracy or susceptibility to suggestion in children? What dynamics affect a child's decision to recant his or her former allegations? How aware are young children of adults' attempts to influence their memories? Which techniques of suggestion are most effective in modifying children's memory reports?

Although those are limitations on the ecological validity of current child witness studies, this does not mean they are not valuable. Goodman, Clarke-Stewart, and their colleagues have shown remarkable creativity in designing research situations or seeking out naturally occurring events that match some of the important characteristics of alleged child abuse incidents. In a related area, we have learned a great deal in recent years about the memory of adult eyewitnesses (for recent summaries, see Brigham & Spier, in press; Kassin, Ellsworth, & Smith, 1989; Wells & Loftus, 1984), even though the match between the research settings and the real-world situations with which many researchers were concerned—violent crimes—is also limited. Experimenters cannot rob, assault, or terrorize adult eyewitnesses any more than they could sexually abuse children for the sake of science. Nevertheless, as with adults, the findings of creatively designed laboratory studies or studies of children that take advantage of naturally occurring stressful events (e.g., Peters, 1987) can provide valuable information about children as victims in traumatic situations. As researchers become more sensitive to the real-world parallels of greatest interest and design their studies to highlight them, and pay close attention to theoretical issues, laboratory research can yield results of high theoretical and practical relevance.

References

Belli, R. F. (1989). Influences of misleading postevent information: Misinformation interference and acceptance. *Journal of Experimental Psychology: General, 118,* 72–85.

Brigham, J. C. (1989). Disputed eyewitness identifications: Can experts help? *The Champion, 8*(5), 10–18.

Brigham, J. C., & Spier, S. A. (in press). Opinions held by professionals who work with child witnesses. In H. R. Dent & R. Flin (Eds.), *Children as witnesses.* Chichester: Wiley.

Ceci, S. J., Ross, D. F., & Toglia, M. P. (1987). Age differences in suggestibility: Narrowing the uncertainties. In S. J. Ceci, M. P. Toglia, & D. F. Ross (Eds.), *Children's eyewitness memory* (pp. 57–78). New York: Springer-Verlag.

Goodman, G. S. (1984). Children's testimony in historical perspective. *Journal of Social Issues, 40*(2), 9–32.

Humphrey, H. H. (1985). *Report on Scott County investigations.* Office of the Attorney General of Minnesota.

Jones, D. P. H., & McGraw, J. M. (1987). Reliable and fictitious accounts of sexual abuse in children. *Journal of Interpersonal Violence, 2,* 27–45.

Kassin, S. M., Ellsworth, P. E., & Smith, V. L. (1989). The "general acceptance" of psychological research on eyewitness testimony: A survey of the experts. *American Psychologist, 44,* 1089–1098.

Leippe, M. R., Brigham, J. C., Cousins, C., & Romanczyk, A. (1989). The opinions and practices of criminal attorneys regarding child eyewitnesses: A survey. In S. J. Ceci,

D. F. Ross, & M. P. Toglia (Eds.), *Perspectives on children's testimony* (pp. 100–130). New York: Springer-Verlag.

Loftus, E. F., & Hoffman, H. H. (1989). Misinformation and memory: The creation of new memories. *Journal of Experimental Psychology: General, 118*, 100–104.

Peters, D. P. (1987). The impact of naturally occurring stress on children's memory. In S. J. Ceci, M. P. Toglia, & D. F. Ross (Eds.), *Children's eyewitness memory* (pp. 79–91). New York: Springer-Verlag.

Raskin, D. C., & Yuille, J. C. (1989). Problems in evaluating interviews of children in sexual abuse cases. In S. J. Ceci, D. F. Ross, & M. P. Toglia (Eds.), *Perspectives on children's testimony* (pp. 184–207). New York: Springer-Verlag.

Tversky, B., & Tuchin, M. (1989). A reconciliation of the evidence on eyewitness testimony: Comment on McCloskey and Zaragoza. *Journal of Experimental Psychology: General, 118*, 86–91.

Wells, G. L., & Loftus, E. F. (Eds.). (1984). *Eyewitness testimony: Psychological perspectives*. Cambridge, England: Cambridge University Press.

Zaragoza, M. S., & McCloskey, M. (1989). Misleading postevent information and the memory impairment hypothesis: Comment on Belli and reply to Tversky and Tuchin. *Journal of Experimental Psychology: General, 118*, 92–99.

COMMENTARY: SEXUAL ABUSE AND SUGGESTIBILITY

LUCY S. McGOUGH

The law has long struggled with divining the difference between *facts* and judgments, inferences, conclusions, or opinions, and frankly the difference between *fact* and *interpretation* is often quite illusory. An ordinary (nonexpert) witness is usually cautioned that he or she is to give only the facts not his or her conclusions based on the observed facts. May a witness say that the car was "speeding" or that the woman was "drunk" or "slovenly"? Historically, no, but the precise lines of demarcation are clear only to the likes of Jack Webb when interrogating his garrulous witnesses. In most courtrooms today, the facts–interpretation limitation has been discarded as highly artificial and thoroughly unworkable (McCormick, 1984).

This is the same problem faced in reconciling Goodman's studies with those of Clarke-Stewart. It seems casuistic to maintain that children are reliable as to the facts of their experience but at the same time also to demonstrate their suggestibility to interpretations provided by forceful adults. As the subjects themselves struggled to explain in the Goodman trailer play experiment, there is a vital difference between "bad touching" and "good touching" or, for that matter, "inadvertent touching." There is a point of congruence between these two sets of studies, but the one chosen does not seem supportable.

The body of Goodman's work seems to stand for the proposition that if children have personally experienced a significant event like touching by a stranger, and if they are enabled to reconstruct their experience shortly thereafter, and if this reconstruction occurs in a supportive environment created by a warm, skillful interviewer, then their accounts of the extent, duration, and sequence of the experience core are highly reliable. Presumably Clarke-Stewart and everyone else would agree with this conclusion. And Goodman can be properly credited for her data showing that answers about the touching (or presumably real abuse) are more resistant to suggestion than are peripheral details and that bystanders are more vulnerable than victims.

In the new coin of the realm, ecological validity, we should pause to examine the real world of children's sexual abuse accusations. (I simply note in passing that neither of these series of experiments captures the special dynamics of intra-family abuse that statistically is the most commonly occurring, Herman, 1981; Wells, 1983). The current legal system does little to recreate the kinds of conditions conducive to the elicitation of a reliable account by the child. In an adversarial system of justice, there are few neutral players. Given an authoritarian interviewer (police officer, criminal investigator, parent, or defense counsel), who may be consciously or subconsciously motivated to influence the child's memory; given multiple pretrial interviews; given a child's increased memory-fade over time; and given substantial intervals between the observed events and testimony at trial, substantial impairment of a child's memories seems inevitable. It is beyond the scope of this commentary to do more than sketch the reliability risks inherent in current pretrial procedures (McGough, in press).

Two possible conclusions can be drawn from the Goodman data. The first is that children are amazingly nonsuggestible in a relatively benign interviewing environment. The second is that children can be resistant to suggestibility if and only if a benign interviewing environment is created and maintained until their account is recorded. The first conclusion emphasizes the strength of a child's capabilities, whereas the second underscores their fragility. The first conclusion accepts and even seems content with the current legal processes; the second lays the empirical groundwork for change. The rules and pretrial processes of the legal system will never become more protective of children as long as lawmakers are led to believe that suggestibility is not a substantial risk and that children can take their lumps like any other victim who chooses to go forward with an accusation.

Clarke-Stewart's studies move us one step further along toward unraveling the impact of both the timing of manipulation and the varying sources of sug-gestion. The paradigmatic suggestibility test uses the tester–interviewer as the source of attempted distortion. Furthermore, the alteration of fact is inserted within the questions: for example, "The red car didn't stop at the stop sign, did it?" (Loftus, 1979; Marin, Holmes, Guth, & Kovac, 1979; Duncan, Whitney, & Kunen, 1982). What has been missing from most prior empirical work is the use of a powerful, independent agent of suggestion (Chester's boss) who intervenes between the child's experience and the elicitation of the account. Furthermore, this agent vigorously asserted a version of the facts and insisted on its accuracy rather than more subtly rearranging the facts within a test question.

One of the most intractable real-world problems is to devise a way to staunch or at least measure the flow of influences that occur outside any formally logged interview format. Studies that assign to the interviewer the role as the agent of suggestion account for only part of the potential contamination of a child's story. All sorts of adult actors ordinarily do intervene in a child abuse case, either before any formal record of the accusation is made or after it, and these interactions are rarely disclosed. Two examples are suggestions that are imbedded in the course of an attorney's informal discussions with a client or parent-child interactions about the child's experiences. Clarke-Stewart's work is helpful in discerning what is probably a continuum of suggestiveness, ranging from weak forms to the irresistibly powerful (Ceci, Ross, & Toglia 1987). The innate or educated ability of children to withstand such assaults is a critical topic for continuing study.

To an outsider, both series of experiments converge to underscore the importance of the initial interview for the elicitation of an unbiased account, for the preservation of that version against later potential contamination, and perhaps to inoculate the child against predictable subsequent attempts to interfere with his or her autonomous memory. The recording of an unbiased initial interview of the child is the keystone to reform of the current processes. If a solid record were required to be made in any case involving a child witness, then no matter what pressures were thereafter brought to bear upon the child, the child and the legal system would have a benchmark against which subsequent changes could be evaluated for improper suggestiveness.

References

Ceci, S. J., Ross, D. F., & Toglia, M. P. (1987). Age differences in suggestibility: Narrowing the uncertainties. In S. J. Ceci, D. F. Ross, & M. P. Toglia (Eds.), *Children's eyewitness memory* (pp. 79–91). New York: Springer-Verlag.

Duncan, E. M., Whitney, P., & Kunen, S. (1982). Integration of visual and verbal information in children's memories. *Child Development, 53*, 1215–1223.

Herman, J. (1981). Father–daughter incest. *Women's Mental Health Collective, 12*, 76–80.

Loftus, E. F., (1979). *Eyewitness testimony*. Cambridge, MA: Harvard University Press.

Marin, B. V., Holmes, D. L., Guth, M., & Kovac, P. (1979). The potential of children as eyewitnesses. *Law and Human Behavior, 3*, 295–305.

McCormick on Evidence (1984, 3d ed. E. W. Cleary) at 23–30. St. Paul: West Publishing Co.

McGough, L. S. (in press). Fragile voices: Child witnesses in the American legal system. New Haven: Yale University Press.

Wells, D. M. Expert Testimony: To Admit or Not to Admit, 57 *Florida Bar Journal* 673, n. 14 (Dec. 1983).

CHAPTER 7

CONCERNS ABOUT THE APPLICATION OF RESEARCH FINDINGS:
THE ISSUE OF ECOLOGICAL VALIDITY

JOHN C. YUILLE and GARY L. WELLS

Problems have been associated with the application of psychological knowledge to the criminal justice system since such applications began. The first study of children's eyewitness memory was conducted in order to present the results to a court (for details, see Goodman, 1984). A Belgian psychologist, Varendonck, was hired by a defense lawyer in a murder trial and asked to investigate the malleability of children's testimony. He conducted several studies that he felt demonstrated the unreliability of children's evidence. For example, he asked children to describe a stranger who had appeared in the playground outside of their school. Despite the fact that no stranger had appeared, the suggestion was sufficient for many children to describe the fictitious stranger (Varendonck, 1911). These research results were presented in court in an attempt to discredit the child witnesses in the murder trial.

Varendonck's (1911) publication pioneered two features that have become characteristic of research on children's eyewitness abilities: (a) he emphasized the suggestibility associated with children's testimony and (b) he provided a model for the introduction of research evidence in court. For more than eight decades both aspects of Varendonck's original work have remained controversial. The susceptibility of children to suggestion is the central focus of a current debate in this field, and it prompted the conference that led to this volume. The application of research evidence to actual cases is the focus of this chapter and a secondary theme that prompted the convening of the conference.

The concerns associated with the application of research findings in the courts and other judicial contexts have not changed fundamentally since the time of Varendonck. The basic problem is one of timing: When do researchers reach a sufficient degree of consensus to permit the presentation of a research finding as both reliable and valid? That is, when does a scientific phenomenon or procedure move from controversy to acceptance? This is the problem a U.S. court faced in the 1920s when an attempt was made to offer lie detector evidence in a case. The position taken by that court, since known as the Frye test, was that the majority of professionals in a field must agree about the reliability and validity of a phenomenon or technique before the courts will admit expert testimony concerning that phenomenon or technique.

Varendonck's findings, based on a single set of studies, probably would not have met the Frye test. However, scores of studies of children's eyewitness abilities have been completed in the past 15 to 20 years. Do we have a sufficient data base at present to offer expert evidence to the courts or other systems that must make decisions based on children's evidence? Is the Frye test, or some variant like it, appropriate for the evaluation of psychological knowledge? Can we arrive at a formula or set of rules that will assist us in deciding when our research findings have reached a state of maturity to permit application? What sorts of restrictions and qualifications should we include in our expert opinions? These questions are the focus of this chapter.

HISTORICAL CONTEXT

Researchers of child witnesses have no monopoly in voicing concerns about applying research findings. There have been heated and extensive debates around application issues in the whole domain of psychology. Of particular note, divisions have appeared among psychologists about their appropriate role as experts in the criminal justice system (for a critical review, see Yuille, 1989). Many psychologists have been content, or even eager, to offer expert testimony concerning such diverse topics as the consequences of spousal abuse, the vagaries of eyewitness testimony, and the future dangerousness of convicted offenders. Such eagerness developed early in the history of psychology. Munsterberg, a student of Wundt, the founding father of psychology, wrote a book entitled *On the Witness Stand* (1908). He argued that the research findings from a decade of work on eyewitness testimony in Europe and America had reached a point at which the criminal justice system must pay attention. He called upon police, lawyers, and the courts to incorporate this new knowledge. Wigmore, the leading scholar on evidence at the time, took Munsterberg to task in a very critical review (1909). Wigmore argued that the psychological research was in an immature state and that there might always be limitations to the usefulness of such research for the courts. In effect, Wigmore and Munsterberg defined the extremes of the application debate.

Through the decades of the 1930s, 1940s, and 1950s, academic psychologists became more fascinated with stimulus–response laws and the behavior of rats than with topics like eyewitness memory. As a result, the debate about application in the courts was of little interest. However, when psychologists became intrigued with complex human memory again in the 1960s, the application debate was engaged anew. The debate recently led the leading exponents of opposing views to articulate their views in the *American Psychologist*. Loftus (1983), renewing the Munsterberg position, argued that if the courts want to listen, we have an obligation to present our current state of knowledge of eyewitness testimony. McCloskey and Egeth (1983), adopting a position much like Wigmore's, provided a variety of arguments against presenting expert testimony on eyewitness memory. And, more recently, some researchers have provided evidence indicating that expert testimony regarding numerous aspects of adult eyewitness testimony meets the Frye test (Kassin, Ellsworth, & Smith, 1989).

In summary, the present concern with the proper form and nature of applications of psychological research on children's eyewitness memory has appeared in the context of a long and currently active debate about such applications in general. The fact that the debates about expert testimony have remained heated and unresolved in the area of adult eyewitness research suggests that an immediate resolution of the debate in the domain of children's testimony is not likely. However, there are some special recent problems associated with children's testimony that add new dimensions to the debate.

EVALUATING CHILDREN'S EVIDENCE

Skepticism about children's testimony remained unchallenged for centuries. Our recent and growing understanding of the extent of the sexual abuse of children (e.g., Finkelhor, 1979) necessitated a review of previously held attitudes toward children's testimony, and now the pendulum has swung to another position. The courts are now treating children's evidence as reliable and valid (for a review, see Yuille, King, & MacDougall, 1988). The rate of appearance of children in courts (both family and criminal) has grown exponentially in just a few years. Judges and jurors are faced with the task of evaluating the uncorroborated evidence of a child (most sexual abuse cases involved only the testimony of the victim and the accused), and there is no clear basis for the evaluation. The triers of fact often look to experts to provide information about children's abilities to provide evidence. Thus the ''new'' context of sexual abuse has created a need for knowledge and the courts are looking to psychologists, among others, to assist. To what extent, and in what fashion, can psychologists contribute to the evaluation of children's evidence?

ECOLOGICAL VALIDITY: THE PROBLEM OF DEFINITION

The difficulties associated with applying research results boils down to a core problem: There is a demand for knowledge about children from the courts, and there is an extensive experimental literature on children's eyewitness memory; how useful is that experimental literature to the needs of the court? In other words, to what extent can the research findings be applied to the kinds of court cases in which children testify (mostly, but not only, sexual abuse cases)? The problem of generalizing from a research context to a real-world context has usually been labeled as the problem of ecological validity (see Chapter 1, this volume, for a discussion of the relation between the concepts of ecological validity and external validity).

Each piece of research is conducted at a specific time and in a specific place, with certain constraints, with particular children, and so on. How do the unique features of a given study or set of studies limit the generalizations of the findings to other times, other places, other constraints, and so forth? It is apparent that most researchers have responded to the ecological validity issue by treating it as a design problem: They have viewed ecological validy as a feature of the study itself. The assumption is that one can ensure that the results of a study can be generalized to real-world contexts as long as the study appears to be as realistic as possible. The past 15 years of child witness research demonstrates this assumption. Whereas earlier studies tested children's memory for a story or a sequence of slides, concerns about ecological validity led researchers to the use of videotaped events and then live staged events. More recently, researchers have tested children's memory for actual events (e.g., visits to the dentist, the doctor, etc.).

The conclusion that the realistic appearance of a study meets the concern for ecological validity has missed the mark. Ecological validity is not a quality of the appearance of a research paradigm but rather a concern about how research results are applied. The results of a particular study might prove valid for application in one context and yet not be valid for application in another. Consider, for example, the use of a videotaped event versus a live, staged event in a study. The results from using the latter might be valid if they were being applied to a real context in which a live event had been witnessed. However, if an actual case involved the memory of a security guard who had been watching security video monitors, the results of studies using videotaped events might be of more use.

How and where the research results are applied is the issue, not simply some characteristic of research design.

The basis of this view is best labeled as contextualism: Human behavior can only be understood as contextually relative. Each context in which people act has characteristic social dynamics, an emotional impact, particular demands, certain expectations, and so forth. If we wish to compare two situations (i.e., a research context and a forensic context), our concern must be with the contextural equivalence of the two domains. Each generalization of research findings requires that the person making the generalization can demonstrate the manner in which the two contexts are equivalent, as well as the manner in which they are not equivalent. Stating that a research event was realistic does not address the problem. Instead, it is necessary to evaluate the social, cognitive, and emotional contexts of the research event and compare that evaluation with a similar analysis of the forensic context.

Consider the sexual abuse context as the most relevant example. Imagine that the intent of a researcher is to conduct a study that appears to be like an actual sexual abuse investigation. The parallel to the abuse investigation is that children, during the course of the study, will be asked if they were sexually abused. However, the study involves having a stranger enter a room and interact with the child in a harmless fashion. Later the child is asked, in an age-appropriate fashion, if the stranger sexually abused him or her. The question has little meaning in this context. The question may be the same as that asked in a sexual abuse investigation. But the two contexts are so different that the meaning of the question is changed. It is not appearance that makes the research and forensic contexts equivalent. In fact, in this example, the context changed the critical question. The results of such a study could not be generalized to sexual abuse investigations. How nonabused children answered the sexual abuse question in this research situation may bear no relation to how nonabused children would answer it in the context of a sexual abuse investigation.

In effect, the position advocated here is that a researcher who wishes to apply his or her research findings to a real-world context has the onus to provide the foundations and justifications for the generalization. This represents one of the two positions that can be articulated about this issue. The other position is that it is the responsibility of the critic to provide the objections to the generalization. That is, if a researcher believes that the results of a set of studies can be generalized to some real-world context, then he or she is free to proceed. If a critic perceives some problem with that generalization, it is his or her task to outline the nature of the problem. However, we feel that it is better to err in the direction of caution when applying research findings. When one considers the potential impact of psychological knowledge, caution seems prudent. Premature application is fraught with danger for both the community and for psychology.

Let the researcher exercise caution and accept the responsibility for articulating the grounds for assuming equivalence between contexts.

We do not argue that each context is completely unique. Similarities do and can exist between different natural contexts and between controlled research contexts and forensic domains. However, by articulating the assumptions about similarities and differences between two contexts, the researcher will provide a clear statement of the assumptions made. Although there may never be agreement concerning the rules for comparing contexts, each professional can make his or her rules apparent.

STIMULUS SAMPLING PROBLEMS

Controlled research experiments require numerous decisions about sampling, and the nature of those decisions can have profound implications for generalization. It is not possible to discuss all sampling problems and some, such as the sampling of subjects, are relatively obvious. What might be less obvious, but no less important, is the problem of stimulus sampling. Examples from the research literature help illustrate this point.

One of the criteria that the U.S. Supreme Court listed as critical for evaluating the accuracy of an eyewitness's identification of a suspect is the quality of the eyewitness's pre-lineup description of the culprit. Several researchers, however, have conducted controlled experiments showing that witnesses who gave good pre-lineup descriptions were no more likely than those who gave poor pre-lineup descriptions to accurately identify a previously seen face (e.g., Goldstein, Johnson, & Chance, 1979; Wolfskiel & Brigham, 1985). Wells (1985) noted that these studies used a within-face design, that is, all subjects viewed the same face. Thus these studies could not fully test the Court's hypothesis. Although these studies could determine whether eyewitnesses who are good describers are also good identifiers, they could not determine whether faces that are easy to describe are also easy to identify. In other words, by using only one stimulus face, rather than a broad sample of faces, a source of variation that exists in the natural environment was obscured. Using a sample of 88 target faces, Wells (1985) demonstrated that there is a positive relation between the quality of witnesses' descriptions and the likelihood of accurate identifications. This relationship, however, exists across samples of stimulus faces—there was no description–identification correlation. Across stimulus faces, however, the correlation surfaced.

The point is that it can be misleading to generalize from studies that have used only one example of a stimulus. Even if that stimulus is representative, typical, or average, it fails to capture potentially important variation across stimuli. A similar argument was used recently in examining the perceived credibility of child witnesses. Several studies had been conducted in which adult jurors evaluated the testimony of either a child or adult witness. Some studies showed the child to be perceived as being less accurate than the adult (e.g., Ross, Miller, & Moran, 1987), whereas others showed the reverse (e.g., Leippe & Romanczyk, 1987). Wells, Turtle, and Luus (1989) noted that these studies used only one child and one adult and speculated that these results could be attributed to the particular child and particular adult selected to be used in these studies. Using a sample of 14 young children, 14 adolescents, and 14 adults as stimulus persons, Wells et al. found considerable variance within ages and no differences between ages in perceived credibility as evaluated by 294 subject–jurors. Thus the particular child or adult that researchers happen to select as the stimulus for evaluating perceived credibility can be critical to the results. The solution clearly required stimulus sampling.

The general concern here is that researchers commonly fail to sample stimuli, preferring instead to use one exemplar of the class of stimuli to which they wish to generalize. And, although the failure to sample subjects in appropriate numbers of type is readily detected as a problem for generalization, failure to sample stimuli is commonly not detected as a generalization problem.

CONTROLLED VERSUS FIELD CONTEXTS

Context is paramount in evaluating the appropriateness of generalizations from research findings, and there is an aspect of real-world contexts that is deserving of special attention to exemplify the contrast with controlled research contexts. Natural contexts consist of a large number of complex factors, embedded in an intricate web of relationships. The manner in which the variables change and how they correlate in the natural context stands in contrast to controlled research contexts. In the latter, researchers attempt to control most variables while varying others in a systematic fashion. The controlled variation achieved by randomization or by fixed levels is typically quite different than the natural variation of that factor, and the research variable is embedded in a different context by virtue of the experimental control. A potentially serious limitation of generalizing from a controlled experiment to actual cases exists whenever there are natural confounds that are present in actual cases but are controlled in experiments. Experimenters abhor confounds, but they are part of the fabric of natural environments. An example from eyewitness research demonstrates this point.

Researchers have been concerned with the effects of stress on eyewitness memory (of both children and adults). Studies of stress typically involve the presentation of an event under different stress levels followed by a test for memory of the event. Stress is usually manipulated by either varying some quality of the event (e.g., including a violent action vs. a nonviolent action) or varying another stimulus that produces stress (e.g., the level of white noise the witness experiences while observing the event). This type of research has led to the conclusion that high levels of stress interfere with adults' eyewitness memory (Deffenbacher, 1983). Yuille and Cutshall (1986), however, conducted a field study of people who had witnessed an actual, fatal shooting incident. They found that the memories of those witnesses who reported that they were highly stressed by the event were as detailed and accurate as were the memories of those who reported that they were less stressed. However, in contrast to typical laboratory studies, Yuille and Cutshall (1986) found that stress and involvement were confounded. That is, the stressed witnesses were closer to and more involved in the shooting incident than were the unstressed witnesses.

It may be that, in forensic contexts, stress is a natural confound with other factors, such as how close a witness was to the event. The implications of this type of natural confound can be quite significant. In this case, for example, an expert testifying for the defense might be prone to argue from the experimental studies on stress that the memories of witnesses who reported high stress might not be as accurate as those who reported less stress. But the experimenters, in their attempt to control other variables, did not allow stress to covary with involvement, proximity to the event, opportunity to view, and other such variables. Thus, in actual cases, the witnesses with close-range views of the event and those who were paying the most attention might also be the ones most stressed by their experience. As a result, it could be misleading to suggest that the witnesses who were the most stressed are likely to have the least detailed and least accurate memories.

Controlled research is a necessary component of the research enterprise and often provides the only context in which a phenomenon can be explored. However, the researcher must be aware of the special context of the controlled situation and of the restrictions it may place on the generalization of the findings. The process of generalization can be aided through the use of field research. Of course, field research has its limitations as well, but in combination with controlled research, it produces a firmer foundation for application of findings. One way to look at the application problem is as an empirical question. The extent to which the pattern of results found in controlled studies holds in actual forensic contexts can be evaluated, in many instances, through field research. When field research is possible, the professional wishing to apply research knowledge would be well advised to consider testing the generalizations with a field study in which natural confounds are treated not as an anathema, but as part of the phenomenon to be understood and appreciated.

PSYCHOLOGISTS IN COURT

Psychologists are going to continue to be asked to assist the courts and other systems charged with making decisions based on children's evidence. The decision to provide such assistance should not be taken lightly. If the psychologist's role involves expert testimony, it would be useful to consider the effects of expert psychological testimony regarding eyewitness matters (see Wells, 1986) and be familiar with the various perspectives on the ethics of such testimony. Experimental research with mock juries indicates that expert testimony on eyewitness issues affects the jury deliberation process and the extent to which the jurors are skeptical about the testimony of eyewitnesses (Fox & Walters, 1986; Hosch, Beck, & McIntyre, 1980; Wells, Lindsay, & Tousignant, 1980). These kinds of experimental effects make it likely that expert testimony can affect trial outcomes and, therefore, make it particularly important that the expert testimony is based on reliable and generalizable research.

It should not be assumed that an expert on child witnesses can merely describe some research and then leave it to the court to make judgments about generalizability. There is good evidence to indicate that methodological reasoning of the sort required to make such judgments is not a by-product of law school training and is unlikely to exist among lay jurors (Lehman, Lempert, & Nisbett, 1988). It is the responsibility of the psychologist to acquaint the court with the problems and limitations associated with the generalization of research findings. Any qualities of the research context that limit generalization should be addressed with the same attention as the qualities that permit application.

The adversarial nature of our criminal justice system is one of the problems faced by professionals serving as expert witnesses. Typically the psychologist will be engaged by one of the adversaries and will be encouraged to present the current state of knowledge in a fashion that assists their side of the case. This feature of the law–psychology interaction can mitigate the psychologist's ability to provide a comprehensive picture of the current state of knowledge. One strategy to overcome this difficulty is for the psychologist to adopt the stance of a friend of the court. That is, the psychologist can inform the prosecutor or defense counsel that he or she will present psychological knowledge from the perspective of an educator to the court and not in the service of an adversary. If the lawyer is unwilling to accept psychological services on this basis, those services are perhaps better not offered.

CONCLUSIONS

We addressed several questions about the constraints on application in this chapter. Our answers to those questions are summarized as follows.

1. There is an extensive and growing data base concerning children's eyewitness abilities, and this is reflected in the contents of the present volume. Some of this knowledge is of use to those who must evaluate children's evidence in actual cases.

2. Caution should be used in generalizing from controlled research studies to real-world contexts. The research and forensic contexts must share more than superficial similarities. The variances and covariances among variables that infiltrate actual eyewitness cases are controlled or randomized out in experimental research in ways that can make generalization from experiments to actual cases a risky endeavor under certain circumstances. Whenever possible, a comparison of the experimental research and field contexts should be made and their apparent similarities and differences enunciated.

3. When psycholgists offer expert evidence they should present all of the information, including qualifications and limitations, about a phenomenon.

References

Deffenbacher, K. (1983). The influence of arousal on reliability of testimony. In B. R. Clifford & S. Lloyd-Bostock (Eds.), *Evaluating witness evidence* (pp. 235–251). Chichester, England: Wiley.

Finkelhor, D. (1979). *Sexually victimized children*. New York: Free Press.

Fox, S. G., & Walters, H. A. (1986). The impact of general versus specific expert testimony and eyewitness confidence upon mock juror judgment. *Law and Human Behavior, 10*, 215–228.

Goldstein, A. G., Johnson, K. S., & Chance, J. E. (1979). Does fluency of face description imply superior face recognition? *Bulletin of the Psychonomic Society, 13*, 15–18.

Goodman, G. S. (1984). Children's testimony in historical perspective. *Journal of Social Issues, 40*, 9–31.

Hosch, H. M., Beck, E. L., & McIntyre, P. (1980). Influence of expert testimony regarding eyewitness accuracy on jury decision. *Law and Human Behavior, 4*, 287–296.

Kassin, S. M., Ellsworth, P. C., & Smith, V. L. (1989). The "general acceptance" of psychological research on eyewitness testimony. *American Psychologist, 44*, 1089–1098.

Lehman, D. R., Lempert, R. O., & Nisbett, R. E. (1988). The effects of graduate training on reasoning: Formal discipline and thinking about everyday-life events. *American Psychologist, 43*, 431–442.

Leippe, M. R., & Romanczyk, A. (1987). Children on the witness stand: A communication/persuasion analysis of jurors' reactions to child witnesses. In S. J. Ceci, M. P. Toglia, & D. F. Ross (Eds.), *Children's eyewitness memory* (pp. 156–177). New York: Springer-Verlag.

Loftus, E. F. (1983). Silence is not golden. *American Psychologist, 38*, 564–572.

McCloskey, M., & Egeth, H. E. (1983). Eyewitness identification: What can a psychologist tell a jury? *American Psychologist, 38*, 550–557.

Munsterberg, H. (1908). *On the witness stand*. New York: Doubleday.

Ross, D. F., Miller, B. S., & Moran, P. B. (1987). The child in the eyes of the jury: Assessing mock jurors' perceptions of the child witness. In S. J. Ceci, M. P. Toglia, & D. F. Ross (Eds.), *Children's eyewitness memory* (pp. 142–154). New York: Springer-Verlag.

Wells, G. L. (1985). Verbal descriptions of faces form memory: Are they diagnostic of identification accuracy? *Journal of Applied Psychology, 70,* 619–626.

Wells, G. L. (1986). Expert psychological testimony: Empirical and conceptual analyses of effects. *Law and Human Behavior, 1, 2,* 83–96.

Wells, G. L., Lindsay, R. C. L., & Tousignant, J. P. (1980). Effects of expert psychological advice on human performance in judging the validity of eyewitness testimony. *Law and Human Behavior, 4,* 275–285.

Wells, G. L., Turtle, J. W., & Luus, C. A. E. (1989). The perceived credibility of child eyewitnesses: What happens when they use their own words? In S. J. Ceci, D. F. Ross, & M. P. Toglia (Eds.), *Perspectives on children's testimony.* New York: Springer-Verlag.

Wigmore, J. (1909). Professor Munsterberg and the psychology of testimony. *Illinois Law Review, 3,* 399–445.

Wolfskiel, M. P., & Brigham, J. C. (1985). The relationship between accuracy of prior description and facial recognition. *Journal of Applied Psychology, 70,* 611–618.

Yuille, J. C. (1989). Expert evidence by psychologists: Sometimes problematic and often premature. *Behavioral Sciences and the Law, 7,* 181–196.

Yuille, J. C., & Cutshall, J. L. (1986). A case study of eyewitness memory of a crime. *Journal of Applied Psychology, 71,* 291–301.

Yuille, J. C., King, M. A., & MacDougall, D. (1988). *Child victims and witnesses: The social science and legal literatures.* Ottawa, Canada: Department of Justice.

COMMENTARY: RESEARCH FINDINGS— WHAT DO THEY MEAN?

ELIZABETH F. LOFTUS and STEPHEN J. CECI

Yuille and Wells present five reasonable caveats regarding the hazards of generalizing from an imperfect knowledge base to a particular case at trial. In the first part of this commentary, we briefly address four of their concerns, making some semantic distinctions and offering a few qualifications to what are otherwise reasonable concerns. We conclude with a vignette that is animated by their fifth point regarding the inappropriateness of some expert testimony.

Yuille and Wells state that "ecological validity is not a quality of the appearance of a research paradigm but a concern about how research results are applied." The motivation for this claim appears to lie in a distrust of generalizing from a single study, even if it possesses some degree of face validity. Thus a study of some realistic crime context is an insufficient basis for drawing inferences about other crime contexts. If this is all that Yuille and Wells intend, then it would be hard to quarrel with them as this caution is certainly worth bearing in mind. But the principle that underlies the wording of this point strikes us as bordering on the tautological. If ecological validity has more to do with how research is applied than with the qualities of the research paradigm, then the sequitor ought to be the following question: What is the basis for drawing inferences about the applicability of research? Put this way, it is apparent that the basis for such decisions is precisely an analysis of the qualities of the research in question, including an examination of the overlap between these qualities (cognitive, emotional, and physical) and the qualities of the case. So, although we understand Yuille and Wells's desire to tame the urge to apply a research finding that has been carried out in a paucity of contexts, none resembling the case being tried, we do wonder about the utility of their attempted separation of research design and its application.

Yuille and Wells also made the point that human behavior is tied to specific contexts. It has been known that behavior is tied to specific contexts and, as a result, slight shifts in context have sometimes led to large shifts in outcomes (see Bronfenbrenner, 1979). Yet many psychologists have failed to appreciate the contextual nature of behavior and have erected grand, overarching, theoretical

facades on the basis of highly context-specific findings. Few researchers today
suggest that universal laws of behavior are trans-species, or even trans-situational
within species. Having said this, it strikes us as necessary to add something to
the other side of this argument, lest the reader walk away with the impression
that a contextualist approach to cognition is tantamount to foresaking prediction
across contexts. Amidst the welter of contextual factors that imbue a behavior,
there frequently exists some regularity, a point we shall return to in our concluding
vignette. Contextualists, while endorsing the ever-changing nature of contexts,
believe that regularities of nature often exist and, furthermore, believe in the
ability to accurately chart them in the swirling tides of change (Jaeger & Rosnow,
1988). To be a contextualist is not synonymous with being against prediction or
denying that regularities exist. Nor is it incompatible with being in favor of
controlled research. It means merely that contextual complexity needs to be inserted into our controlled studies and into our explanations of behavior.

A third point that Yuille and Wells made is that decisions about sampling
can have profound implications for making generalizations. In making this point,
Yuille and Wells extend the earlier concern of Brunswick and Lewin regarding
the need to sample not only subjects but also situations, in order to "possess
generality with regard to normal life conditions" (Brunswick, 1943, cited in
Chapter 1, this volume). Although this concern is not a new one for psychologists
(e.g., see Bull's commentary on Chapter 7), it is still a welcome reminder of the
limitations of studying a few individuals' responses to a few stimuli, in a few
settings. Any generalization should reflect such sampling barriers to the reliability
of individual differences, as Yuille and Wells note. In a recent review of the
cognitive research, Schooler has argued that the generalizability of many scientific
findings are problematic because of inadequate care in sampling across subjects
and contexts and the implicit assumption that basic cognitive processes function
invariantly across different socio-demographic groups and social addresses (Schooler,
1989).

Fourth, Yuille and Wells assert that the numerous and complexly interwoven
factors embedded in a natural context stand in contrast to controlled research
contexts and, therefore, the controlled variations achieved by randomization or
by fixed levels is typically quite different from the natural variation of that factor.
They further assert that one of the hazards of generalizing from controlled studies
is that experimentalists abhor confounds. They correctly note that in some natural
contexts variables co-mingle, as in the stressed witness example they describe.
Granted, researchers often have neglected to consider such naturally occurring,
correlated, independent variables. Who can deny this? But the problem is not one
of too much controlled research. In the example mentioned, it is possible to
experimentally covary stress and witness involvement in a controlled manner to
determine whether these factors stand in positive, neutral, or negative relationship
to eyewitness accuracy. Reduced to this level of analysis, the so-called problem

of too much controlled research (i.e., the proclivity of experimentalists to randomize out covariances among variables) is actually a problem of too little controlled research. This is not to say we disagree with the spirit of Yuille and Wells's enjoinder to link controlled research to field research. The latter can be useful not only as a means of testing hypotheses but also in generating them. But the complexity of the everyday world is no basis for inferring that correlated variables ought not be disentangled and examined for their unique and interdependent contribution to behavior.

According to Yuille and Wells, when psychologists are asked to offer expert testimony, they should thoroughly consider the qualities of the research context that limit generalization to the case. This fifth point is perhaps the glue for Yuille and Wells's entire argument—it entails all of the aforementioned points (generalization, ecological validity, sampling, and controlled research limitations). We address it, therefore, in a fashion that incorporates all of these earlier issues that were addressed out of context.

Consider a prototypical study of children's eyewitness testimony (Davies, Stevenson-Robb, & Flin, 1988). The youngest children in this study were 7- and 8-year-olds whose performance was compared to that of older children (9–10 and 11–12). All subjects interacted with a visitor to their school for about five minutes. Children, in groups of four, helped the visitor set up equipment in connection with a to-be-delivered talk on road safety, with different children being assigned different tasks (e.g., arranging the projector). Two weeks later, each child was questioned about the visitor and asked to attempt an eyewitness identification from a 12-picture array. Among other results, the investigators found that when the array did not contain the perpetrator, the youngest children made significantly more false identifications (88%) than did older children (60%).

In view of Yuille and Wells's caveat regarding overgeneralization by expert witnesses, what can we conclude from Davies et al.'s finding? One of the first questions that we might ask is whether other studies also demonstrate that younger children are more likely than older children to pick someone out of a perpetrator-absent photo array. Certainly not every study has shown this. Indeed, a study that appeared in the same volume as did Davies et al.'s showed no effects of age on the false identification rate in perpetrator-absent lineups. Yarmey (1988) had young children (aged 4 to 8), older children (9 to 10), and adults watch four minutes of videotape about an abduction of an 8-year-old boy. One day later children were asked to identify the victim and abductor from six-person target-absent photo arrays. No significant age differences in false identifications were found. Despite the existence of contrary findings such as this one, Davies et al. (1988) concluded their review of the target-absent lineup research by noting that their results "broadly replicate the existing literature and underline the problems of the urge to choose among the youngest subjects" (p. 127).

Let us suppose that we have a body of literature that shows that 7-year-old children make more false identifications from target-absent lineups than do older children. Suppose we say that approximately 20 studies show this effect. Let us further suppose that there exist occasional other studies (say a total of 3) that fail to show significant age-related decrements in performance and that we as researchers are not sure why this disparity among studies exists. Nonetheless, with 20 of 23 (87%) of the studies revealing the age-related pattern, we feel confident about the conclusion of Davies et al. (1988). Consider the following example.

A lawyer calls Dr. Child Researcher (CR) one day. The lawyer is handling a case in which a 7-year-old child and her 12-year-old sister both witnessed an armed robbery at Toys-R-Us. The two girls stood exactly the same distance away and viewed the thief for the same amount of time. Both girls later try to identify the thief from an eight-person photo array. The 7-year-old picks number 6, who is the defendant; the 12-year-old picks no one. The lawyer asks about the research on target-absent lineups and Dr. CR tells her about the Davies et al. findings. "Great," she says, "87% of studies find that younger children are less accurate than older children; then you will testify that the 7-year-old is probably mistaken." Of course, Dr. CR must decline, but is there anything legitimate that Dr. CR can tell the court?

The strong pattern of results constitutes a legitimate foundation for a statement to the effect that "Numerous studies have compared the ability of children about 7 years of age to older children in their ability to identify briefly seen strangers from target-absent photo arrays. The majority of these studies show that younger children make more false identifications." It would not be false, inappropriate, illegal, or unethical if such a statement were made in court by Dr. CR. Doing so is consistent with an expert witness's role as an educator of the jury and trier of fact, provided that she takes into consideration all relevant research and not just that subset that is most favorable to her client. In the example at hand, for instance, it would be important to educate the jury about the baseline error rates for the two age groups. Even if 7-year-olds are inferior to 10-year-olds, the difference may be so small as to be of little practical (as opposed to statistical) significance.

Some researchers, however, might argue that Dr. CR should not generalize from this body of research to the present case. After all, none of the 23 studies mentioned in the literature was conducted in a Toys-R-Us store, and none used an eight-person photo array. The studies were quite different from the conditions of observation and testing in the case. If behavior is contextually relevant, then we should not generalize across contexts. Yet, we argue that when a finding has been seen in a wide variety of stimulus settings, albeit simulations, we are encouraged to believe that it will occur when a few stimulus parameters are different. Our basis for this belief has to do with the role that theory plays in generating studies, including the above-mentioned alterations in stimulus settings. When someone reports that *a* and *b* are causally related under certain, specifiable conditions, a theory may lead one to predict that they will be unrelated under different conditions (e.g., delay intervals, types of stimuli, etc.). In other words, most research questions are theoretically motivated. Thus a theory is a vehicle for bridging the gap between controlled laboratory research and a specific real world application.

An obvious example is the forgetting curve. Suppose that the 7-year-old robbery witness made an identification 84 days after her visit to Toys-R-Us. Her older sister picked no one from the photo array four days after the visit. Although we probably have no single study in which delay interval of precisely 84 days following a theft in a toy store was examined, we can still say with confidence that the memory trace for the culprit would not have improved over that period of time. We know that memory is stronger after 4 days than after 84 days because of empirical and theoretical work that tells us so. We do not need to have tests at every level of a variable or every possible combination of variables to be able to predict how these variables would work in a new situation.

The foregoing example speaks to the power of theories: At their core, scientific theories are means for escaping a rigid situationalism that, if endorsed, would argue that no study is relevant to any other unless it was an exact replication of its procedures, motives, age groups, settings, and so forth. It goes without saying that if psychologists really believed this were the case, they would be forced to summarize the relevance of the entire corpus of scientific theory and findings for court cases with the song title "I've Got Plenty of Nothing"! Such a characterization of the value of empirical research is not only overly pessimistic but deeply misconceived.

References

Bronfenbrenner, U. (1979). *The ecology of human development.* Cambridge, MA: Harvard University Press.

Davies, G., Stevenson-Robb, Y., & Flin, R. (1988). Tales out of school: Children's memory for an unexpected event. In M. M. Gruneberg, P. E. Morris, & R. N. Sykes (Eds.), *Practical aspects of memory: Current research and issues* (pp. 122–127). Chichester, England: Wiley.

Jaeger, M. E., & Rosnow, R. L. (1988). Contextualism and its implications for inquiry. *British Journal of Psychology, 79*, 63–75.

Schooler, C. (1989). Social structural effects and experimental situations: Mutual lessons of cognitive and social science. In K. W. Schaie & C. Schooler (Eds.), *Social structure and aging: Psychological processes* (pp. 129–147). Hillsdale, NJ: Erlbaum.

Yarmey, A. D. (1988). Streetproofing and bystanders' memory for child abduction. In M. M. Gruneberg, P. E. Morris, & R. N. Sykes (Eds.), *Practical aspects of memory: Current research and issues* (pp. 112–116). Chichester, England: Wiley.

COMMENTARY: THE ISSUE OF RELEVANCE

RAY BULL

Deese concluded his 1972 book, *Psychology as Science and Art*, by saying that "one aspect of the future of psychology about which we can have no doubt whatever is that its influence will grow because society has nowhere else to turn for guidance and direction than to the social sciences in general and psychology in particular" (p. 107). Over 10 years ago Clifford and I used this quotation to commence our concluding chapter in *The Psychology of Person Identification* (1978). There can be no doubt that over these last 10 years Deese's prediction has come true with regard to witnessing and, more recently, with child witnesses in particular. The chapter by Yuille and Wells does make a worthwhile contribution to the debate. However, I am surprised that their chapter fails to mention recent articles by Monahan and Walker (1988) and Walker and Monahan (1987), which have proposed new ways for psychological research, in particular research on witnessing, to be used by criminal justice systems.

Yuille and Wells make the point that research findings need to be "both reliable and valid," and they follow this by usefully mentioning the Frye test's requirement that professionals in a field must agree about reliability and validity. Unfortunately, they did not indicate explicitly whether validity specifically includes relevance. A body of research findings could meet the requirements of what constitutes reliability and validity without being relevant. Additionally, although professionals in a field could possibly agree on reliability and many traditional aspects of validity, are they (in this case, psychologists) best placed to determine relevance to a particular legal, judicial, or trial issue? (King's 1986 book on the role of psychology in court addresses this issue and is essential reading for all researchers on child witnesses, although few seem aware of it.)

Yuille and Wells argue that "ecological validity is not a quality of the appearance of a research paradigm but rather a concern about how research results are applied." Later they suggest that "a researcher who wishes to apply his or her research findings to a real-world context has the onus to provide the foundations and justifications for the generalization." Be that as it may, Yuille and Wells appear to have missed the point that many psychological experts on witnessing who testify in court (at least in several countries—using either the adversarial or inquisitorial system) often speak about research other than their own. This being the case, who is responsible for the generalization—surely not the original re-searcher? As Monahan and Walker (1988) argued the court should decide in such cases, and they offer useful suggestions for bringing this about. Monahan and Walker suggested that research findings presented in court are neither legislative facts (that concern general questions of law and policy) nor adjudicative facts (that pertain only to the case at hand) but are used to construct a frame of reference or background context for deciding issues crucial to the resolution of a case. They have called this new use of social science in law the creation of social frameworks.

Walker and Monahan (1987) pointed out that these social frameworks are typically offered (in the United States) by one of the parties through the oral testimony of expert witnesses for evaluation and application by a jury. They suggested

> a very different procedural scheme for dealing with social science used as a social framework: the research either may be offered by one of the parties in a written brief or located by the trial judge; it should be evaluated by the judge according to accepted common law principles; and only then should it be conveyed to the jury, by instruction of the judge. (Walker & Mona-han, 1987, p. 560)

I would like to know Yuille and Wells's views on such a suggestion, given that aspects of it already occur in Europe (e.g., see Spencer, Nicholson, Flin, & Bill, 1990).

Yuille and Wells do suggest that "it is better to err in the direction of caution when applying research findings." Laudable as this is, I would have preferred that their chapter address squarely the issue of what psychologists being asked to testify in court should do if there is good reason to believe that the court or jury holds views, or a lawyer presents arguments, for which (a) there exists no support from psychological research and (b) the research that does exist suggests an op-posing view. Rarely does the court or jury have no view on child witnesses and the factors pertaining to a particular case prior to the case.

In addition, the greatest impact of research on child witnesses is not on court testimony but is on pretrial events (e.g., involving parents, caregivers, police, and decisions to prosecute); over past decades decisions about pretrial events have been influenced by prejudices and ignorances concerning children's accounts. Furthermore, several countries recently have changed their laws and legal practices to reflect a change in the belief that child witnesses are very unreliable or sug-gestible (Spencer et al., 1990). Such changes have often been based on full reviews of the extant research literature (e.g., Hedderman, 1987). Even though much of the research cited lacked ecological or external validity, are we to assume, from Yuille and Wells's argument, that such changes are premature?

Yuille and Wells make good points concerning the sampling of stimuli and the confounding of variables in natural settings. In 1978 Clifford and I made a strong plea for this to occur in witness research, a plea that has not been as successful as we had hoped. Yuille and Wells argue that field research should be combined with research on the same topics conducted in controlled (e.g., laboratory) settings. One problem with the cases in which most children testify is that ethically neither field nor controlled research could be set up directly on that topic. That is, Yuille and Wells say that the kinds of court cases in which children testify are "generally but not only sexual abuse cases." Even though work by Flin and me in Scotland (Flin & Bull, 1990) reveals that here children testify more frequently in cases involving murder and attempted murder than in cases involving sexual abuse, valid field research in this type of case might prove to be as unattainable as it seems to be for sexual abuse.

Thus many court cases involving child witnesses will inevitably require generalizations from somewhat similar, but essentially different, research settings. The real issues are how these generalizations are made, who makes them, and who assesses them. Should this be psychologists? As stated earlier, Monahan and Walker have some useful ideas that fit well with Yuille and Wells's strategy that the psychologist "present psychological knowledge from the perspective of an educator to the court and not in the service of an adversary." This already has to happen in countries that have the inquisitorial system of criminal justice (for an account of this issue with regard to child witnesses see Spencer et al., 1990) and, in my experience, has happened in Britain as well. For many years I have been concerned about psychologists publicly "spending most of their time saying how wrong their colleagues have been" (Bull, 1982, p. 336). The chapter by Yuille and Wells makes a worthwhile contribution to reducing the frequency of such naysaying.

References

Bull, R. (1982). Can experimental psychology be applied psychology? In S. Canter & D. Canter (Eds.), *Psychology in practice* (pp. 57–73). Chichester, England: Wiley.

Clifford, B., & Bull, R. (1978). *The psychology of person identification*. London: Routledge.

Deese, J. (1972). *Psychology as science and art*. New York: Harcourt, Brace, & Jovanich.

Flin, R., & Bull, R. (1990). Child witnesses in criminal prosecutions. In J. Spencer, G. Nicholson, R. Flin, & R. Bull (Eds.), *Children's evidence in legal proceedings* (pp. 85–97). London: Hawksmere.

Hedderman, C. (1987). *Children's evidence: The need for corroboration* (Home Office Research and Planning Unit Paper No. 41). London: Home Office.

King, M. (1986). *Psychology in and out of court: A critical examination of legal psychology*. Oxford, England: Pergamon Press.

Monahan, J., & Walker, L. (1988). Social science research in law: A new paradigm. *American Psychologist*, *43*, 465–472.

Spencer, J., Nicholson, G., Flin, R., & Bull, R. (1990). *Children's evidence in legal proceedings*. London: Hawksmere.

Walker, L., & Monahan, J. (1987). Social frameworks: A new use of social science in law. *Virginia Law Review*, *73*, 559–598.

CHAPTER 8

EXPERIMENTAL STUDIES OF INTERVIEWING CHILD WITNESSES

HELEN R. DENT

Many factors outside the control of an investigator, such as age (Goodman & Reed, 1986) and intelligence (Brown, 1974) have been found to exert some influence on the quality of children's eyewitnessing abilities. Different aspects of interviewing, including small changes in the form of questions (Dale, Loftus & Rathbun, 1978), use of misleading suggestion (King & Yuille, 1987), context reinstatement (Wilkinson, 1988) and provision of peer support (Moston, 1987), have also been found to affect the amount and accuracy of children's recall. These factors are normally under the control of an investigator and, perhaps for this reason, are an obvious and frequent target of research into eyewitnessing.

Early experimental investigations of the reliability of child witnesses reached the common conclusion that children were both unreliable and were much more suggestible than adult witnesses (see Goodman, 1984, for a review of this work). Recent experimental studies have reached more disparate and complicated conclusions, ranging, for example, from finding that 6-year-old children are just as resistant to suggestion as adults (Marin, Holmes, Guth, & Kovac, 1979), to the finding that 6-year-olds (Goodman & Reed, 1986) and 9-year-olds (Cohen & Harnick, 1980) are less resistant to suggestion than adults. For good reviews of these and other recent studies, see Hedderman (1987) and Zaragoza (1987). One obvious reason for the disparity in such research findings is the difference in research design and methodology employed by the various experimenters. For example, Marin et al. (1979) used a delay interval of 10 or 30 minutes following a brief staged argument between the experimenter and a confederate. Their interview consisted of free recall followed by 20 objective questions and one leading question. Goodman and Reed (1986) interviewed their subjects four or five days after they interacted for five minutes with an unfamiliar man. Their interview included 4 suggestive questions, 1 correctly leading questions and 17 objective questions. Cohen and Harnick (1980) interviewed subjects immediately after they watched a 12-min black and white film of petty theft. This interview contained 11 leading and 11 nonleading questions. A week later, subjects were asked 22 questions of similar content but in a multiple choice format. In the face of such variety in procedure, it is not surprising that these and other studies have produced apparently different findings.

In an area where advice is being sought from psychologists by police, lawyers, and other professionals regarding the optimal treatment of child witnesses, it is particularly important to aim for consistency in methodology between experiments and repetition of findings in order to increase the reliability of the results on which advice is based. The purpose of this chapter is to attempt to do so in a small way by presenting findings from a series of six studies by the author with similar research design and methodology. The results from these studies will be presented in the following thematic sections: levels of prompting and accuracy, the type of material recalled, the skill of the interviewer, and the developmental level of the interviewee.

METHOD

The design and procedure of these experiments consisted of a film or staged event followed by an interview. The film lasted for four minutes and showed a car being stolen. The staged events consisted of brief (two to five minutes) interruptions in children's classrooms with one, two or three actors interacting with the teacher. One simple scenario involved a workman wearing overalls and carrying a tool bag who came to check the door and window catches. A more complicated event involved four actors (three men and a woman) who interacted with each other as well as the teacher. In all but one of the studies, the interview consisted of questions phrased by the experimenter but posed by a confederate and were of the form free recall, general questions or specific questions. General and specific questions could also be called open-ended and closed respectively. A couple of examples of general questions used in one study, are, ''Can you tell me what the man looked like?'' and ''What did the woman do while she was in your classroom?'' Corresponding specific questions were, ''What color was the man's hair?'' and ''Did the woman say anything to your teacher?'' In the odd study, the interviewers were given free rein and asked to obtain as accurate recall as possible from each child. The ages of the children in each study were 9–11 years, and 8–12 years for the children with mental disabilities. In one study adults were also included as subjects.

Attempts to Minimize Suggestibility

The studies using experimenter-generated questions were designed to minimize suggestibility in the following ways. First, the interviewers had not seen the film or events and so were unable to prompt the children inadvertently. Second, they informed the children that they did not know what had occurred. This was intended to have the effect of decreasing the extent to which the children felt they were being tested, lessening the inherent suggestibility of questions posed, making the task meaningful to the children and increasing the likelihood that the interpretation of the task was as the experimenter intended. Third, the instructions to the children were designed to be as unambiguous and comprehensible as possible and fourth, the children were explicitly instructed to say "I don't know" if unsure of the answer to a question. An extract from one set of instructions illustrates the attempt to achieve these four aims:

> I want to find out what they did while they were in your classroom and what they looked like. You see I don't know, so I want you to help me. I'm going to ask you some questions and I want you to give me the best answers you can. Just tell me everything you can remember. Don't make anything up and don't worry if you can't remember, or you can't answer a question, just say you don't know.

A fifth strategy used to minimize suggestibility was to avoid repetition of questions. This ploy is often used in forensic situations to reduce interviewees' confidence in their answers. A sixth strategy was, not surprisingly, to avoid the use of overtly leading and, where possible leading forms of question as identified by Muscio in 1916 and Dale et al. in 1978. Finally, the children were interviewed on home ground (their own school), were assured that the exercise was not a test and that it did not matter how much or little they could remember. These strategies for minimizing suggestion were not built into the study that focussed on interviewer behavior since those interviewers were given a free rein and were not given any guidance on interview technique.

The reason for going into so much detail on the attempts made to reduce suggestion in these experimental studies is to define clearly that context in which the data should be evaluated. The purpose of the meeting that gave rise to this publication was to explore the suggestibility of children as witnesses. In the context in which children perform as witnesses, few if any of the strategies mentioned are used to minimize suggestion and some are used either deliberately or inadvertently to enhance suggestion. Some examples would be the use of leading questions; an imposing social context (police station or courtroom); repeated questioning and the status of the interviewer. The data presented here will provide some indication of how children perform when strong attempts have been made to reduce the impact of such factors and provide a more conducive atmosphere than the one Alice in Wonderland found herself in when the King said "Give me your evidence and don't be nervous or I'll have you executed on the spot" (Carroll, 1865).

RESULTS AND CONCLUSION

Levels of Prompting and Accuracy

The first theme of this chapter concerns levels of prompting and accuracy. The data relevant to this come from one of the studies with experimenter generated questions (Dent & Stephenson, 1979). Children aged 9–11 years and of normal intelligence were randomly assigned to one of three interview conditions, free recall (condition one), general questions (condition two) and specific questions, (condition three). They were interviewed on five occasions after watching a film of a car theft. The first interview took place immediately after the film (session one), the second interview a day later (session two), and the third interview two days later (session three). The fourth interview was given two weeks (session four), and the fifth two months (session five) after seeing the film. The children in the specific questions condition answered the same set of 46 specific questions on all five sessions. Children in the other two conditions, however, gave free recall or answered 10 general questions only on sessions one and two. On sessions three, four, and five they answered the 46 specific questions. The children's responses were scored from a checklist of 90 points of information contained in the film. It would have been possible but extremely unlikely for the subjects to have scored this number of correct points in any of the experimental conditions.

Table 1 shows the mean numbers of correct and incorrect points of information recalled by the children in each subject group. It is clear that the children who answered specific questions gave more correct points and hence a more complete account of the incident than the children who answered general questions or gave free recall. Conversely, the children who gave free recall, produced a smaller number of incorrect points and hence a more accurate account of the incident, than children who answered general or specific questions. When the children in the free recall and general questions conditions answered specific questions in experimental sessions three, four, and five, their numbers of correct and incorrect points increased to the level given by children in the specific questions condition. This would seem to indicate that the pattern of results obtained in sessions one and two was due to the experimental condition rather than the subject group. Analyses of variance showed there to be statistically reliable differences

Table 1.

MEAN NUMBERS OF CORRECT AND INCORRECT POINTS OF INFORMATION
IN REMEMBERED BY CHILDREN IN TWO TESTING SESSIONS

Condition	Mean correct points		Mean incorrect points	
	Session I	Session II	Session I	Session II
1. Free recall (*n* = 12)	14.16	17.75	1.42	1.67
2. General questions (*n* = 9)	22.0	23.67	3.00	3.89
3. Specific questions (*n* = 9)	34.0	34.44	8.22	7.89

Note. Data are from An Experimental Study of the Effectiveness of Different Techniques of Questioning Child Witnesses by H. R. Dent and G. M. Stephenson (1979), *British Journal of Social and Clinical Psychology, 18*, 41–51. Copyright 1979, adapted by permission.

between conditions when free report and general questions were used, but not when all groups simply answered specific questions. This indicates that children's recall is facilitated by the increased cueing in specific questions but that the increase in suggestions created by posing more specific questions also has a detrimental effect on accuracy. This finding has been consistent throughout all similar studies conducted by the author (Dent, 1978, 1986, 1987) and so could be considered robust.

The Type of Material Recalled

Another robust finding, discovered by chance in this same study (Dent & Stephenson, 1979) was that children appear to be more suggestible about certain types of information than others. Specifically, the children were more adversely affected in the specific questions condition on recall of the appearance of the people and the car seen in the film, than about the sequence of events and activities of the actors. Table 2 shows the mean percentages of errors made by the children when describing people and objects and when narrating events.

Apart from when free report was used (condition one, sessions one and two) it can be seen that a greater proportion of errors was made when answering either general or specific questions about appearance than about the sequence of events. This seems to indicate, particularly since no errors were made on description in the free report condition, that descriptive information may be more susceptible than event information to the suggestion inherent in greater levels of cueing. Different levels of suggestibility may be found to operate for other categories of information such as speech or written information. It would certainly be useful to know this for the forensic situation.

Table 2.

MEAN PERCENTAGES OF ERRORS MADE BY CHILDREN WHEN DESCRIBING
PEOPLE AND WHEN NARRATING EVENTS

	Condition					
	1. Free recall		2. General questions		3. Specific questions	
Session	People	Events	People	Events	People	Events
1.	0	10.0	29.93	7.2	38.03	11.11
2.	0	9.03	40.14	7.49	38.24	10.13
3.	37.93	17.77	39.48	12.27	42.98	10.28
4.	36.78	14.48	39.72	10.78	41.64	12.93
5.	55.23	16.36	34.68	9.68	39.98	10.31

Note. Data are from An Experimental Study of Effectiveness of Different Techniques of Questioning
Child Witnesses by H. R. Dent and G. M. Stephenson, 1979, *British Journal of Social and Clinical
Psychology*, *18*, 41–51. Copyright 1979, adapted by permission.

The Skill of the Interviewer

In addition to the level of prompting and the type of material recalled, the skill
of the interviewer appears to have some bearing on the susceptibility of children
to suggestion. An experiment was carried out by Dent (1982) to investigate this
factor using 12 interviewers. They comprised three senior police officers, three
school teachers, three parents, and three voluntary youth workers. They were told
the general aims of the study, but were not informed that their interviewing styles
would be a focus of attention. Each interviewer individually saw five children
from classrooms in which an incident had been staged the previous day. The
incident was fairly complex and involved three men and a woman who interacted
with each other and the teacher, and delivered and removed items from the
classroom. The interviewers were not given any instructions on how to interview
the children but were asked to obtain as complete and accurate recall of the incident
as possible. The mean number of correct points obtained by each interviewer
ranged widely from 48–8 and the mean incorrect points ranged from 1–10. The
most surprising finding from this study was that two of the interviewers (both
school teachers) obtained a combination of high correct and low incorrect points
despite giving little time for free recall, using few general, many specific and
some leading questions. This may have been because they used other techniques,
for example cognitive context reinstatement, which facilitated the children's recall,
but may also have been due to their ability to judge how and when to use more
suggestive questions. They also avoided falling into the trap of phrasing questions
to elicit information that was consistent with their preconceived notion of what

Table 3.

MEAN ACCURACY PERCENTAGES FOR TOTAL (DESCRIPTIVE AND EVENT)
INFORMATION RECALLED

Subjects	Free recall	General questions	Specific questions
Children with mental disabilities (n = 78)	80	80	66
Children with normal intelligence (n = 102)	87	82	74
Adults (n = 64)	90	84	83

Note. Data are from *An Experimental Study of the Comparative Reliability of Child and Adult Witnesses* by H. R. Dent, 1987, London: Home Office. Copyright 1987, adapted by permission.

happened in the event, an activity strongly associated with inaccurate recall. It would be worth investigating whether school teachers as a group do possess good forensic interviewing skills and, if so, what elements of their training and experience particularly promoted these.

The Developmental Level of the Interviewee

A final factor that has some influence on suggestibility is the developmental level of the interviewee. This was examined by a study Dent (1987) with the following subject groups, children (9–11-years-old) and adults (16–41-years-old) of normal intelligence and mildly mentally handicapped children (8–12-years-old) in which free report and experimenter generated general and specific questions were used to elicit recall of a staged event. The event was designed to be credible to adults as well as comprehensible to the mentally handicapped children. Two actors interrupted classrooms in schools and adult education institutions claiming to be monitoring noise levels in classrooms and stress in teachers. During the incident, which lasted for two minutes, one actor emptied the contents of her briefcase as she searched for a stopwatch.

The results of this study, as seen in Table 3, show all three subject groups to have a similar level of accuracy when minimal or moderate levels of prompting were used, as in free report or general questions. However, when greater cueing was used in the form of specific questions, the three groups differed significantly in their levels of accuracy, with adults being the most and mentally handicapped children the least accurate. The same pattern of results was found when descriptive recall for the appearance of the actors and the objects was analyzed separately from total recall.

When the data were examined in greater detail, it became apparent that the children benefitted more from prompts than did the adults. Their recall was much less complete in the lower cueing conditions (free recall and general questions) but of a similar level of completeness when greater cueing was used (specific questions). Unfortunately the children's increase in completeness was accompanied by a marked decrease in accuracy. This indicates a need for great care in interviewing children to enable them to recall as much and as accurately as possible. The data also indicate that greater care is needed when interviewing children than adults, but that children are capable of as accurate recall as adults.

This experiment, reported by Dent (1987), does not provide the solution to how to obtain recall of maximal completeness and accuracy from children. The study examining interviewer behavior (Dent, 1982) has indicated that prior training and experience with children may enhance interviewer performance. Other recent research, particularly the exciting work on reinstating physical contexts with pre-school children (Wilkinson, 1988) and on peer support in interviews with 10-year-olds (Moston, 1987), indicates that there are a variety of factors that may have a positive influence on the completeness and accuracy of children's memory for events. Such variables deserve a closer scrutiny in future research.

The data presented and discussed in this paper indicate that children are capable of being good eyewitnesses, but that their recall appears to be more vulnerable to various distorting influences in the interview situation than does adult recall. The problem that faces courts, lawyers and all professionals involved is that the forensic situation is replete with these influences, particularly the use of high levels of prompting, and it will take major changes in the education of the professionals and in courtroom procedure, to provide an effective remedy.

References

Brown, A. (1974). Strategic behavior in retardate memory. In N. R. Ellis, (Ed.). *International Review of Research in Mental Retardation*. New York: Academic Press.

Carroll, L. (1865). *Alice in Wonderland*.

Cohen, R. L., & Harnick, M. A. (1980). The susceptibility of child witnesses to suggestion. *Law and Human Behavior*, *4*, 201–210.

Dale, P. S., Loftus, E. F., & Rathbun, L. (1978). The influence of the form of the question on the eyewitness testimony of pre-school children. *Journal of Psycholinguistic Research*, *7*, 269–277.

Dent, H. R. (1978). *Investigation of juvenile and adult testimony and identification evidence*. Doctoral thesis: University of Nottingham, England.

Dent, H. R. (1982). The effects of interviewing strategies on the results of interviews with child witnesses. In A. Trankell, (Ed.). *Reconstructing the past*. Stockholm, Sweden: P. A. Norstedt and Sons.

Dent, H. R. (1986). Experimental study of the effectiveness of different techniques of questioning mentally handicapped child witnesses. *British Journal of Clinical Psychology*, *25*, 13–17.

Dent, H. R. (1987). *An experimental study of the comparative reliability of child and adult witnesses*. Final report of project support by Grant No. 48716 from the Home Office Research and Planning Unit.

Dent, H. R., & Stephenson, G. M. (1979). An experimental study of the effectiveness of different techniques of questioning child witnesses. *British Journal of Social and Clinical Psychology*, *18*, 41–51.

Goodman, G. S. (1984). Children's testimony in historical perspective. *Journal of Social Issues*, *40*, 9–31.

Goodman, G. S., & Reed, R. S. (1986). Age differences in eyewitness testimony. *Law and Human Behavior*, *10*, 317–332.

Hedderman, C. (1987). *Children's evidence: the need for corroboration*. London: Home Office. (Research and Planning Unit Paper No. 41).

King, M. A., & Yuille, J. C. (1987). Suggestibility and the child witness. In S. J. Ceci, M. P. Toglia & D. F. Ross, (Eds.). *Children's Eye Witness Memory*. New York: Springer-Verlag.

Marin, B. V., Holmes, D. L., Guth, M., & Kovac, P. (1979). The potential of children as eyewitnesses. *Law and Human Behavior*, *3*, 295–305.

Moston, S. (1987, September). *The effects of the provision of the social support in child interviews*. Paper presented at the meeting of the British Psychological Society Developmental Section Conference, York, England.

Muscio, B. (1916). The influence of the form of a question. *British Journal of Psychology*, *8*, 351–386.

Wilkinson, J. (1988). Context effects in children's event memory. In M. Gruneberg, P. Morris & R. Sykes (Eds.). *Practical Aspects of Memory: Current Research and Issues*, Volume 1. Chichester: John Wiley and Sons.

Zaragoza, M. S. (1987). Memory, suggestibility and eyewitness testimony in children and adults. In S. J. Ceci, M. P. Toglia & D. F. Ross, (Eds.). *Children's Eyewitness Memory*. New York: Springer-Verlag.

COMMENTARY: PUTTING INTERVIEWING IN CONTEXT

PETER A. ORNSTEIN

To a considerable extent, the testimony provided by children in legal settings depends on the interviewing skills of those who question them. Assuming that children are being asked about events that have been experienced or witnessed, the skilled examiner is able to establish a context in which accurate recall is fostered and the possibilities of distortion are minimized. Doing so, however, is not an easy task, and some of the complexities of the matter are presented by Dent in her treatment of a series of laboratory studies of children and adults who have been exposed to films or staged events.

From my perspective, Dent's report provides us with a treatment of an interesting and informative set of experiments, as well as an understanding of the need for programmatic studies of interviewing. However, my reaction to this chapter is that the issues discussed here could profitably be placed in a broader context, one that is both more developmentally focused and theoretically grounded. Given the major developmental changes that take place across the preschool and elementary school years, it does not seem productive to talk about the interviewing of a homogeneous class of "children." In addition, there is an obvious linkage between the variables that are important in the context of interviewing and those that are central to contemporary analyses of memory and cognition. Thus, the issues regarding the interviewing of children of different ages can be profitably placed in the broader framework of what is known about cognitive development.

COGNITIVE DIAGNOSIS

The developmental literature suggests that the task of the interviewer is one of "cognitive diagnosis," just as the task of the laboratory researcher is one of diagnosing age-related changes in children's competence in reasoning, memory,

Preparation of this chapter was supported in part by grant MH 43904 from the National Institute of Mental Health. Much appreciation is expressed to Patricia Clubb for helpful comments on an earlier draft of this chapter.

147

and other cognitive domains (see Flavell, 1985; Folds, Footo, Guttentag, & Orn-stein, 1990). But diagnosis is not easy, even with the controls that can be applied in the laboratory. The difficulty of assessment stems from the high degree of context specificity that characterizes children's performance in a broad range of cognitive tasks. We know that performance can vary substantially from setting to setting and hence that our estimates of children's abilities can also vary markedly, depending on the situation in which we choose to make our judgments (Folds et al., 1990; Ornstein, Baker-Ward, & Naus, 1988). For example, 8- and 9-year-olds are usually not thought to be skillful in the use of strategies for remembering, but our impressions of their abilities can be altered significantly by relatively minor variations in task parameters. Indeed, in highly "supportive" contexts, young children can be shown to be quite strategic. Furthermore, the younger the child, the greater the variability in performance across settings (Folds et al., 1990; Ornstein et al., 1988).

These contextual variations in performance no doubt arise because of age differences in children's fundamental cognitive skills, their understanding of the social settings in which assessments take place, and their feelings of ease and comfort with the adults who meet with them. In general, laboratory performance is best when the conditions of support provided by the experimenter compensate for children's inabilities to carry out various cognitive operations on their own. Thus, for example, because active multi-item rehearsal requires the retrieval of previously presented items, and young children may have difficulty with speeded retrieval, performance is facilitated by leaving to-be-remembered items visible after they are initially presented (Ornstein, Medlin, Stone, & Naus, 1985).

THE INTERVIEW CONTEXT

The implication of these findings is that the conditions established by the inter-viewer can have a profound effect upon children's reports. Thus the diagnosis that is made may be tied to the context for interviewing, and this linkage may be greater for younger as opposed to older children. Moreover, at some level, the skilled interviewer must tailor the interview conditions specifically for each in-dividual child, based on an analysis of cognitive and linguistic abilities, under-standing of the proceedings, and level of stress. The critical nature of choices made by the interviewer is reinforced by one fundamental reality that must always be kept in mind: A different impression of the young child might be obtained under altered conditions of interviewing. Because of this, a number of fundamental issues must be dealt with by potential interviewers.

When Should the Child be Questioned?

The timing of the interview must be considered by interviewers, even if it is not always under their direct control. Not only is it essential to have knowledge of the delay between an event and a subsequent interview, but also it is important to keep track of the child's experiences during the interval. Both the passage of time and a variety of intervening experiences can have an impact on the status of the resulting memory trace.

In the absence of reinstating events, the strength of a trace decreases with time, thereby making access and successful retrieval more difficult. Moreover, the initial memory traces of young children, typically weaker in comparison with those of older individuals, may undergo more rapid decay (see, e.g., Brainerd, Kingma, & Howe, 1985). In addition, as the delay interval increases, there is a greater likelihood of interference with the existing trace. Regardless of which position is taken in the debate on whether inconsistent postevent information alters the actual structure of the memory trace (see, e.g., Loftus 1979; McCloskey & Zaragoza, 1985), repeated conversations about an event have the potential to interfere with children's recall of information about that event. Furthermore, the likelihood of this interference varies inversely with age (Ceci, Ross, & Toglia, 1987; Zaragoza, 1987).

Accordingly, in planning an interview it is crucial to know the length of time that has elapsed, as well as the individuals who have interacted with the child in this interval. In the context of the legal system—especially given the reality of children being questioned repeatedly by police, physicians, nurses, social workers, psychologists, and lawyers over long periods of time—it seems likely that children's reports can come to be combinations of their own fading memories and the points of view of others. Even without the intention to mislead, adults who question children must recognize that the interview process itself has the potential to distort children's memories.

Where Should the Child be Interviewed?

Children are questioned in many places, for example, in police stations, emergency rooms, mental health facilities, lawyers' offices, judges' chambers, and in open court. Obviously, these locations vary substantially in terms of the degree to which a child is likely to feel comfortable and the extent to which available cues may facilitate recall. Thus, it is essential to take the setting into account, because the location of an assessment can have a measurable impact on performance. For example, even the recall performance of adults is enhanced if memory is assessed in the situation in which the materials were initially presented (e.g., Godden & Baddeley, 1975).

As a general principle, it seems likely that memory will be facilitated as the interview context comes to resemble the situation in which the event was experienced. However, a possible limiting condition to this proposed relationship may be the extent to which the initial setting can elicit negative feelings and thus interfere with performance. And at a more general level, interviewers must be sensitive to the fact that some locations (e.g., courtrooms) may simply be intimidating to younger children and are thus not optimal settings in which to access children's knowledge and retention.

How Should the Child be Questioned?

Interviewers must also think carefully about the structure of the interview, as the form of the questions directed to children can have a substantial impact on their performance. For example, Dent and her colleagues, as well as others (e.g., Ornstein, Gordon, & Larus, in press) have shown that young children generate more information in response to specific yes–no types of questions than when given open-ended questions. However, this enhanced recall is accompanied by greater possibilities of error and distortion.

Other features of the questions directed to children are also important, such as the choice of language used in the inquiry. In some situations, young children may fail to understand completely the words and the linguistic constructions employed by their adult inquisitors (see Dale, Loftus, & Rathbun, 1978). Furthermore, the tendency of examiners to repeat their questions may lead young children to change their responses. In addition to the possibilities of distortion mentioned earlier, young children may interpret repeated questions about a single episode as a sign that the interviewer feels that there is some problem with their ''stories.'' As a consequence, children may change their reports to meet what they perceive to be the expectations of the interviewer (see, e.g., Siegal, Waters, & Dinwiddy, 1988).

What are the Child's Expectations?

The issue of children's responses to repeated questioning leads to consideration of a more general matter, namely, that of the extent to which the interviewer and the child share a common set of assumptions about the task before them. The entire interview process rests on the establishment of shared expectations, and the obtained data may be difficult to interpret if this is not the case. For example, consider how traditional interpretations of preschoolers' performance on Paigetian class-inclusion tasks must be modified when it is realized that these young children often interpret the experimenter's instructions in a manner that is inconsistent with what was intended, thereby leading them to be performing what is functionally a quite different task (see Donaldson, 1978).

Within the context of interviewing, it is important to gauge the degree to which the child and examiner agree on just what it means to provide information about a previous experience. To what extent may a child assume that the adult examiner already has knowledge of the event and, therefore, that it is not necessary to provide a full report? That this may be important is suggested by a recent study of metamemory (Best & Ornstein, 1986) in which children provided more information to a younger child in a tutorial paradigm than they did to an adult experimenter using a standard questionnaire procedure.

THE NEED FOR GUIDELINES FOR INTERVIEWERS

One thing that has not been considered directly in this brief commentary is the question of who is doing the interviewing. Yet it should be clear from this discussion that many people come to question children about their experiences. Obviously, these individuals may differ greatly in their interviewing skills and their knowledge of children. Thus some interviewers are quite able (even gifted) in their ability to establish rapport with children, whereas others are not able to put them at ease. And some interviewers are able to adjust their questioning to fit the characteristics of individual children. Given this variability, the conclusions reached are often likely to differ.

But more is at stake than possible differences in the cognitive diagnoses made by interviewers who may differ in skill. Because we are dealing with a sequential process, later interviewers may be handicapped in that they have to contend not only with the passage of time but also with the possibly negative impact of earlier questioners. The consequences of this potential contamination cannot always be specified, but they are unlikely to be positive. For example, it is the diagnosis of an early interviewer (e.g., a hospital social worker) that may lead to the initiation of a legal action, but it is the diagnosis of a later interviewer (e.g., a judge) that may determine the outcome of a case. And other things being equal, it is likely that the early interviewer has a better chance of establishing an accurate record of the event in question than does the later interviewer.

Given the complex network of factors that can affect the interview process, what can be done to increase the accuracy and thoroughness of children's reports? One possibility is to initiate attempts to standardize the interview process. Although much remains to be learned, we know enough to begin to develop protocols for interviewing and to provide guidelines for individuals who are likely to interact with children in the context of the legal system. These guidelines should include information about the major variables that can affect children's reports and suggest procedures for structuring interactions with potential witnesses. In addition, the guidelines should stress the importance of minimizing the number of individuals who are given permission to question a child and the necessity of formally keeping track of these interactions. Ultimately, the development, evaluation, and distribution of such interview guidelines may increase the likelihood that children's reports are based on their own memories.

References

Best, D. L., & Ornstein, P. A. (1986). Children's generation and communication of mnemonic organizational strategies. *Developmental Psychology*, *22*, 845–853.

Brainerd, C. J., Kingma, J., & Howe, M. L. (1985). On the development of forgetting. *Child Development*, *56*, 1103–1119.

Ceci, S. J., Ross, D. F., & Toglia, M. P. (1987). Suggestibility of children's memory: Psycholegal implications. *Journal of Experimental Psychology: General*, *116*, 38–49.

Dale, P. S., Loftus, E. F., & Rathbun, L. (1978). The influence of the form of the question on the eyewitness testimony of preschool children. *Journal of Psycholinguistic Research*, *7*, 269–277.

Donaldson, M. (1978). *Children's minds*. New York: Norton.

Flavell, J. H. (1985). *Cognitive development* (2nd ed.). Englewood Cliffs, NJ: Prentice-Hall.

Folds, T. H., Footo, M., Guttentag, R. E., & Ornstein, P. A. (1990). When children mean to remember: Issues of context specificity, strategy effectiveness, and intentionality in the development of memory (pp. 67–91). In D. F. Bjorklund (Ed.), *Children's strategies*. Hillsdale, NJ: Erlbaum.

Godden, D. R., & Baddeley, A. D. (1975). Context-dependent memory in two natural environments: On land and underwater. *British Journal of Psychology*, *66*, 325–331.

Loftus, E. F. (1979). *Eyewitness testimony*. Cambridge, MA: Harvard University Press.

McCloskey, M., & Zaragoza, M. S. (1985). Misleading postevent information and memory for events: Arguments and evidence against memory impairment hypotheses. *Journal of Experimental Psychology: General*, *114*, 381–387.

Ornstein, P. A., Baker-Ward, L., & Naus, M. J. (1988). The development of mnemonic skill. In F. E. Weinert & M. Perlmutter (Eds.), *Memory development: Universal changes and indvidual differences* (pp. 31–50). Hillsdale, NJ: Erlbaum.

Ornstein, P. A., Gordon, B. N., & Larus, D. M. (in press). Children's memory for a personally experienced event: Implications for testimony. *Applied Cognitive Psychology*.

Ornstein, P. A., Medlin, R. G., Stone, B. P., & Naus, M. J. (1985). Retrieving for rehearsal: An analysis of active rehearsal in children's memory. *Developmental Psychology*, *21*, 633–641.

Siegal, M., Waters, L. J., & Dinwiddy, L. S. (1988). Misleading children: Causal attributions for inconsistency under repeated questioning. *Journal of Experimental Child Psychology*, *45*, 438–456.

Zaragoza, M. S. (1987). Memory, suggestibility, and eyewitness testimony on children and adults. In S. J. Ceci, M. P. Toglia, & D. F. Ross (Eds.), *Children's eyewitness memory* (pp. 53–78). New York: Springer-Verlag.

CHAPTER 9

ASSESSMENT OF CHILDREN'S STATEMENTS OF SEXUAL ABUSE

DAVID C. RASKIN and PHILLIP W. ESPLIN

Throughout the Cornell conference, Suggestibility of Children's Recollections, considerable attention was devoted to questions about the accuracy of children's recollections and the extent to which such recollections may be influenced by suggestions, especially from adults (e.g., Chapter 6, this volume). Although accuracy of witness accounts may be the critical issue in many types of investigations, such as bystanders' accounts of a crime, the major problem in sexual abuse investigations is not the child's ability to provide an accurate account. The most important question concerns the child's motivation to provide the account and the credibility of that account. The underlying issue is not whether the child is capable of providing an accurate description of the witnessed events in a situation in which the child has no motive to misrepresent. Instead, the validity of children's allegations of sexual abuse frequently turns on whether a child who may have reasons to misrepresent the events or the perpetrator has provided a credible account (Raskin & Steller, 1989). Criteria-based content analysis (CBCA) of the child's statement is designed to address this problem (Raskin & Esplin, in press; Steller & Koehnken, 1989).

In order to understand the rationale and need for CBCA, one must consider psychological factors that shift the focus of concern from the probable accuracy of witnesses' statements to their credibility or validity. In general, a statement may be obtained from a disinterested witness who was a bystander to the events (e.g., a bank robbery) or an interested witness who was a direct participant (e.g., a victim of rape or sexual abuse). The motives for the witnesses to provide an account of the events may differ markedly for these two situations, and the validity of the accounts may be substantially influenced by motivational factors.

The disinterested bystander is motivated primarily to assist the investigators in apprehending an unknown perpetrator and does not expect to gain any other benefit. Concern is focused on how the conditions of observation and the interview techniques may have affected the accuracy of perception, memory, retrieval, and identification (see Raskin, 1989). The situation is considerably different when an interested witness has motives for revenge or has a relationship with the accused that might form the basis for an exaggerated or fabricated accusation. For example, a teen-age child might provide a false account in order to escape from undesired parental control over social activities and contacts. In recent years, particular problems have arisen in intrafamilial sexual abuse cases involving divorce, custody, or visitation disputes (Raskin & Yuille, 1989). In such contexts, children may be influenced to make false accusations of sexual abuse in order to assist one parent in prevailing against the other in the domestic dispute.

CRITERIA-BASED CONTENT ANALYSIS

Assessment of the validity of allegations of sexual abuse made by child witnesses requires special techniques that go beyond the traditional examination of factors that may affect the accuracy of an account provided by a disinterested witness. The CBCA technique is specifically designed to assess the validity of accounts provided by witnesses whose motives may lead to false accounts and accusations or to whom another interested party may have suggested or pressured them to provide an invalid account. The CBCA approach to these problems is based on pioneering work by Undeutsch (1989), who originated a procedure he called *statement reality analysis* in the 1950s. The method consists primarily of a content analysis of a witness's statement based on the premise that accounts of self-experienced events differ in content and quality from statements based on invention or fantasy. This premise has been referred to as the Undeutsch hypothesis (Steller, 1989). Content analysis of children's statements of sexual abuse developed over decades of application in tens of thousands of sexual abuse cases in Germany (Undeutsch, 1989; Wegener, 1989), and it has recently been systematized (Steller & Koehnken, 1989) and incorporated into a broader procedure known as *statement validity assessment* (Rasklin & Esplin, in press). The purpose of this approach is to differentiate statements based on a child's actual experience of sexual abuse from those that contain substantial invention or fabrication concerning sexual abuse.

Application of CBCA requires that a relatively complete statement be obtained as soon as possible from the child who has disclosed a sexual abuse incident. This statement is elicited by a trained interviewer using a structured interview designed to maximize the amount of information provided by the child and to minimize contamination of its content by the interviewer and by other significant adults or previous interviewers (Rasklin & Esplin, in press). The main approach is to obtain as much free narrative as possible from the child without imposing unnecessary structure. This statement should reflect the child's knowledge and memory of the event, as described by the child. Because it is well known that accuracy is highest with free-recall procedures, direct questions are asked after completion of the free-narrative phase, and only when necessary. Leading questions and suggestions are inappropriate, except when deliberately used toward the end of the interview to assess the child's susceptibility to suggestion. The entire interview is tape-recorded and transcribed for later analysis.

The content and quality of the statement are analyzed using the transcript of the interview and the CBCA criteria. The results of CBCA comprise the major data from which inferences are made regarding the likelihood that the child's description was derived from direct experience of the events, as opposed to being invented or fabricated. The outcome of the CBCA is then considered together with other information to provide an overall assessment of the validity of the statement. Thus the content of the statement is evaluated, not the general credibility of the child witness.

CBCA employs 19 specific content criteria organized into five categories, as shown in Table 1. The list of criteria begins with general characteristics of the statement as a whole, progresses to increasingly specific criteria, and ends with another general criterion. These criteria were derived and organized by Steller and Koehnken (1989) from the extensive European literature on statement analysis. In applying each of the criteria in CBCA, the evaluator considers whether or not a witness who may be misrepresenting the events could and would be able to invent and produce a statement with the content and qualities present in this statement. This is especially useful when analyzing a statement obtained from a child who has limited knowledge and experience in sexual matters. Such a person would have great difficulty fabricating and relating an account that would satisfy the content criteria. When applying the criteria, it is necessary to consider the age, experience, and cognitive capacity of the witness.

CBCA begins with a thorough examination of the entire statement to assess the presence or absence of the first three general characteristics; one must note when examples of specific criteria are encountered. For the statement to be considered realistic, it must have a logical structure and contain a quantity of details that are meaningful in describing the alleged sexual events. It must be kept in mind that a relatively simple sexual incident described by a young and inexperienced child tends to have simpler structure and fewer details than does an account of complex and repeated sexual acts provided by an older, more experienced child. Unstructured production is also very important because it refers to the style and sequence of descriptions characteristic of accounts generated from actual memory of an experience. However, an overly structured account may lack free-narrative

Table 1.

CONTENT CRITERIA FOR ANALYZING WITNESSES' STATEMENTS

Criteria for Analyzing General Characteristics

1. Logical structure. Is the statement coherent? Is the content logical? Do the different segments fit together? (Note: Peculiar or unique details or unexpected complications do not diminish logical structure.)
2. Unstructured production. Are the descriptions unconstrained? Is the report somewhat unorganized? Are there digressions or spontaneous shifts of focus? Are some elements distributed throughout? (Note: This criterion requires that the account is logically consistent.)
3. Quantity of details. Are there specific descriptions of place or time? Are persons, objects, and events specifically described? (Note: Repetitions are not counted.)

Criteria for Analyzing Specific Contents

4. Contextual embedding. Are events placed in spatial and temporal context? Is the action connected to other incidental events, such as routine daily occurrences?
5. Descriptions of interactions. Are there reports of actions and reactions or conversation? (Note: Verbatim reproduction of conversation is also scored under criterion 6.)
6. Reproduction of conversation. Is conversation reported in its original form? (Note: Use of unfamiliar terms or quotes are especially strong indicators, even when attributed to only one participant.)
7. Unexpected complications during the incident. Was there an unplanned interruption or an unexpected complication or difficulty?

Criteria for Analyzing Peculiarities of Content

8. Unusual details. Are there details of persons, objects, or events that are unusual, yet meaningful in this context? (Note: Unusual details must be realistic.)
9. Superfluous details. Are peripheral details reported that are related to the situation but that do not contribute directly to the allegation?
10. Accurately reported details misunderstood. Did the child correctly describe an object or event but interpret it incorrectly?
11. Related external associations. Is there reference to an event or conversation of a sexual nature that is related in some way to the incident but that did not occur within the incident?
12. Accounts of subjective mental state. Did the child describe feelings or thoughts experienced at the time of the incident?
13. Attribution of perpetrator's mental state. Is there reference to the alleged perpetrator's feelings or thoughts during the incident?

Criteria for Analyzing Content Related to Motivation

14. Spontaneous corrections. were corrections offered or information added to material previously provided in the statement? (Note: Responses to direct questions do not qualify.)
15. Admitting lack of memory. Did the child indicate lack of memory or knowledge of an aspect of the incident?
16. Raising doubts about one's own testimony. Did the child express concern that some part of the statement seems incorrect or unbelievable? (Note: Merely asserting that one is telling the truth does not qualify.)
17. Self-deprecation. Did the child describe some aspect of his or her behavior related to the incident as being wrong or inappropriate?
18. Pardoning the perpetrator. Did the child make excuses for the alleged perpetrator or fail to blame the alleged perpetrator when an opportunity occurred?

(continued)

Table 1. (*Continued*)

Criteria for Analyzing Offense-Specific Elements of Content
19. Details characteristic of the offense. Are there elements that are common to this type of offense? (Note: Details contrary to common knowledge are especially strong indicators.)

---

[1]Adapted from Steller, M. & Koehnken, G. New York: Springer Publishing.

description, caused by the child's limited cognitive or expressive abilities or by the interviewer imposing too much structure. Therefore, unstructured production is not an absolute requirement for a valid statement.

The next two categories of criteria refer to progressively more specific contents of the statement. They describe contents that provide the concreteness and vividness characteristic of actually experienced events. Contextual embedding and interactions are expected to be present in valid accounts, but other criteria may occur less frequently. Although the validity of the statement is strongly reinforced by the presence of some criteria, their absence does not necessarily invalidate the statement. This is especially true for reproduction of conversation, unexpected complications, unusual details, accurately reported details misunderstood, related external associations, and accounts of subjective mental state. Recent data regarding the expected frequency of occurrence of the various criteria are presented later in this chapter.

The next general category of criteria refers to contents related to the motives of the witness; a fabricating witness is not expected to incorporate such contents into the account. Making spontaneous corrections, admitting lack of memory, and raising doubts might draw the attention of the interviewer to the possibility that the witness is insincere, and a witness acting out of revenge or a selfish motive for personal gain is unlikely to engage in self-deprecation or to minimize the damage to the falsely accused. Thus a lying or coached witness is expected to attempt to maintain the basic story without modification; to try to answer all questions, even if that requires additional fabrication; and not to raise doubts about the believability of the story, blame oneself for the events, or minimize negative characterizations of the perpetrator.

The category of offense-specific elements is based on the professional literature and experience of investigators and other professionals involved in the area of sexual abuse. Sexual acts with children have characteristic patterns and elements that enable an experienced evaluator to recognize a description that is consistent with typical sexual abuse incidents. Many of these characteristics are contrary to laypeople's suppositions, and such content is not likely to appear in statements of children who have not experienced such events. For example, incestuous relationships typically progress over time, beginning with relatively benign sexual acts and expressions of affection and escalating to more serious sexual acts, such as intercourse and sodomy. Valid accounts of incest usually include a typical progression, whereas fictitious statements often include fully executed, serious sexual acts during the first incident.

SCIENTIFIC BASIS AND ECOLOGICAL VALIDITY OF CBCA

Although CBCA developed out of more than 30 years' experience in actual cases of sexual abuse in Germany (Undeutsch, 1989; Wegener, 1989), only recently have scientific studies examined the validity of the method (Steller, 1989). Two basic approaches to validation have been taken: (a) controlled naturalistic study of children's accounts of events that approximate many critical characteristics of sexual abuse and (b) analysis of accounts obtained from child witnesses in actual investigations of sexual abuse. In both types of studies, statements obtained from the children consisted of verified descriptions of actually experienced events and others that were most likely invented or fabricated. The validity of CBCA is evaluated in terms of the extent to which the criteria discriminate between valid descriptions and fictitious accounts.

Before describing some of the recent scientific research on CBCA, it is important to point out some basic requirements for ecologically valid studies of children's statements concerning sexual abuse (see Chapter 1, this volume) and how these studies differ from many others that are erroneously offered for such purposes (e.g., Chapter 6, this volume). As Steller (1989) has clearly pointed out, meaningful and generalizable attempts to approximate sexual abuse experienced by a child must incorporate three characteristics: direct involvement of the witness, loss of control, and negative emotional tone (although the latter may not be present when relatively benign sexual acts are performed with a child who does not understand their actual meaning). In addition, researchers should attempt to incorporate novel aspects into the incidents to be described by the children so that prior experience is not likely to provide the child with a basis to fabricate a credible account or to know what types of inventions the researchers are likely to reject.

To generalize the research findings to sexual abuse situations, in which frequently witnesses are motivated to misrepresent important aspects of the events, it is crucial that researchers obtain statements from children who have been motivated to misrepresent and have also been induced to make misrepresentations that they believe will be accepted by an adult. Failure to incorporate these crucial elements is a fatal methodological flaw that may render research findings not only useless, but is likely to mislead evaluators of statements given by children in sexual abuse cases. For example, following an actual genital examination by a physician, Saywitz, Goodman, Nicholas, & Moan (1989) failed to get children to comply with the suggestive question, ''She (the doctor) didn't have any clothes on, did she?'' This result provides no information about the suggestibility of children in actual sexual abuse cases. Five-year-olds know that doctors do not take off their own clothes during an examination, and the child has no reason to expect that a mentally competent adult would believe such a statement! The majority of normal children would be reluctant and embarrassed to make such an absurd claim to an adult in almost any circumstance, not just during an artificial research interview.

Although some researchers and professionals concerned with sexual abuse believe that the studies by Goodman and her colleagues demonstrate that children are invariably resistant to suggestions of sexual abuse, their results tell us nothing about the suggestibility of children regarding statements of sexual abuse in the real world. Unlike the situation in the physician's examining room, with which almost all children have relevant experience and no motive to misrepresent, sexual abuse is generally unfamiliar to children. The alleged sexual abuse situation may include motives to misrepresent, persistent attempts by one or more powerful and significant adults to influence the child, and suggestive interview techniques that lead the child to make statements that the child believes the interviewer wants to hear and will also believe. Some or all of these factors are frequently present in sexual abuse investigations, and lack of knowledge and failure to understand these processes do not excuse unwarranted generalizations from research that lacks many of the critical elements that are required for external validity.

RESEARCH ON CBCA

Two recent studies have examined the validity of CBCA and its utility in discriminating between children's descriptions of self-experienced events and statements produced by disingenuous attempts to convince the interviewer that an event was actually experienced. One of these studies applied CBCA to the contents of children's true and invented stories in a storytelling competition (Steller, Wellershaus, & Wolf, 1988), and the other assessed the ability of CBCA to discriminate between confirmed descriptions given by children who were victims of sexual abuse and highly doubtful statements by children who alleged sexual abuse (Rasklin & Esplin, in press).

Steller et al. (1988) employed a storytelling competition with a total of 98 schoolchildren from first and fourth grade. They were asked to tell two stories, one concerning an event they had actually experienced and one that they invented. To satisfy the requirements described earlier, topics included receiving an injection, undergoing a surgical operation, giving a blood sample, having dental work performed, suffering an accident that required medical treatment, being physically beaten by another child, and being attacked by a dog or other animal. The children were given instructions to choose from these categories and to come back in a week to tell their two stories, one that they had actually experienced and one that they made up. Their actual experiences were verified independently by their parents, and the children were motivated by prizes to provide two believable stories.

The two statements were obtained through blind interviews and then transcribed. Graduate students trained in CBCA, although they were not highly experienced, performed CBCA ratings. For each story, they rated the presence or absence of each criterion. Analyses of the data indicated that only the medical stories seemed to differ with regard to the criteria, possibly because of the low frequency of occurrence of the other types of stories and because children who had not experienced such events may have possessed knowledge from observing them happen to others.

Among the general criteria, logical structure and quantity of details discriminated significantly between the self-experienced and invented stories. The criterion of unstructured production did not discriminate because it was misinterpreted by the raters as being the opposite of logical structure. All of the criteria in the categories of specific contents and peculiarities of content, except the perpetrator's mental state, significantly discriminated between the two stories and generally confirmed the underlying hypothesis of CBCA. Attributions of the perpetrator's mental state and the motivational criteria may have been less appropriate to the situations described by the children than to actual sexual abuse.

The first scientific field study of actual sexual abuse cases was recently reported by (Esplin, Houed, & Raskin, 1988). They applied CBCA to 40 sexual abuse statements obtained from children aged 3 to 15 years who were referred for professional evaluations by Esplin and Raskin. Because assaults by strangers seldom involve motives for a child to misrepresent the events, all of the accused were either family members or people with whom the child was acquainted. The confirmed statements were obtained from 20 children in cases in which 18 of the 20 perpetrators confessed to the allegations prior to any discussions of plea bargains, and 16 of the 20 included definite physical evidence of vaginal or anal trauma. Thus 14 cases had full confessions and physical evidence, 4 had only confessions, and 2 had only physical evidence.

The 20 doubtful statements were more difficult to identify and confirm. They were obtained from cases in which all 20 of the alleged perpetrators persistently denied the allegations and never made any admissions, and there was a subsequent recantation by the child or a lack of prosecution, judicial dismissal, or a specific finding by the court that no abuse had occurred. In 19 of the 20 doubtful cases there was no corroborating evidence; in the single case with physical evidence, the child later admitted to naming the wrong perpetrator. In addition, polygraph examination results were available on 14 of the 20 alleged perpetrators, all of which indicated truthful outcomes regarding their denials of the allegations. We feel that these criteria indicate a high probability that the doubtful statements were invented and that the confirmed statements were based on memory of self-experienced incidents of sexual abuse.

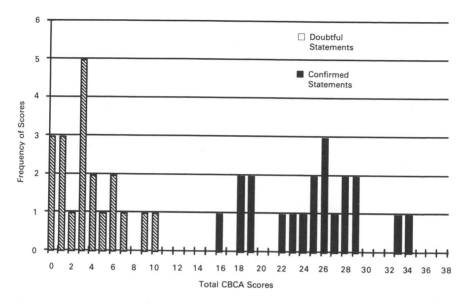

Figure 1.   Frequency distribution of total criteria-based content analysis (CBCA) scores for the confirmed and doubtful statements of sexual abuse made by 40 children aged 3 to 15. Data are from Application of Statement Validity Assessment by P.W. Esplin, T. Houed, and D.C. Raskin, June, 1988. Paper presented at NATO Advanced Study Institute on Credibility Assessment, Maratea, Italy.

Transcripts of the 40 interviewers were evaluated by Houed, who had received extensive training in CBCA and had no knowledge concerning the cases. She reviewed the typed transcripts and assigned scores for each of the 19 content criteria. If a criterion was not present in the statement, it received a score of 0; if it was present, it received a score of 1; if it was strongly present, it received a score of 2. The scores for each statement were summed to provide a total possible score of 38, and the frequency distributions of total scores for the two groups are shown in Figure 1.

The mean score was 24.8 for the confirmed statements and 3.6 for the doubtful statements, which differed significantly, $t(38) = 16.53, p < .001$. Figure 1 indicates that the distributions of total scores for the two groups did not overlap, ranging from 16 to 34 for the confirmed statements and from 0 to 10 for the doubtful statements. Thus the overall results obtained with CBCA clearly differentiated the two groups of statements and provided strong confirmation for the method.

The frequency of occurrence of the 19 criteria in the confirmed and doubtful statements was examined, and the results are presented in Table 2 as percentages for each group. Inspection of these results indicates clear support for the utility of most of the 19 content criteria. In line with the CBCA hypotheses, criteria 1,

Table 2.

PRESENCE OF CRITERIA-BASED CONTENT ANALYSIS (CBCA) CRITERIA IN
CONFIRMED AND DOUBTFUL STATEMENTS OF SEXUAL ABUSE MADE BY
40 CHILDREN AGE 3 TO 15

CBCA criterion	% of confirmed statements	% of doubtful statements
1	100	55
2	95	15
3	100	55
4	100	35
5	100	30
6	70	0
7	70	0
8	95	0
9	100	5
10	5	5
11	5	0
12	90	30
13	40	0
14	100	10
15	75	35
16	10	0
17	25	0
18	55	5
19	100	30

Note. Data are from Application of Statement Validity Assessment by P. W. Esplin, T. Houed, and
D. C. Raskin, June, 1988. Paper presented at NATO Advanced Study Institute on Credibility assessment, Marakea, Italy.

3, and 19 were present in all confirmed statements and criterion 2 was present in
all but one. It is of interest to note that criteria 1 and 3 were also present in about
half of the doubtful statements, but criterion 2 was present in only a few of them.
Some of the other criteria occurred very frequently in the confirmed statements
but with only moderate frequency in the doubtful statements (criteria 4, 5, 12,
and 15), whereas many other criteria appeared almost exclusively in the confirmed
statements (6, 7, 8, 9, 13, 14, 17, and 18). A few criteria were seldom present
(10, 11, and 16), and the surprising occurrence of criteria 10 and 18 in a doubtful
statement was explained when the child later admitted to substituting the perpetrator, which is the most difficult type of case for CBCA and other assessment
procedures.

CONCLUSIONS

The results of these recent scientific studies lend strong support to the underlying
principles and hypotheses of CBCA. There is little doubt that children's descrip-

tions of their own experiences of sexual abuse and events with similar features differ in content and quality from statements that are invented, and the CBCA method is a very useful tool for discriminating between such statements in actual cases of sexual abuse. We must reject unsupportable assertions, such as "there is currently no evidence that children . . . can be led by parents or others to report falsely such events" (Goodman & Helgeson, 1988, p. 110) and "we know that children do not make up stories asserting they have been sexually molested" (Faller, 1984, p. 475). Psychologists must resist making claims that not only lack scientific support but also are clearly contradicted by data obtained in ecologically valid studies.

Erroneous representations based on irrelevant laboratory research must be replaced by effective methods for assessing the validity of children's statements about sexual abuse. In actual cases, the task is to obtain and analyze all of the available information using techniques that permit valid inferences about the extent to which the child's statement represents memory of self-experienced events. We need psychologically sound procedures that provide a scientifically supportable basis for discriminating between valid statements made by children and those that result from other sources of information, suggestive interviews, and improper influences by others. CBCA combined with an overall validity assessment (Rasklin & Esplin, in press) has been employed successfully in criminal investigations and judicial proceedings to support statements by children who had been sexually abused and has also served as an important tool to uncover and ameliorate many serious problems caused by fictitious allegations.

References

Esplin, P. W., Houed, T., & Raskin, D. C. (1988, June). *Application of statement validity assessment*. Paper presented at NATO Advanced Study Institute on Credibility Assessment, Maratea, Italy.

Faller, K. C. (1984). Is the child victim of sexual abuse telling the truth? *Child Abuse & Neglect, 8*, 473–481.

Goodman, G. S., & Helgeson, V. S. (1988). Children as witnesses: What do they remember? In L. E. A. Walker (Ed.), *Handbook on sexual abuse of children* (pp. 109–136). New York: Springer Publishing.

Raskin, D. C. (Ed.) (1989). *Psychological methods in criminal investigation and evidence.* New York: Springer Publishing.

Raskin, D. C., & Esplin, P. W. (in press). Statement validity assessment: Interview procedures and content analysis of children's statements of sexual abuse. *Behavioral Assessment.*

Raskin, D. C., & Steller, M. (1989). Assessing the credibility of allegations of child sexual abuse: Polygraph examinations and statement analysis. In H. Wegener, F. Loesel, & J. Haisch (Eds.), *Criminal behavior and the justice system: Psychological perspectives* (pp. 290–302). New York: Springer-Verlag.

Raskin, D. C., & Yuille, J. C. (1989). Problems in evaluating interviews of children in sexual abuse cases. In S. J. Ceci, D. F. Ross, & M. P. Toglia (Eds.), *Perspectives on children's testimony* (pp. 184–207). New York: Springer-Verlag.

Saywitz, K., Goodman, G. S., Nicholas, E., & Moan, S. (1989, April). *Children's memories of genital examinations: Implications for cases of child sexual assault.* Paper presented at the meeting of the Society for Research on Child Development, Kansas City, MO.

Steller, M. (1989). Recent developments in statement analysis. In J. C. Yuille (Ed.), *Credibility assessment* (pp. 135–154). Dordrecht, The Netherlands: Kluwer.

Steller, M., & Koehnken, G. (1989). Criteria-based statement analysis. In D. C. Raskin (Ed.), *Psychological methods in criminal investigation and evidence* (pp. 217–245). New York: Springer Publishing.

Steller, M., Wellershaus, P., & Wolf, T. (1988, June). *Empirical validation of criteria-based content analysis.* Paper presented at the meeting of the NATO Advanced Study Institute on Credibility Assessment, Maratea, Italy.

Undeutsch, U. (1989). The development of statement reality analysis. In J. C. Yuille (Ed.), *Credibility assessment* (pp. 101–120). Dordrecht, The Netherlands: Kluwer.

Wegener, H. (1989). The present state of statement analysis. In J. C. Yuille (Ed.), *Credibility assessment* (pp. 121–134). Dordrecht, The Netherlands: Kluwer.

COMMENTARY: ASSESSING THE CREDIBILITY OF WITNESSES' STATEMENTS

LUCY S. MCGOUGH

The purpose of this comment is to locate the claims of criteria-based content analysis within the context of the current American legal system. To a rather remarkable degree, courts have received expert testimony explaining the special behaviors of children who are sexual abuse victims as a class or group. Such testimony can be very powerful, restraining and reorienting the tribunal toward an empathic assessment of the child's delay, ambivalence, and trauma. In the words of one court, psychologists can explain the atypical reactions of child abuse victims so that what the court or jury might otherwise "attribute to inaccuracy or prevarication" may be viewed as "merely the result of immaturity, psychological stress, [or] societal pressures" (*State of Arizona v. Lindsey*, 1986).

However, only a handful of courts would now permit any expert to go one step further and testify whether a particular child victim's statement is reliable or not (for cases that have permitted such testimony, see, e.g., *State of Hawaii v. Kim*, 1982; *State of Minnesota v. Myers*, 1984; *State of Montana v. Geyman*, 1986). The usual justification for denying the receipt of such testimony is that there has been no showing that experts can determine the reliability of abuse victims' statements with a "high degree of reliability" (*State of Utah v. Rimmasch*, 1989). Obviously what Raskin and Esplin have attempted in this research is to fill in this missing predicate.

The lengthy debate over the merits of most states' refusal to accept such expert testimony appears elsewhere (see, e.g., McCord, 1987; Roe, 1985; Serrato, 1988; Note, *Georgetown Law Journal*, 1985). Here I can only briefly sketch some of the justifications. In the Anglo-American legal system, witness credibility is a question of fact to be determined by the jury or, in most cases, by the court alone, based on an assessment of the witness's demeanor and the flaws, inconsistencies, and holes pointed out by the cross-examiner. The fact finder's assessment occurs at a single trial at which both the accuser and the accused are present. To a lawyer, the most striking feature of criteria-based content analysis is how many of its criteria would be found in any standard text on cross-examination and closing arguments on witness credibility (see, e.g., Goldstein, 1985).

As Raskin and Esplin point out, social scientists on the Continent have pioneered work in assessing the validity of a witness's report and are now familiar, welcomed assistants in that legal system. In the Anglo-American system, however, the idea that an expert can be trained to determine the truthfulness of a statement (or of a witness) and is a better fact finder than a layperson is still considered alien and heretical. Legal critics would be quick to point out that such expert testimony would become in Platonic terms, a form upon a form: The reliability of a witness (his or her statement) is being vouched for by an expert whose own reliability then comes into issue. That is a very inefficient process if there is to be a trial. How has that particular individual been trained and what is his or her personal track record for reliability? How would we continue to evaluate the reliability of the criteria rater? Such expert testimony is but a short theoretical step from the use of a lie detector machine's recording, still nearly universally ignored as nonprobative (McCormick, 1984).

Having made the conventional arguments, we should also consider two very pragmatic ones. It is not likely that we will abandon our adversarial system of justice for the accusatory or inquisitorial civil law system in which cases proceed based on written affidavits from witnesses and experts, to be later reviewed by a tribunal wholly removed from the disputants. Furthermore, any reform that relies on the creation and use of experts in trials in which the sexual abuse of children is an issue is an expensive one. It would take an army of experts to serve the thousands of divorce, custody, dependency, and criminal actions that involve allegations of abuse.

Those comments aside, the current data on the reliability of criteria-based credibility assessment seem promising. There are two uses to which this methodology could be put immediately. First, trained experts can be very helpful to prosecutors (or counsel in civil cases) in determining whether to go forward with a case pivoting on a child's allegations. Likewise, experts might convince counsel for the abusing adult to recommend a plea bargain or the settlement of a civil dispute. Content-based criteria analysis is especially appealing because it can operate after the fact of contamination to avoid an unjust result when for whatever reason, the child's account is now unreliable. Second, the methodology could be very helpful in properly training those who interview children.

Apparently Raskin and Esplin would espouse the long view that trial processes will not be substantially improved until American law accepts the use of experts in assessing witnesses' credibility. Certainly the greater use of properly trained experts to provide guidance to the court or jury in evaluating reliability is supportable. However, short of a wholesale revamping of American trial processes, I think there are easier, less expensive reforms within our reach. One reform is relaxing the hearsay ban to permit consideration of a child's early, out-of-court statements and neutrally recorded videotaped accounts in both civil and criminal cases. Rethinking the effectiveness of typical cross-examination for child witnesses and revising its scope is another. There are ample empirical data to back up the need for each of these reforms, and they can be accomplished within the confines of our current adversarial system.

I think the authors of this volume would agree that, to borrow Gilligan's memorable phrase, children "speak in a different voice" (Gilligan, 1982). I think we would also agree that changes must be made with the current legal evidentiary rules and processes so that those voices that speak reliably can be properly credited and, more important, so that children can be empowered to become their most reliable selves. We disagree only about how that new city is to be reached. Methodological differences, or even cross-discipline differences in the reasons for our travel ought not obscure the common journey. Heart, courage, and brains are all that are needed on the yellow brick road.

References

Gilligan, C. (1982). In a different voice: Psychological theory and women's development. Cambridge and London: Harvard University Press.

Goldstein Trial Technique (2d ed. Lane, 1985). Wilamette, Illinois: Callaghan & Co. (Chaps. 18–22).

McCord, Syndromes, Profiles and Other Mental Exotica: A New Approach to the Admissibility of Nontraditional Psychological Evidence in Criminal Cases, 66 Oregon Law Review 19 (1987).

McCormick on Evidence (3d ed. Cleary, 1984) 206 (pp. 622–637) (collecting cases and scientific studies on polygraph testing and empirical studies, citing among others, the work of conference participants Jack Brigham, Ray Bull, Elizabeth Loftus, David Raskin, and Gary Wells).

Note, The Unreliability of Expert Testimony on the Typical Characteristics of Sexual Victims, 74 Georgetown Law Journal 429 (1985).

Roe, Expert Testimony in Child Sexual Abuse Cases, 40 University of Miami Law Review 97 (1985).

Serrato, V., Note: Expert Testimony in Child Sexual Abuse Prosecutions: A Spectrum of Uses, 68 Boston University Law Review 115 (1988).

State v. Geyman, 729 P.2d 475 (Mont. 1986).

State v. Kim, 64 Haw. 598, 645 P.2d 1330 (1982).

State v. Lindsey, 149 Ariz. 472, 474, 720 P.2d 73, 75 (1986).

State v. Myers, 359 N.W.2d 604 (Minn. 1984).

State v. Rimmasch, 775 P.2d 388 (No. 30760, dec. May 17, 1989, Supreme Court of Utah).

COMMENTARY: IS THIS CHILD FABRICATING? REACTIONS TO A NEW ASSESSMENT TECHNIQUE

GARY L. WELLS and ELIZABETH F. LOFTUS

Raskin and Esplin have described a procedure for assessing children's statements of sexual abuse. They argue, and we agree, that a statement provided by a disinterested witness (such as a bystander to a robbery) can differ markedly from that provided by a direct participant (such as a sexual abuse victim) in that the former is less likely than the latter to be influenced by motivational factors. Criteria-based content analysis (CBCA) is an attempt to discriminate between statements of child witnesses that result from self-experienced events and statements that result from suggestions by other people, fantasy, or other forms of invention. Although we applaud Raskin and Esplin's goal of trying to establish a method of identifying genuine reports and uncovering fictitious allegations, we have concerns about CBCA with regard to the adequacy of its current empirical support, the ability of the technique to partition individual and age-related differences in linguistic abilities from validity-related differences, and the potential problem of overbelief of the results of CBCA on the part of judges and juries. We begin our commentary with an evaluation of the empirical support for CBCA.

Raskin and Esplin describe two studies that they claim support the validity of CBCA. In one study children related one true and one false story in a storytelling competition (Steller, Wellershaus, & Wolf, 1988). The other study used transcripts of 20 "confirmed" and 20 "doubtful" sexual abuse cases (Esplin, Houed & Raskin, 1988). Raskin and Esplin emphasize the latter study more than the former, probably for several reasons. Among other problems with the Steller et al. study is the fact that the CBCA ratings produced significant differences between the true and fabricated stories only for a subset of the stories (the medical stories), raters misinterpreted the meaning of logical structure, the perpetrator's mental-state criterion did not differ between stories, and the general set of conditions that Raskin and Esplin describe as needed for external validity are not all met in the Steller et al. study.

Greater emphasis is placed on the study of Esplin et al. (1988). In this study CBCA was applied to 40 sexual abuse statements made by children aged 3 to 15 years. The statements were categorized into 20 confirmed and 20 doubtful. The confirmed cases were classified as such because of a confession by the accused ($n = 18$) or physical evidence that the child was abused ($n = 16$). Some ($n = 14$) had both a confession and physical evidence, some ($n = 2$) only physical evidence, and the others ($n = 4$) only confession evidence. The doubtful cases were classified as doubtful because the accused persons denied the acts ($n = 20$), the child recanted, or there was no prosecution, a judicial dismissal, or a court finding that no abuse had occurred. In addition, 14 of the 20 accused in the doubtful cases passed a polygraph exam.

Transcripts of the children's sexual abuse statements were evaluated by one evaluator for each of the 19 content criteria in the CBCA. The resulting data are among the most impressive we have ever encountered in a psychological study. Total scores summed over the 19 criteria produced a perfect, non-overlapping discrimination between the 20 confirmed and 20 doubtful cases. Indeed, no score in the doubtful set was above 10, and no score in the confirmed set was below 16.

The Esplin et al. (1988) findings are subject to an alternative interpretation. Assume, hypothetically, that many of the 20 doubtful cases of sexual abuse were in fact true cases of sexual abuse. Assume further that the critical difference between the child victims in the doubtful cases were children who were unconvincing. They might be unconvincing, even though sexual abuse occurred, for any number of reasons. For example, these children might have deficiencies in logical reasoning, they might have been frightened to the extent that they could not process peripheral detail, they might have poor verbal skills, and so on. Because they are unconvincing witnesses, prosecutors might be unlikely to press charges (lack of prosecution), judges might feel that conviction is unlikely (judicial dismissal), and defense attorneys might be unlikely to advise their clients to admit to the charges (no confessions and persistent denial by the accused). Indeed, the child's frustration at being able to articulate the events and convince adults could even result in false recantations. If this set of conditions exists, then it should not be surprising that the cases in which there was lack of prosecution or judicial dismissal or denial by the accused are precisely the ones in which the children's statements came out poorly on the CBCA.

We know of no good way to rule out this alternative interpretation. The major problem is that judicial dismissal, lack of prosecution, and persistent denials by the accused are judgments that are made by judges, prosecutors, and accused people, and these judgments can be influenced significantly by the convincingness of the victim–witness. Because scores on the CBCA depend on factors such as logical structure, quantity of details, reproduction of conversation, accounts of subjective mental states, and other factors correlated with convincingness, there is the risk of "classification circularity." By this we mean that the same factors that cause low scores on the CBCA also cause the case to be classified as doubtful.

The classification circularity problem can be related to another concern that we have with CBCA. Although Raskin and Esplin note that "when applying the criteria, it is necessary to consider the age, experience, and cognitive capacity of the witness," we seriously question the ability of people to assess cognitive capacity without the aid of formal, standardized tests. Furthermore, few people fully understand age-related changes in language. The way that a 4-year-old describes an incident is not the way a 12-year-old would describe the same incident, and the simple instruction to CBCA users to "consider" age is not sufficient assurance when the claim is that this is a scientific technique. Returning to the classification circularity problem, for example, we wonder if the 20 doubtful cases tended to be younger children than the 20 confirmed cases. Accused people may be less likely to admit sexual contact with a 4-year-old than with a 15-year-old, prosecutors may be less likely to put a 4-year-old than a 15-year-old through the ordeal of a trial, and 4-year-olds may be less likely to achieve good scores on the CBCA. At the very least we need to know that scores on the CBCA are not influenced by the age of the witness.

Another concern with the study of Esplin et al. (1988) is that the data are based on only one evaluator. Although it was claimed by Raskin and Esplin that the evaluator had no knowledge of the cases and, thus, used only the transcripts, it is difficult for us to understand how that could have guaranteed under the circumstances. These circumstances include the fact that the evaluator lived in the same city were the cases occurred and knew one of the chief investigators. As well, her training in CBCA should give her a natural interest in and attention to any of these cases that appeared in the media and a tendency to interact with and discuss local cases with professionals. If so, then recognition of a case and the use of information extraneous to the transcripts while evaluating the transcripts could occur at any number of levels. Such influences need not have occurred knowingly or at a level that would allow her to articulate the influence or name the case. Our point is that we would like to have guarantees that evaluators *could not* rather than *did not* have knowledge of the cases being evaluated. Relatedly, if CBCA is a technique that is being advocated for wider use, and this seems to be the intent of its developers, then we must have studies that assess variance across evaluators. After all, validity cannot exceed reliability, and, in this case, we have concerns about inter-evaluator reliability. What level of inter-evaluator reliability can we expect from use of the CBCA, and what type and extent of training is needed to achieve that level?

Questions can also be raised about the extent to which the 40 cases used in the Esplin et al. study are representative of cases of alleged sexual abuse. Presumably, some selection was involved in order to achieve exactly 20 confirmed and 20 doubtful cases. In an attempt to select cases that were as confirmed as possible and as doubtful as possible, we suppose that there were cases that represented neither extreme. That is, we presume that many cases of alleged sexual abuse cannot be clearly classified as confirmed or doubtful. Because these cases were not part of the data in the Esplin et al. study, a problem emerges in the area of practical application. Specifically, in actual cases of alleged sexual abuse for which we might want to use the CBCA, we cannot restrict our assessments to only confirmed and doubtful cases; either we do not yet have such categorical information or, if we do, access to this information makes it somewhat unnecessary to use the CBCA on those cases. Thus our practical concern is not with the cases that are either confirmed or doubtful but rather with the uncertain cases, which are not the cases on which the Esplin et al. data are based.

What kind of study would be convincing? Suppose there were 1,000 cases, some doubtful, some confirmed, and some in between. Suppose then that a random sample of 20 of each were selected. If these were subjected to CBCA and several truly blind evaluators were to produce nearly perfect discrimination of the three types of statements, then we would be impressed. Until such time, strong conclusions about truth or lying based on the current, rather small amount of empirical research is premature.

Finally, we have concerns about how CBCA will be used and how it will be presented. For reasons that we outlined in the previous paragraphs, we do not believe that the empirical data justify making conclusions of an absolute nature about individual cases. Statements in court to the effect that a particular child's statement is true or false are not justified at this time. It might be acceptable to say that a particular child's statement has many of the qualities that are (or are not) consistent with what is thought to be an event that was actually experienced by the child. But an expert using CBCA should also acknowledge some of the limitations to current scientific evidence, including the fact that most of the scientific conclusions are based on only one study thus far. Indeed, at this point we are not convinced that CBCA would pass the Frye test of being generally accepted as reliable and valid by the relevant community of scientists. At this time we believe that the CBCA might be better relegated to the role of an investigative tool. After it receives more scientific support, and the kinds of problems that we have outlined have been addressed, CBCA might be justified as a powerful technique for courtroom use.

References

Esplin, P. W., Houed, T., & Raskin, D. C. (1988, June). *Application of statement validity assessment.* Paper presented at NATO Advanced Study Institute on Credibility Assessment, Maratea, Italy.

Steller, M., Wellershaus, P., & Wolf, T. (1988, June). *Empirical validation of criteria-based content analysis.* Paper presented at the meeting of the NATO Advanced Study Institute on Credibility Assessment, Maratea, Italy.

COMMENTARY: RESPONSE TO WELLS, LOFTUS, AND MCGOUGH

DAVID C. RASKIN and PHILLIP W. ESPLIN

We appreciate the thoughtful and challenging comments by psychologists Wells and Loftus and legal scholar McGough. They have pointed to legitimate problems concerning some of the criteria for selecting cases for the "doubtful" group, the relation between ages of the subjects and the obtained differences in criteria-based content analysis (CBCA) scores in the two groups, the extent to which our cases represent the full range of sexual abuse cases, and the interrater reliability of CBCA. Their critiques have caused us to reevaluate the design of our field study, reexamine the data, and clarify some of the findings. However, we believe that other aspects of the critiques are in error. The latter include their speculation that the results were contaminated by possible knowledge of the case facts by the blind CBCA interpreter, their treatment of the accuracy and admissibility of polygraph results and our use of them as a criterion for case selection, and investigative uses of CBCA and admissibility of court testimony based on CBCA.

We agree that selection of doubtful cases by using nonprosecution or dismissal of charges creates the appearance of circularity between the selection criteria and the CBCA results. Although all subjects in the doubtful group were drawn from cases in which the accused made no admissions and there was no successful prosecution, the latter characteristic was not necessary for selection of the doubtful statements. In fact, the cases were not selected on the basis of lack of successful prosecution.

In order to eliminate the appearance of criterion circularity, we removed two subjects from the doubtful group by including only the 18 subjects who satisfied at least two of the following criteria that were independent of the child's analyzed statement: lack of medical evidence (19), recantation (15), and truthful polygraph result on the accused (14). Eleven subjects met all three criteria, 3 lacked a recantation, and 4 lacked a polygraph test result. After eliminating any potential circularity, the CBCA results remain the same; there is no overlap between the groups. Thus the CBCA results cannot be explained away by the claim that the doubtful cases were selected merely because the children's statements were unconvincing, because the quality of statements played no role in their assignment to either group.

Multiple criteria are often necessary in field research to increase the accuracy of case assignments to groups, but our use of polygraph test results as an important and independent criterion is totally ignored by Wells and Loftus and maligned by McGough, who stated that polygraph evidence ''is nearly universally ignored as nonprobative (McCormick, 1984).'' McGough not only overstates the arguments presented in McCormick, but her conclusion is wrong. Polygraph tests may exceed 90% accuracy when properly performed and interpreted (see Raskin, 1989), and they are not universally ignored. They are almost universally relied on for national security purposes and criminal investigations (Raskin, 1986), and they are admissible as evidence in 6 of the 11 federal circuit courts and in the courts of 20 states (Morris, 1989). Law enforcement agencies all over the United States rely heavily on polygraph tests as investigative tools, and prosecutors frequently use their results in making dispositional decisions, especially in cases of alleged sexual abuse of children. Given their accuracy and independence from other criteria, it makes a great deal of sense to use polygraph assessments of the credibility of denials by the accused as one of several criteria for assessing the validity of children's statements in field research (Raskin & Steller, 1989).

Wells and Loftus correctly note that our sample may not be representative of the complete range of sexual abuse cases. Obtaining such a sample was clearly beyond the scope of this study, but failure to sample the full range of cases from definitely confirmed to definitely invalid says nothing about the ability of CBCA to differentiate the groups employed in this study. We used extreme groups in this first field study of the validity of the CBCA technique because it would make little sense to proceed if we could not discriminate between extreme groups. Houed is presently completing a larger study that sampled a broader range of cases.

Wells and Loftus point out the possible confounding of age differences in the two groups and the contents and qualities of their statements. Although the tendency of the doubtful group to contain younger subjects ($M = 6.9$ years) than did the confirmed group ($M = 9.1$ years) was nonsignificant, $t(38) = 1.95, p > .05$, there were substantially more subjects under age 5 in the doubtful (8) than in the confirmed group (1). Regardless of age differences between the groups, even the highest CBCA score for a doubtful statement was lower than the lowest CBCA score for a confirmed statement. Therefore, the differentiation of the two groups by means of CBCA cannot be attributed to the fact that there were more younger subjects in the doubtful group.

If we consider only the statements from children at least 5 years old, the ages of the doubtful ($M = 8.8$ years) and confirmed ($M = 9.6$ years) groups are comparable, and the CBCA scores clearly differentiated between the statements in the two groups. However, the small number of preschool children in the confirmed group precludes any definitive statement about the ability of CBCA to differentiate valid and invalid statements by children under age 5. Larger samples of statements from children of ages 3 and 4 are needed to test the efficacy of CBCA on preschool children, and such data are currently being analyzed by Houed. Because cognitive, linguistic, and expressive abilities are substantially less developed in preschool children, their statements generally tend to be less complete and of lower quality. Special interview procedures and analytic methods may be required to discriminate valid from invalid statements elicited from preschool children.

Wells and Loftus also raise concerns about the interrater reliability of CBCA. Unfortunately, we were not able to make such an assessment in this first field study. However, other data shed light on the question. Steller (1989) reported a moderate amount of interrater agreement on individual CBCA criteria, even though the raters were undergraduate students who received only 90 minutes of training. Houed has recently analyzed data from six CBCA raters on 10 cases, and interrater reliabilities ranged from .82 to .96. These data argue that the interrater reliability of CBCA is quite satisfactory.

Wells and Loftus speculate that our CBCA assessments were not really blind. They claim that because the rater lived in the same city as Esplin and had received training from him, she may have learned about the case facts from news accounts or discussions with Esplin and was thereby influenced in her CBCA scoring of the transcripts. Not only is this mere speculation, but it is incorrect. Of the 40 cases, 30 were from outside the Phoenix area, the cases were not reported by the media because they involved minors, and neither of the authors provided any case facts or group assignments to the evaluator. The CBCA results were based exclusively on the contents of the statements.

McGough claims that we believe that "trial processes will not be substantially improved until American law accepts the use of experts in assessing witness credibility," and she argues that the use of CBCA is tantamount to a credibility assessment of the truthfulness of a witness's statement, which is inadmissible in American courts. This characterization of our position is not correct; we do not advocate the use of CBCA as the basis of expert testimony that a child is or is not truthful. Such conclusions would be inappropriate, they are generally inadmissible, and such testimony might violate ethical admonitions to avoid offering opinions on the ultimate issue.

It is our position that proper interview techniques combined with CBCA and statement validity assessment analysis are best employed as investigative tools to increase the quality of information available to decision makers, such as police investigators, caseworkers, attorneys, and prosecutors. Careful attention to the results of these procedures should increase the accuracy of decisions to file criminal charges, to proceed with a formal prosecution, to remove a child from the home, to grant custody or terminate visitation rights, and so forth.

Expert testimony based on CBCA should be given only when administrative procedures have failed and there is a need to assist the trier of fact in understanding the evidence. Under these circumstances, it is proper to educate the trier of fact about appropriate and inappropriate interview techniques and the contents of statements that are consistent or inconsistent with accounts derived from actual experience. The expert may also comment on the evidence in the specific case as it relates to the appropriateness of the interview techniques and the contents of the obtained statements. The final judgment of the validity of the statement is reserved for the trier of fact.

Expert testimony based on CBCA as was just described is consistent with the rules of evidence and the growing body of case law regarding expert testimony by psychologists (see Doyle, 1989). We see no reason why criminal courts should not accept it, and we have testified in this manner in many courts around the country. These include courts whose evidentiary requirements range from the relatively permissive standards of domestic relations proceedings, to the intermediate level of criminal juvenile proceedings, to the strictest requirements of the criminal courts. Some of this testimony has been presented at the direct request of the courts.

We recognize that our first field validation study is far from perfect, but we are confident that this research and the studies in progress will demonstrate that CBCA provides major advances over many approaches that are currently employed in sexual abuse investigations. A methodology that elicits from a child a complete and uncontaminated statement and formally assesses its validity can produce great benefits to children and society. We feel that appropriate use of CBCA can provide substantial protections for children by preventing sexual victimization, by assisting professionals in successfully prosecuting perpetrators, and by minimizing the risk that children may be exploited by adults who attempt to influence their statements for their own purposes.

References

Doyle, J. M. (1989). Legal issues in eyewitness performance. In D. C. Raskin (Ed.), *Psychological methods in criminal investigation and evidence* (pp. 125–147). New York: Springer Publishing.

Morris, R. A. (1989). The admissibility of evidence derived from hypnosis and polygraphy. In D. C. Raskin (Ed.), *Psychological methods in criminal investigation and evidence* (pp. 333–376). New York: Springer Publishing.

Raskin, D. C. (1986). The polygraph in 1986: Scientific, professional, and legal issues surrounding applications and acceptance of polygraph evidence. *Utah Law Review, 1986*, 29–74.

Raskin, D. C. (1989). Polygraph techniques for the detection of deception. In D. C. Raskin (Ed.), *Psychological methods in criminal investigation and evidence* (pp. 247–296). New York: Springer Publishing.

Raskin, D. C., & Steller, M. (1989). Assessing the credibility of allegations of child sexual abuse: Polygraph examinations and statement analysis. In H. Wegener, F. Loesel, & J. Haisch (Eds.), *Criminal behavior and the justice system: Psychological perspectives* (pp. 290–302). New York: Springer-Verlag.

Steller, M. (1989). Recent developments in statement analysis. In J. C. Yuille (Ed.), *Credibility assessment* (pp. 135–154). Dordrecht, The Netherlands: Kluwer.

CHAPTER 10

CONCLUDING COMMENTS

GRAHAM DAVIES

SUGGESTIBILITY: TRAIT OR STATE?

In a recent study (Davies, Tarrant, & Flin, 1989), my colleagues and I asked 6-to 7- and 10- to 11-year-old children to interact with a stranger playing the role of a public health official. A week later we questioned the children about the incident and asked them to compile a composite picture of the stranger's face. Among our participants was one child whom I shall call (in deference to his native country) John Macleod. John seemed very unsure when we reminded him about the stranger at the school. He did not remember very much about his appearance, but after some effort he completed a composite face with which he was satisfied. It was duly rated by judges alongside the other children's composites and proved an average to poor likeness. It was only at this point that we discovered there were two John Macleod's in the class—and the one who had seen our health official was not the child we had later tested!

Many psychologists would readily see this incident as an example of suggestibility in a child witness. But to what extent is such behavior a reflection of some formal characteristic endemic in children? Or the nature of the situation and mode of questioning adopted by the interviewer? This issue of whether suggestibility represents a trait or a state was rarely addressed directly at the conference, Suggestibility of Children's Recollections, yet must lie at the heart of any debate over the nature of children's suggestibility.

A few psychologists (e.g., Gudjonsson & Clark, 1986), but many lawyers, believe in suggestibility as a trait. Increase in age and mental maturity are matched

177

by a corresponding waning in suggestible behavior. However, there is little evidence for a single all-pervasive characteristic of this kind invested in children. A former student of mine recently reviewed the literature on suggestibility as a trait (Baxter, 1990). Like previous reviewers (Coffin, 1941; Krech & Crutchfield, 1948), he could find little evidence to support the unified view.

As a result of their analysis of the scores of 60 adults on 12 separate measures of suggestibility, Eysenck and Ferneaux (1965) identified two factors they called primary and secondary suggestibility. Performance on a fidelity of report task, the measure most akin to eyewitnessing, was unrelated to primary suggestibility, which they identified with susceptibility to hypnosis, but did form part of a cluster of measures they called gullibility. However, Baxter reported that whereas later research has vouchsafed the existence of their primary factor, secondary suggestibility has not been readily replicated: As yet there appear to be no reliable correlates of performance on witness-related tasks. Echoing earlier reviewers, Baxter concluded that the degree of suggestibility exhibited by an adult or a child is mainly determined by situational factors: "It may be that the situations in which child witnesses are interviewed are often particularly suggestive, rather than that child witnesses are particularly suggestible" (Baxter, 1990, p. 404). If this analysis is correct, then the responsibility for suggestibility passes from the child witness to the adult interviewer.

THE THREE MEANINGS OF SUGGESTIBILITY

A second issue highlighted by the anecdote and reflected in the contributions to this volume is the very different meanings that are attributed to the term *suggestibility*. In its most common form it is interpreted as essentially a cognitive phenomenon: The child's memory is more malleable than that of an adult and thus more subject to inaccuracy and invention (Loftus & Davies, 1984). This theme is reflected in this volume in the studies of the impact of postevent misinformation on subsequent recall (Zaragoza, Chapter 3) and the effect of questioning style and phrasing on the amount of accuracy of information elicited (Goodman & Clarke-Stewart, Chapter 6; Dent, Chapter 8).

However, researchers from Binet (1900) and Bartlett (1932) onward have acknowledged that cognition cannot be divorced from social and affective components, least of all in the study of vulnerable witnesses being interrogated by adults. The social dimension of suggestibility is reflected in studies of compliance: the readiness of a weak and less empowered juvenile to go along with the opinions and implications of the more powerful adult. By manipulating the age of the questioner (Ceci, Ross, & Toglia, 1987; Toglia's commentary on Chapter 3, this volume) or the warmth and supportiveness of questioning (Goodman & Clarke-Stewart, Chapter 6) researchers probe this aspect of suggestibility. Also subsumed

within the social dimension, but a theme absent from this volume is conformity—
the tendency of the witness to conform to the views of the majority even when
these are at variance with the person's own initial perceptions (Sigston & White,
1975). Some recent research from my own laboratory demonstrates that children
are more likely to make errors in recall of events if they hear four of their peers
give the wrong answer than if they hear one, and this tendency is greater in 7-
year-olds than in 13-year-olds (Baxter & Davies, 1987).

This typology of suggestibility has potential practical as well as theoretical
implications. If all or part of suggestibility is social or affective in origin then it
opens up the possibility of later recovery of testimony, given sympathetic and
skilled interviewing techniques. Even when an experimenter is ostensibly acti-
vating the cognitive dimension of suggestibility, but using an adult questioner to
confront a child, it is not always possible to eliminate the social dimension,
especially when the dependent variable proves susceptible to such social manipulations (Ceci et al., 1987; Moston & Engleberg, in press). Most studies reported
in this volume ostensibly concerned themselves with the cognitive aspect of suggestibility. However, an exclusive focus on the latter violates ecological precepts
and risks the drawing of inappropriate solutions.

SUGGESTIBILITY AND COGNITION

If suggestibility is not a trait but a state, how does it map onto our conception of
cognitive process? Is it possible to specify where and what mental mechanisms
might produce suggestible behavior? I can identify two major areas of research
that are well represented in this volume: first, the predominantly theory-driven
studies of memory development and, second, the largely problem-driven literature
on eyewitness testimony. As Lindberg (Chapter 4) has pointed out, both may be
subsumed into the classic three-stage conception of memory (encoding, storage,
and retrieval). It is profitable to consider each of these stages in turn and relate
factors operating within them to potential sources of suggestibility effects in
children.

Can suggestibility be a product of inadequate encoding of information by
the child? As Brainerd and Ornstein (Chapter 2) remind us, children become more
proficient with age in attending to and internalizing relevant aspects of their
environment, and that process is guided by growing knowledge of the world.
Loftus and Davies (1984) speculated that the more impoverished the representation
of an event, the more vulnerable the memory was to distortion from external
influence. Although demonstrations of an inverse relation between suggestibility
and total recall for children of different ages is a value, a far more critical test of
the hypothesis would be to demonstrate a similar effect within a given age group.
An impoverished encoding view would also be compatible with an inverse relation

between measured intelligence and suggestibility. Here again, there may be some support from between-group comparison (Dent, 1986; Pear & Wyatt, 1914), but the crucial within-group data are unavailable.

In adults, success in inducing suggestible responding is greatly influenced by the perceived centrality of the events to be manipulated; postevent suggestions are more powerful on peripheral than on central items (Loftus, 1979a). Numerous anecdotes and some experimental research (Parker, Haverfield, & Baker-Thomas, 1986) suggests that the focus of attention of young children may differ from that of adults in their perceptions of the same scene. To the extent that there is a trade-off between attention to central and peripheral aspects of an event (Wells & Leippe, 1981), young children's representation of its critical elements could be more impoverished and, therefore, more susceptible to "infilling" through suggestion.

Another conception from the cognitive literature that is particularly relevant to child abuse is the idea of scripts—patterns of behavior in the child's life that follow a fixed sequence (Nelson, 1986). Children as young as 2 years of age show evidence of constructing and retrieving from such memories and display obvious irritation when some element of ritual is omitted or altered (Nelson & Ross, 1980). Much theoretical debate hinges on whether only a generic script is available in memory, or whether records of each individual experience are retained (Morton, 1990). If generic memories are the norm in young children, then suggestibility effects might well occur when a child must disentangle a particular incident from the general abuse scenario ("What happened on Christmas Eve last year when you visited Grandpa?"). A child who recalled an element from the generic memory, which for some reason was incompatible with agreed events on that particular occasion, might well risk being labeled "suggestible."

Vulnerability to suggestion could also be accelerated during the storage phase of memory. The list-learning studies reviewed by Brainerd and Ornstein (Chapter 2) suggest that rates of spontaneous forgetting from long-term memory may slow with increasing development. Such a process would accelerate loss of information from an already impoverished representation. However, as Flin (commentary on Chapter 2) points out and Brainerd and Ornstein readily agree, the relevance of such studies to autobiographical memory needs to be demonstrated. Moreover, there is always the risk that repeated prompting and questioning, particularly from an interested party, may lead to the kind of postevent misinformation effects discussed by Zaragoza (Chapter 3).

The debate between Zaragoza and Toglia over whether postevent suggestions actually weaken or eliminate original memories has important implications for the child suggestibility debate. As yet, no researcher has demonstrated that suggestions assimilated by a child during a retention period can be reversed, although this process has been observed in adults (Bekerian & Bowers, 1983; Gibling & Davies, 1988). The question must arise, however, of whether young children have the metacognitive skills necessary for using techniques such as guided memory or mental reinstatement (Geiselman & Padilla, 1988). In the meantime, much light might be shed on the theoretical mechanisms underlying postevent suggestions by disinterring the extensive verbal learning literature on pro- and retroactive interference, which in its experimental paradigms and theoretical concerns bears many startling parallels to the contemporary debate (e.g., Kausler, 1974).

The retrieval stage represents a major potential source of suggestibility for the child. As Dent (Chapter 8) demonstrates, children's free accounts are often sparse but generally reliable. The results of direct questioning, conversely, frequently result in an inverse relation between age and accuracy. This trend is normally accelerated if direct or leading questions are employed. It is useful to speculate about the source of the inaccurate information furnished by the child. Some may be a direct result of the kinds of social pressures highlighted earlier, whereby a more powerful adult is perceived by the child as expecting a positive answer (a failing on the part of the adult rather than the child as my introductory anecdote illustrates). Both Dent (Chapter 8) and Baxter (1990) point to ways of reducing the social chasm between child and interrogator through having interviewers stress their lack of knowledge of events and ignorance of the right answers.

However, it seems unlikely that social factors alone will explain all the errors that children may make under direct questioning. Orthodox laboratory studies of children's free recall clearly point to an improvement with age in the effectiveness and exhaustiveness with which information is retrieved from memory (Kobazigawa, 1974). However, attempts to show widespread differences in proficiency of memory monitoring between younger and older children have proved surprisingly unsuccessful (e.g., Johnson & Foley, 1984). Nevertheless, the possibility that young children might be hampered in their ability to retrieve the source of information is worthy of further research (Ceci et al., 1987). Children can on occasion show a difficulty in distinguishing between original memories of an event and what they were subsequently told or thought (see Davies & Baxter, 1988), and this could produce suggestible responses (Toglia, Commentary on Chapter 3).

Children, however, can under some circumstances use externally available contextual cues to remarkable effect in retrieving memories. Wilkinson (1988) has shown that children of 3 and 4 years of age can exhibit major improvements in recall if questioning about a sequence of events takes place at the locations and in the sequence in which they occurred. However, the luxury of being able to recreate such scenarios so completely and systematically is rarely available to the investigator as opposed to the researcher.

In summary, a variety of cognitive mechanisms could produce the suggestibility effect in children through immaturities in the memory processing system. The source of problems could lie at encoding, storage, or retrieval or in any combination of these. However, any analysis in these terms needs always to take into account the realities of autobiographical memory in general and memory for abusive incidents in particular. Laboratory research can provide a useful fund of powerful theoretical ideas, but its findings need always to be related to the realities of sexual abuse.

SUGGESTIBILITY AND ECOLOGICAL VALIDITY

As Ceci notes in Chapter 1, one of the major themes of the Cornell Conference on the Suggestibility of Children's Recollections, was the degree to which current research paradigms (and by implication, results) were representative of the circumstances about which children might later testify. Although his own research suggests that there are few if any features that apply to all such situations, there are some that are sufficiently common and potentially powerful in their effects as to demand investigation. Some may serve to enhance memory, others to confuse and weaken it. Again, it is useful to consider these features in terms of the encoding, storage, and retrieval cycle.

One factor operating at the encoding phase, which has received a good deal of attention in these pages, is stress and its impact on recall and suggestibility to leading questions. There are the apparent differences in results obtained by Goodman (Chapter 6) on the one hand and Peters (Chapter 5) on the other. The issues that these findings raise and the methodological differences underlying them have been vigorously debated both in the commentaries on their respective chapters and in the contribution of Yuille and Wells (Chapter 7). It is hoped that these exchanges will serve usefully to refine the research agenda.

Goodman's pioneering work has done much to demonstrate that children are not necessarily poor witnesses and that high levels of stress do not necessarily lead to compliant responding. She was the first to seek out naturally occurring stressful situations and has included among her questions those typically asked in abuse inquiries. Yuille, Wells, and others argue that this is an unnatural juxtaposition and that questions of abuse are unlikely to arise from visits to the doctor or school clinic. As Ceci in Chapter 1 reminds us, abuse comes in many colors, and potential abusers do take advantage of privileged positions, whether as health care professionals, youth leaders, or professional babysitters. However, abuse by strangers is the exception rather than the rule. The ingenious studies of Peters appear to demonstrate that there are circumstances and situations in which the pattern of findings reported by Goodman do not apply. What is now required is application of the new methodologies revealed by these researchers to a wider range of scenarios. What happens, for instance, when children are asked leading questions about the behavior of friends or relatives as compared to total strangers? Until such a web of findings is accumulated, perhaps all researchers should take the advice of Yuille and Wells and refrain from making expansive generalizations, whether in the media or on the witness stand.

Stress is only one feature of abuse and, as Raskin and Esplin (Chapter 9) remind us, not a necessary corrolary. They cite involvement and loss of control as additional common themes. Goodman's work suggests that involvement may well assist the processes of recall as may the stereotyped nature of repeated abusive acts by the same person on a single child. Furthermore, such incidents frequently occur at set locations (e.g., grandpa's house) and are prefaced by consistent events (e.g., bathing and kissing goodnight). All of these factors should militate in favor of a rich and elaborated script memory well embedded in everyday events and thus readily triggered by external cues or sympathetic questioning (Todd & Perlmutter, 1980).

Turning to storage factors, there are a number of features of abuse cases that are not well represented as yet in the research literature and whose impact on suggestible responding remains to be explored. There is the effect of very long delays on recall highlighted by Flin (Commentary on Chapter 2) and by Goodman (Commentary on Chapter 5). Studies of children's autobiographical memory demonstrate that preschoolers are capable of recalling landmark events from early childhood with reasonable precision (Cole & Loftus, 1987). Such memories could be perpetuated and strengthened through a process of repeated reminiscence. Clinical research on the long-term memory of adults who have suffered abuse as children may shed light on whether rehearsal or repression is the norm for this type of experience (e.g., Herman & Schatzow, 1987).

Once abuse is suspected or detected, there is often repeated questioning by different agencies, and, once again, little is known of its impact on recall. One study (Dent & Stephenson, 1979) showed little impact of repeated questioning concerning a filmed incident over an 8-week interval. As Flin emphasizes and Clarke-Stewart's work reminds us, objective questioning when abuse is suspected is not the norm, and the long-term impact of suggestive questioning needs further exploration.

Most concerns about suggestibility focus on the final retrieval phase of memory. Here again, stress reappears in an institutionalized form if the child must give evidence in the alien and intimidating atmosphere of a conventional courtroom. Although there is some evidence that cross-examination may have value to triers of fact in determining the accuracy of child witnesses (Turtle & Wells, 1988), there is no evidence that the stress of a courtroom appearance is at all diagnostic. The caring concensus is that children will perform better in situations that permit out-of-court testimony such as a video-link arrangement (Davies, 1988), although as yet, no data are available as to its effectiveness.

Raskin and Esplin describe a refinement of a system used extensively in Germany as a method assessing credibility that can dispense with the witness stand: witness statement analysis. The method seems full of promise to judge from its early results, but it will be necessary to show that it can outpace the intuitive judgments of an untutored professional before it will gain widespread acceptance. In England and the United States, however, it seems likely that it will be used as a preliminary screening device rather than having the results entered as evidence; such expert comments on witness's credibility are explicitly banned by the courts (McGough, Commentary on Chapter 6; Melton & Limber, 1989).

However, the major source of allegations of suggestible responding lies in the style of interviewing and methods of questioning. To date, most research paradigms have tended to employ well-structured incidents about which children are interviewed in an objective fashion by friendly adults who are aware of what actually occurred. The interviewer knows what are appropriate questions and can afford to be dispassionate about the answers received. However, the realities of child abuse are frequently at variance with these assumptions. As Clarke-Stewart reminds us, the situation for the child can be ambiguous and ill-understood. The initial questioner frequently is a caregiver who is far from unconcerned or un-committed as to what the child has to say. The interviewer does not know what occurred and may have skeptical or unfounded expectations. As Dent's (1982) early study demonstrated, suggestive responses may well be the result.

Research is urgently needed that touches on these issues and Clarke-Stewart's Chester the Molester paradigm breaks new ground. As with all such work, Clarke-Stewart's work raises as many questions as it answers. Would similar effects have occurred with an older sample of children? Would the children have been just as compliant if it was their dolls who had been sprayed and polished or if Chester had acted in a similar manner toward the children themselves? How permanent was the reshaping of their perceptions following biased questioning? Could careful questioning, aided if necessary by enactment or the use of cues, have still recovered a residual memory? These are but a few of the questions provoked by this important new line of research.

Wilkinson's studies (1988) demonstrate that cues and enactment can be powerful facilitators of recall. However, the privilege of knowing precisely what had occurred and where is frequently unavailable to the interviewer. When only approximate cues are available, will these facilitate recall or act as triggers for fantasy? This is one of the allegations most often made against the most common aid employed by child abuse investigators, the anatomically correct doll. The function of such dolls appears to be ill-defined in clinical practice. Some therapists see them merely as communication aids for the child who is unable or unwilling to describe what occurred; others see them as a form of stimulus support to facilitate memory. And others see them as an instrument of fantasy and play through which children will communicate their repressed feelings and preoccupations (see Westcott, Davies, & Clifford, 1989, for a review). More research is required to identify the precise functions that dolls can and cannot serve in interviews and so refine the tactics for their deployment and use (Goodman & Aman, 1990).

CONCLUSIONS

There are now ample demonstrations that situations can be constructed in such a way that children can be induced to respond in a suggestible or compliant manner. However, as the work of Loftus and others has long since demonstrated, intelligent adults too can be vulnerable to suggestion in laboratory-based eyewitness tasks (Loftus, 1979b). What needs to be specified by research is when and under what conditions and by how much are children as vulnerable or more vulnerable to suggestion than adults. Even then, this would not be a basis for excluding testimony, but rather aiding the training of investigators and the procedures they should follow. The implication, for instance, of Clarke-Stewart's findings is the importance of early interviewing with objective questions, rather than the exclusion of young children's testimony from the courts of law.

I have noted some of the stages of memory in which suggestion could occur and have alluded to some of the many mechanisms that could produce the effect. I have also noted some of the important differences between such contemporary experimental research and the realities of child abuse. Some might seek to reduce suggestibility effects, others to exaggerate them. All alternatives deserve to be explored. However, such exploration is unlikely to be achieved purely through traditional experimental methods. Already, psychologists are working close to the boundaries of what is ethically acceptable research, and some of the full horrors of abuse are almost by definition unsimulatable. As Yuille and Wells observe, what is required is the supplementation of traditional experimental studies by actual case studies and cohort analyses in the manner of recent studies of adult eyewitnessing (Macleod, 1987; Yuille & Cutshall, 1986). Only by a symbiosis of experimental and observational research methods are psychologists likely to construct a comprehensive picture of the social and cognitive determinants of suggestibility.

References

Bartlett, F. C. (1932). *Remembering: A study in experimental and social psychology.* Cambridge, England: Cambridge University Press.

Baxter, J. (1990). The suggestibility of child witnesses: A review. *Applied Cognitive Psychology, 4,* 393–408.

Baxter, J., & Davies, G. (1987). *Conformity and the child witness.* Paper presented at the meeting of the Society for Research in Child Development, Baltimore, MD.

Bekerian, D. A., & Bowers, J. M. (1983). Eyewitness testimony: Were we misled? *Journal of Experimental Psychology: Learning, Memory and Cognition, 9,* 139–145.

Binet A. (1900). *La suggestibilité.* Paris: Schleicher.

Ceci, S. J., Ross, D. F., & Toglia, M. P. (1987). Suggestibility in children's memory: Psycho-legal implications. *Journal of Experimental Psychology: General, 116,* 38–49.

Coffin, T. E. (1941). Some conditions of suggestion and suggestibility: A study of certain attitudinal and situational factors influencing the process of suggestion. *Psychological Monographs*, *53*(4).

Cole, C. B., & Loftus, E. (1987). The memory of children. In S. J. Ceci, M. P. Toglia, & D. F. Ross (Eds.), *Children's eyewitness memory* (pp. 178–208). New York: Springer-Verlag.

Davies, G. M. (1988). Use of video in child abuse trials. *The Psychologist*, *1*, 20–22, 169–170.

Davies, G. M., & Baxter, J. (1988). *Children's ability to distinguish fact from fantasy*. Paper presented at the meeting of the NATO Advanced Study Institute on Credibility Assessment, Maratea, Italy.

Davies, G. M., Tarrant, A., & Flin, R. (1989). Close encounters of a witness kind: Children's memory for a simulated health inspection. *British Journal of Psychology*, *80*, 415–429.

Dent, H. (1982). The effects of interviewing strategies on the results of interviews with child witnesses. In A. Trankell (Ed.), *Reconstructing the past* (pp. 279–297). Stockholm: Norstedt & Sons.

Dent, H. (1986). An experimental study of the effectiveness of different techniques of questioning mentally handicapped child witnesses. *British Journal of Clinical Psychology*, *25*, 13–17.

Dent, H. R., & Stephenson, G. M. (1979). An experimental study of the effectiveness of different techniques of questioning child witnesses. *British Journal of Social and Clinical Psychology*, *18*, 41–51.

Eysenck, H. J., & Ferneaux, W. D. (1965). Primary and secondary suggestibility. *Journal of Experimental Psychology*, *35*, 485–503.

Geiselman, R. E., & Padilla, J. (1988). *Interviewing child witnesses with the cognitive interview*. Unpublished manuscript.

Gibling, F., & Davies, G. (1988). Reinstatement of context following exposure to post-event information. *British Journal of Psychology*, *79*, 129–141.

Goodman, G. S., & Aman, C. (1990). Children's use of anatomically detailed dolls to recount an event. *Child Development*, *61*, 1859–1871.

Gudjonsson, G., & Clark, N. (1986). Suggestibility in police interrogation: A social psychological model. *Social Behavior*, *1*, 83–104.

Herman, J. L., & Schatzow, E. (1987). Recovery and verification of memories of childhood sexual trauma. *Psychoanalytic Psychology*, *4*, 1–14.

Johnson, M. K., & Foley, M. A. (1984). Differentiating fact from fantasy: The reliability of children's memory. *Journal of Social Issues*, *40*, 33–50.

Kausler, D. H. (1974). *Psychology of verbal learning and memory*. New York: Academic Press.

Kobazigawa, A. (1974). Utilization of retrieval cues by children in recall. *Child Development*, *45*, 127–134.

Krech, D., & Crutchfield, R. S. (1948). *Theory and problems of social psychology*. New York: McGraw-Hill.

Loftus, E. (1979a). *Eyewitness testimony*. Cambridge, MA: Harvard University Press.

Loftus, E. F. (1979b). Reactions to blatantly contradictory information. *Memory & Cognition*, *7*, 368–374.

Loftus, E. F., & Davies, G. M. (1984). Distortions in the memory of children. *Journal of Social Issues*, *40*, 51–67.

Macleod, M. (1987). *Psychological dynamics of the police interview*. Unpublished doctoral dissertation, Aberdeen University, Scotland.

Melton, G. B., & Limber, S. (1989). Psychologist's involvement in cases of child maltreatment. *American Psychologist*, *44*, 1225–1233.

Morton, J. (1990). The development of event memory. *The Psychologist, 3*, 3–10.

Moston, S., & Engleberg, T. (in press). The effects of social support on children's eyewitness memory. *Applied Cognitive Psychology*.

Nelson, K. (1986). *Event knowledge: Structure and function in development*. Hillsdale, NJ: Erlbaum.

Nelson, K., & Ross, G. (1980). The generalities and specifics of long-term memory in children. In M. Perlmutter (Ed.), *Children's memory: New directions for child development* (No. 10, pp. 87–101). San Francisco: Jossey-Bass.

Parker, J. F., Haverfield, E., & Baker-Thomas, S. (1986). Eyewitness testimony of children. *Journal of Applied Social Psychology, 16*, 287–302.

Pear, T. H., & Wyatt, S. (1914). The testimony of normal and mentally defective children. *British Journal of Psychology, 3*, 388–419.

Sigston, A., & White, D. G. (1975). Conformity in children as a function of age level. *British Journal of Social and Clinical Psychology, 3*, 388–419.

Todd, C., & Perlmutter, M. (1980). Reality recalled by preschool children. In M. Perlmutter (Ed.), *Children's memory: New directions for child development, No. 10*, (pp. 69–85). San Fransisco: Jossey-Bass.

Turtle, J. W., & Wells, G. L. (1988). Children versus adults as eyewitnesses: Whose testimony holds up under cross-examination? In M. M. Gruneberg, P. E. Morris & R. N. Sykes (Eds.). *Practical aspects of memory: Current research and issues, Vol. 1* (pp. 27–33). Chichester: Wiley.

Wells, G. L., & Lieppe, M. R. (1981). How do triers of fact infer the accuracy of eyewitness identifications? Memory for peripheral detail can be misleading. *Journal of Applied Psychology, 66*, 682–687.

Westcott, H., Davies, G. M., & Clifford, B. R. (1989). The use of anatomical dolls in child witness interviews. *Adoption and Fostering, 13*, 6–14.

Wilkinson, J. (1988). Context effects in children's event memory. In M. M. Gruneberg, P. E. Morris & R.N. Sykes (Eds.). *Practical aspects of memory: Current research and issues, Vol. 1* (pp. 107–111). Chichester: Wiley.

Yuille, J. C., & Catshall, J. (1986). A case study of eyewitness memory of a crime. *Journal of Applied Psychology, 71*, 291–301.

INDEX

Age. *See also* Development
    CBCA validity and, 170, 173–174
    identification accuracy and, 131–132
    long-term memory and, 149
    memory impairment and, 33, 41
    memory processes and, 17–18, 50–54,
      181
    stress and recall correlations, 78–79, 83–
      84, 86, 87
    suggestibility and, 50–54, 58
Anxiety. *See also* Stress
    scales for, 64, 79, 87, 90
Arousal. *See* Stress
Attentional focus, stress and, 84
Attorney-client interactions, 116
Authority, and child suggestibility, 38

Bartlett, F. C., 43
Benaji, M., 26
Boring, E., 8
Brainerd, C., 10–19, 21–23, 24, 26, 179, 180
Brigham, J., 110–113
Britain, 136
Bronfenbrenner, U., 4–5
Bull, R., 134–136
Bussy, K., 90
Bystanders
    motivations of, 154, 168
    suggestibility of, 94–95

Ceci S., 1–9, 31–36, 41–43, 129–133, 182
Central information, 50, 52–54, 180
Chester the molester study, 57, 99–103, 184
Children's testimony research. *See* Research
Clarke-Stewart, A., 57, 92–104, 106–109,
    110–113, 115–117

Classification circularity problem, for CBCA,
    170, 172
Clinical situations
    environment of, 97
    genital contact reporting, 98–99, 107–
      108, 158–159
    long-term retention studies, 13
    stress and recall studies, 66–67, 74, 79,
      86, 88, 89, 90, 91
Coexistence hypothesis, 41, 43
Cognitive development. *See* Development
Cognitive diagnosis, 147–148
Cognitive processes, suggestibility and, 179–
    182
Commission errors
    clinical genital contact, 98, 107–108
    long-term recall and, 97–98
    misinformation and, 37
    sexual abuse field study, 160
    sexual terminology and, 96
    target-absent lineups and, 88
Compliance, 101–103, 178
Confrontational stress, live lineups and, 67–70,
    75
Constructive memory, 14, 43–44
Content analysis. *See* Criteria-based content
    analysis
Context, 4, 129–130. *See also* Ecological
    validity
    controlled vs. natural, 124–125, 130,
      131, 135–136
    cross-situational regularities and, 130
    generalizing across, 132
    research applicability vs., 121–122
Controlled research. *See* Laboratory research
Controversy, and scientific truth, 8
Coy v. Iowa, 70, 90–91